11/96

D0175082

97/ ЖЖ   99/1

|

97

GAYLORD MG

VOLCANO
AND
MIRACLE

Also by Gustaw Herling

The Island
A World Apart

GUSTAW HERLING

Selected and Translated by

RONALD STROM

VIKING

VOLCANO

AND

MIRACLE

A Selection of Fiction and Nonfiction from

THE JOURNAL
WRITTEN AT NIGHT

VIKING
Published by the Penguin Group
Penguin Books USA Inc., 375 Hudson Street, New York, New York 10014, U.S.A.
Penguin Books Ltd, 27 Wrights Lane, London W8 5TZ, England
Penguin Books Australia Ltd, Ringwood, Victoria, Australia
Penguin Books Canada Ltd, 10 Alcorn Avenue, Toronto, Ontario, Canada M4V 3B2
Penguin Books (N.Z.) Ltd, 182–190 Wairau Road, Auckland 10, New Zealand

Penguin Books Ltd, Registered Offices:
Harmondsworth, Middlesex, England

First published in 1996 by Viking Penguin,
a division of Penguin Books USA Inc.

10 9 8 7 6 5 4 3 2 1

Grateful acknowledgment is made for permission to reprint an excerpt from "Through-out Our Lands" from *Collected Poems* by Czeslaw Milosz. Copyright © 1988 by Czeslaw Milosz. Reprinted by permission from The Ecco Press.

Library of Congress Cataloging-in-Publication Data
Herling-Grudziński, Gustaw, 1919–
    [Dziennik pisany nocą. English. Selections]
    Volcano and Miracle : a selection of fiction and nonfiction from The journal
written at night / Gustaw Herling ; translated by Ronald Strom.
      p. cm.
    ISBN 0-670-85482-4 (alk. paper)
    1. Herling-Grudziński, Gustaw, 1919– —Biography. 2. Authors, Polish—20th
century—Biography. 3. Herling-Grudziński, Gustaw, 1919– —Translations into English. I. Strom, Ronald. II. Title.
PG7158.H4462A33213   1996
891.8'.537—dc20   95-21207

This book is printed on acid-free paper.
♾
Printed in the United States of America
Set in Garamond 3
Designed by Katy Riegel

CONTENTS

CONTENTS

INTRODUCTORY NOTE

Volcano and Miracle is a selection of fiction and prose writings from Gustaw Herling's masterwork, the *Journal Written at Night*, which has been appearing for more than a quarter century in the émigré Polish monthly *Kultura*. (Six volumes of the collected *Journal* have been published in Polish.) *The Journal* is written in diary form, but it is not autobiography. The author is a peripheral figure, whose occasional appearance is not unlike the self-portraits Renaissance artists sometimes set monogram-like in a discreet corner of their vast frescoes. The *Journal* is an account of events and reflections that offer the occasion for this great writer to continue rethinking and reimagining the human condition. The individual entries are finished works in themselves, but they are identified only by date, standard practice in journal and diary writing. Descriptive titles have now been provided for convenient reference.

The present selection, which might well have been subtitled "Calamities Natural and Unnatural," takes its title from the Neapolitan tale *The Miracle*, in which life is suspended between the natural threat of Mount Vesuvius and the perhaps unnatural hope that a saint's blood will liquefy. Much of Herling's fiction and nonfiction is concerned with human fate and conduct between these two poles. Reason considers the cruel threat of natural disaster and unnatural disaster, man's own evil action; and imagination glimpses miraculous hope in moments when man struggles to keep faith with some transcendent good.

The locus of Herling's imaginative fiction and reasoning nonfiction ranges from a southern Italian village reduced to rubble by earthquake to slave labor camps in Siberia, the streets of revolutionary Naples in the seventeenth century, and the placid avenues of nineteenth-century Turin, where Nietzsche conceived his anti-Christ.

Gustaw Herling-Grudzinski (Eastern European readers know him by his full name) was born in 1919 in Kielce, in central Poland, the fourth child of a flour and saw mill owner. A fledgling writer and student of literature, Herling had finished his second year at the University of Warsaw when Hitler invaded Poland. After Poland's defeat, he was one of the founders of the first anti-Nazi underground organization. In 1940 he was captured by the NKVD in eastern Poland, then under Soviet occupation, and spent two years in a Soviet slave labor camp on the White Sea. His experiences there are described in the classic *A World Apart*, first published in English in 1951, with an introduction by Bertrand Russell. After his release he joined the Polish army organized in Russia and went to the Middle East and then to Italy, where at the Battle of Monte Cassino he was awarded the highest Polish military honor. It was only at the end of the war that he could go back to writing. In Rome he took part in founding the Polish monthly *Kultura*, which was conceived as a forum for independent thought and imagination beyond the reach of communist tyranny. The magazine still exists, and continues to publish books as well, under the directorship of its first editor, Jerzy Giedroyc. *Kultura*'s catalogue includes such distinguished authors as Czeslaw Milosz and Witold Gombrowicz, as well as Gustaw Herling.

After the war Herling lived in London and Munich and finally settled in Naples. His writings were strictly banned in Poland for nearly forty years, but since the fall of communism, all of his works have been published in several editions in his homeland.

VOLCANO
AND
MIRACLE

1 9 7 0

Naples, April [Earthquake Italian style]

In July 1883 I had been in Casamicciola (Ischia) for several days with my father, my mother, and my sister Maria in a pension called Villa Verde, in the upper part of the town, when on the evening of the 29th the terrible earthquake occurred. I remember that we had finished dinner and were all together in a room that gave onto a terrace: my father was writing a letter, I was across from him reading, and my mother and my sister sat side by side talking in a corner, when a long somber rumble was heard, and at the same moment the building collapsed on top of us. In a flash I saw my father rise to his feet and my sister throw herself into my mother's arms. Instinctively I leapt to the terrace, which split open beneath my feet, and I lost consciousness. It was late at night when I came to, buried to my neck, the stars shining overhead, and I saw yellowish earth around me, and I could not figure out what had happened, and I seemed to be dreaming. After a while I realized what had happened, and I remained calm, which happens in great disasters. I called for help for me and my father, whose voice I heard not far from me. Despite all my efforts I could not extricate myself. Towards morning, two soldiers dug me out, if I remember rightly, and laid me on a stretcher in the open air. . . . Only some days later were my father, my mother, and my sister found dead under the rubble, my sister and my mother clinging to each other.

1

GUSTAW HERLING

This is an extract from Benedetto Croce's *Memorie della mia vita*, a small volume published in a limited edition. The future Neapolitan philosopher was sixteen years old the year of the tragedy in Casamicciola. He survived it with a broken right arm and a crushed femur, injuries that left him with a sort of partial paralysis. Psychic injuries, even after losing almost all one's family (Croce's brother was not with them on holiday and was spared), are not a usual topic of conversation for people who live in a region that has been volcanic for centuries and who tread such an untrustworthy portion of the earth's crust, staring every day at the cone of Vesuvius and looking again and again toward Pompeii, Herculaneum, and the smoky fumaroles of the Solfatara outside Pozzuoli. There is something on the order of an atavism of natural calamities in these parts.

I took my first steps on the soil of Italy in 1944 in the glare of an eruption of Vesuvius, in a rain of ash under an ominously darkened sky. I will never forget the faces of the inhabitants hastily evacuated from villages that had been declared unsafe because of the streaming lava, faces frozen in an expression of resignation and acceptance. Anyone who stays here or chooses to settle here must have an innate or acquired sense of the fragility of the earth and of human life.

Croce's brief description of the earthquake on Ischia leaves out details mentioned in other accounts. The inhabitants had a foreboding of impending danger, but they did not speak of it, in hopes that at the last moment it might vanish; and they did not want to scare off the tourists and summer residents at the height of the season. Despite the fine sunny weather, the sea had been extremely rough for several days, and away from the shore it churned like boiling water and occasionally hurled shoals of dead fish up to the surface. The most reliable omen is fish cooked alive in the sizzling depths, and when they rise to the surface, the foamy surge bears them along like a coating of white leaves of different shapes and sizes.

That is what it was like in Pozzuoli this year in early March, or at least so it seemed. Volcanology is not considered too exact a science. It offers hypotheses and forecasts *cum grano salis,* and the practical worth of its measurements and analyses—obviously despite its aspirations but perforce in the eyes of the population directly concerned —often boils down to scarcely more than a ceremonious little reading of volcanic coffee grounds. As long as the gauges of the volcanological observatories registered day by day the changing humor of the menace looming over Pozzuoli, the sixty thousand inhabitants were in no hurry for mass exodus. A fisherman tipped the scale. He came to shore at dawn one day after a night's fishing and did not even bother to tie up his boat but rushed off in the direction of the still-closed *municipio.* Along the way he woke the sleeping people with a shout, an age-old shout about an age-old sign: the net he hauled up was full of dead fish. Only then did people start packing their belongings. Exactly half of the inhabitants, thirty thousand people, left Pozzuoli. Twenty-five thousand of them left willingly, and five thousand were forced. The forced evacuation involved the "Land Quarter," the Rione Terra, an agglomeration of the oldest houses on the heights of the spur of the promontory that extends farthest into the sea. From a distance the Rione Terra looks like an enormous stony mass of swallows' nests one next to the other clinging fast to the rock. It was here that cracks were seen running up the front of some of the houses, and it was here that a tremor hardly stronger than those registered only by sensitive seismographs was in a few minutes to turn the dwelling place of five thousand people (fishermen and their families, for the most part) into a tomb in the form of a heaped mound of rubble. The lanes in and out were cordoned off, the windows were boarded up, and all that remained among the abandoned walls were a few vagrant cats and the police patrol guarding the possessions the evacuees had not been able to carry away by hand.

Pozzuoli is about fifteen kilometers from Naples (on the Domitian Way in the direction of Rome), in an area of the volcanic region of the Bay of Naples that is so sensitive and so potentially active that aside from the port for vessels ferrying automobiles to Ischia, the site of Saint Januarius' decapitation (with traces of blood on the stone block), and the place of Sophia Loren's birth (without any particular traces), two curiosities always attract tourists: the steamy bubbling "jaws" of the Solfatara and Monte Nuovo, a hill that a quake drove up or rather spewed out of the earth in a single night in 1538 and is now grown over with green pines around the edge of its dormant crater. A phenomenon endemic to Pozzuoli and its environs is called *bradisismo* in Italian, from the Greek words *bradys* ("slow") and *seismos* ("shock"). The phenomenon consists in the slow rise and fall of the earth's crust. According to one school of volcanologists, it is the work of underground gases alternately pushing and withdrawing, while another school argues that it is the result of the fiery forge of magma under Vesuvius bursting in all directions. Whatever the case, Pozzuoli, an exceptionally "plastic" area, is a nerve center of the process, while in the event that the second theory were correct, a violent revival of the volcano would not spare Naples on its way to Pozzuoli, since Naples is built on spongy tufa. Actually *bradisismo* is not cause for excessive concern when the earth's crust moves slowly and uniformly. But irregularity or acceleration augurs the possibility of cataclysm. An acceleration was registered in Pozzuoli, and an unusual one at that. Since ancient times the city's volcanological thermometer has been the Serapeum, the Temple of Serapis, built below sea level in the second century before Christ. The bradyseism register can be read on the columns, their bases immersed in water. In the course of twelve centuries, until the tenth century after Christ, the earth's crust rose and fell a total of six meters, or one meter of bradyseism per century. In these last months, an upward movement of one meter has been registered on the columns of the Serapeum, which has now risen out of the water. Clearly, one meter per century is a different matter than one meter in a few months. Which is what caused the volcanologists' alarm. But had it not been heightened by the alarm of the fisherman, the inhabitants of Pozzuoli would have continued in their atavistic indifference to the earth rising up beneath their very feet.

What are things like a month later? I found an odd psychological situation in Pozzuoli—an earthquake that never was. It is not just that the majority of the evacuees have returned (except for the walled-off Rione Terra); that the town's two renowned markets, the fish and the fruit and vegetable markets, are doing better business than ever; that the streets and cafés are as crowded as before; and that the port has come back to life, with workmen cutting out new niches for ships' gangplanks in the stone pier, which has risen a meter. Conversation is marked by a symptomatic note of resentment and suspicion, namely, "Did they trump up an earthquake that never happened? Who trumped it up?" A shrug of the shoulders, a knowing wink. The mystery was clarified to some degree when a young fisherman who until the forced evacuation had lived with his wife and two children in the Rione Terra agreed to take me there by a secret passage.

The Rione Terra was deserted, except for the Vescovado, where the bishop, together with a small group of priests and nuns, remained at his post for the spiritual protection of the absent, himself under the protection of heaven. Crushed window glass covered the pavement in the lanes, paper peeled in strips from the walls, and objects reduced to scrap metal sat in the corners of the vacated dwellings, and at every step cats cringed fearfully in holes in the walls. My guide, perhaps because the police had forcibly removed him from his old family home in the Rione Terra, was the very personification of Pozzuoli's general skepticism. *"Ma che terremoto, ma che terremoto,"* he said over and over. "What earthquake!"

"What about the cracks in the wall of this house in front of us?"

"A truck was trying to maneuver and ran into it full force."

"And that fisherman with his net full of dead fish?"

"The bastard lied, they bought him off. He stayed away from shore for three days and kept his net under water the whole time, so how could fish stuck in the net not die? We smashed his face in for that."

"Who bought him off?"

"It's hard to say, but it is a fact that there are guys going around here now offering good prices for houses in the Rione Terra. What do they want with houses if the land is so dangerous? Just what do they want? Until now no one has ever managed to demolish the Rione Terra, but what a windfall it would be for real estate speculators, one of the best views in the whole bay! So then (he winked) maybe this land isn't so dangerous after an earthquake that never was."

Of course one ought to be at least skeptical of Pozzuoli's skepticism after an "earthquake that never was," but if I were a director I would shoot a film here, *Earthquake, Italian Style*, after Pietro Germi's excellent *Divorce, Italian Style*. A panoramic luxury hotel has risen from the finally demolished rubble of the Rione Terra, the Hotel Monte Nuovo. Some time later the phenomenon of bradyseism becomes intense, a team of volcanologists raise the alarm, the bay like a giant cauldron is cooking the fish, and fissures appear in the walls of the old houses. But people have learned their lesson, and no one pays any attention. One torrid summer night Pozzuoli sinks into the ground with its bishop in the Vescovado and its masterpiece of panoramic hotel architecture in the Rione Terra. It would be a modern version of the fairy tale of the boy who cried wolf, and, for the informed and acute observer, not without its relevance to Italian politics.

GUSTAW HERLING

Maisons-Laffitte, September [Natalie Herzen and Nechayev]

On the hundredth anniversary of Alexander Herzen's death we have been given a fragment of his daughter Natalie's diary, now deposited in the Paris Bibliothèque Nationale. The first publication in the original Russian and in French translation appeared in *Cahiers du monde russe et soviétique*, with an introduction by Professor Michael Contino, and the English translation in the May issue of *Encounter*. The excerpt consists of the entries from May 28 to July 7, 1870, but what Natalie Herzen talks about is the period just after her father's death in Paris on January 21. In early February she went to Geneva to visit the bereft Ogarev. And there she met Nechayev. This is the very period about which Franco Venturi said in *Il populismo russo*: "At least for a while [Nechayev] won over Herzen's daughter and the old Ogarev, got money from them and thus took into his own hands a new edition of *Kolokol* ('The Bell'). The first issue of this 'organ of Russian liberation, founded by A. I. Herzen,' came out April 2, 1870, the sixth and last on May 9 the same year." These dates make it easy to infer that once the brief Nechayevian chapter of the orphaned Herzen family was finally over, Natalie Aleksandrovna must have felt she needed to re-capitulate it.

Is Venturi right when he says that Nechayev succeeded in "winning over" the daughter of the founder of *Kolokol*? The text of her diary does not justify such a categorical statement, even if it is qualified by the proviso "at least for a while." While Natalie was influenced by Ogarev, who, aside from his slightly senile enthusiasm, yielded to Bakunin's influence, she actually treated Nechayev with mistrustful caution and at the same time refrained from preconceived judgments. She gave him a chance. She was ready to help the cause as much as she could, even if the cause were henceforth to be embodied in the person of that young man with "the air of a bandit," whose "expression was striking in its energy, malice, and cruelty." The utmost of her benevolence in regard to Nechayev is summed up in these words: "He killed a spy though, and that was a good thing. What energy he has, he is a fanatic. He does indeed see nothing except his goal." Something in these words sounds forced, a note of conditional approval "in spite of." Of course, in spite of the impatient angry snarls of her father, who, before dying, had lumped Ogarev as he had become, Bakunin, and Nechayev together in the same basket and labeled it "delirium tremens." So that was the most Natalie could say. Everything else in her diary is a violent duel with Nechayev.

Remember, this was Nechayev's second sojourn abroad. The young man announced himself to the émigrés as leader and plenipotentiary of a widespread clandestine organization in Russia. His attitude toward Bakunin had been submissive and full of the reverence a disciple owes his master, but this time there was a touch of indulgent superiority, not to say scorn. Nechayev's version of the murder of the student Ivanov, which was accepted as pure truth by the uninformed émigré circles, was based on the idea that it was an inevitable act of revolutionary terror carried out against an agent provocateur. And that is not all. Nechayev also brought off one of the masterpieces of his great talent for deception or mythomania: his claim that he had been lucky enough to find refuge abroad after a dramatic flight from the Peter and Paul fortress. It is not so surprising, then, that a hero's halo was set on his head. The glint of this halo blinded Natalie to some degree.

But not very much and not very long. Nechayev laid a systematic, premeditated, and obstinate siege; he went so far as to woo her and may even have proposed (an unusual step for a voluntary revolutionary ascetic!). Step by step he reeled in his line, hoping to land his catch. The line was to draw Natalie into "organizational work," to persuade her to become one of "us" in the name of the revolution against "parasitic life," against the "sterile and antiquated traditions in which she grew up." The catch, of course, was Herzen's money and the daughter's agreement to let her name appear as the editor of the new *Kolokol*, while it was actually edited by Nechayev.

Natalie quickly roused herself from indecision. After all, Nechayev "was preaching the most terrible hypocrisy, with his repeated assertions that 'the end justifies the means.'" After all, that is "pure Jesuitism!" Nechayev calmly agreed: "Yes, of course it is. . . . The Jesuits were most intelligent and ingenious people. There has never existed another society like theirs. One should just take all their rules from beginning to end and act according to them—changing the aim, of course." Herzen's daughter was surprised and frightened by this dec-laration and wondered how Ogarev could let himself be identified with a system that allowed "eavesdropping, opening other people's letters, lying." She asked Ogarev directly and learned from his answer that "there are times when it is necessary to lie."

Nechayev initiated her into other secrets of those special times. Everything, literally everything, must be judged from the point of view of its usefulness to the cause. Whoever is not with us is against us. Confidence in our friends, deception and destruction for our ene-mies. What about the mischief and spying? Words, just words: the product of sentimental superstition. Ordinary human sentiments, fam-ily affections, principles of honesty and rectitude? Fetters of conven-tion, good only for the wastebasket. Natalie became increasingly convinced that she could have nothing in common with these "re-pugnant methods." "They had shown me a marvelously constructed machine, given me the handle, and asked me to help them turn it, saying that it would produce cheap bread or flour for the people, but after some time I found that they had tricked me, and that I was helping to manufacture a kind of poisonous paste which caused suf-fering to the friendly, the indifferent, and the hostile alike."

The diary extract does not make it unequivocally clear whether Herzen's daughter consented, willingly or not, to the continuation of *Kolokol* in its new form with the old title, or whether instead she did not have the necessary legal rights to make a formal protest. In any case she rejected the proposal to put her name to *Kolokol* without a moment's hesitation. In the end she made a total break with Ne-chayev. Natalie locked herself in her house, refused to see him, and would not receive his emissary. Ogarev hurried round, seriously con-cerned about Natalie, because he knew what Nechayev was capable of in an access of rage. He obtained the rest of the funds for the magazine and signed a receipt for the money. "Poor Ogarev," the author of the diary sighs. Then, in the final lines of the published fragment, she asks the ultimate question about Nechayev: "Is he a fanatic or an unscrupulous crook? Was he sincere when he tried to convince people of the necessity for his Polish-Jesuitic system of deceit and mystifi-cation, or are they all of them the ignoble instruments of the Russian Government?"

Two years later, in a letter to Masha Reichel, Natalie Herzen warned her: "Be very cautious with all these Russians who have recently arrived. . . . A new type of man *à la* Nechayev is forming among them, a kind of revolutionary Jesuit, who is ready for every vileness in order to achieve his goal, *i.e.,* the revolution in Russia."

Nechayev is so associated in my imagination with Peter Verkhovensky in *The Devils* that it is hard to make out the actual historical personage behind the literary figure. Dostoevsky himself wrote: "I do not know Nechayev, or Ivanov, or the circumstances of this murder. Even if I did, I would not make use of the knowledge. I take only the complete act. What I imagine may be totally different from what actually happened, and my Peter Verkhovensky may not resemble Nechayev at all; yet I believe that my imagination has created the person, the type, that matches the crime."

Verkhovensky is a cross between satanic charlatan and sordid little intriguer: deep down, there is ultimately not a trace in him of the "ideality," however abstract and pathologically obsessive, that devours, for example, Shigalyov (it is significant that Shigalyov, at the moment of action, draws back from the ambush laid for Shatov-Ivanov). Verkhovensky is absorbed exclusively by the grand devilish game. If Natalie Herzen's question regarded him, there would be no doubt whatsoever that "energy, malice, and cruelty" were the components of that perfect incarnation of the "unscrupulous villain." In any case, here it is fanaticism that follows in the wake of villainy and not vice versa. This is quite clear when after "our meeting" Verkhovensky explains the philosophy of "Shigalyovism" to Stavrogin. Stavrogin says, "So then you are not a socialist at all, but a man with enormous political ambition?" And Verkhovensky replies, "I am a rogue and not a socialist. . . . I am just a villain."

Nechayev was surely different in many respects. There is no reason to doubt the evidence Venturi cites. Aleksandra Zasulich, for example, considered *The Devils* "a stupid caricature of Nechayev and generally of all of us"; she remembered Nechayev as a "simple Russian boy, looking like a worker, a bit unsure of himself in a city. He did not give himself airs at all, he liked to joke and had a hearty laugh." So what? It is not the external appearance, what memory carries away from rather fleeting contact, that matters, but the type: that "new type of man *à la* Nechayev" remarked by Natalie Herzen, that new type of criminal created by Dostoevsky in connection with the murder of Ivanov. There is no denying that the behavior of the historic Nechayev, from the moment of his arrest and trial in 1872 until his death in the Peter and Paul fortress ten years later, gave the fanatic a lugubrious dignity. So it is legitimate at most to grant that, as long as Nechayev was free, unlike Verkhovensky, it was the villainy that followed in the wake of fanaticism.

And ultimately that was clear to Bakunin, the coauthor with Nechayev of the *Catechism of the Revolutionary*, in which the model revolutionary is asked to break with the "ethics of this world," to behave in accordance with a single principle: "everything that allows the triumph of the revolution is moral, and everything that stands in its way is immoral." According to Venturi, Bakunin long saw the shadow of his own ideas in Nechayev but froze in horror and fear when that shadow suddenly appeared before him in flesh and blood. When the truth came out about the murder of Ivanov, when the network of conspirators "in their groups of five" was revealed as almost totally invented by Nechayev, Bakunin decided to excommunicate him at least partially. He defended Nechayev as "one of those fanatics who doubt nothing and fear nothing," but he also called him a "very dangerous fanatic," led by his fanaticism "to turn into a total Jesuit." The reason is that Nechayev "gradually became convinced that the only way to create a serious and indestructible society is to ground it in Machiavelli's politics and fully embrace the system of the Jesuits: only violence for the body, only lies for the soul. Truth, mutual trust, real and lasting solidarity exist only between a dozen people who form the society's sanctum sanctorum. All the rest are to serve as blind instruments, as soulless material in the hands of this dozen who have reached an agreement among themselves. It is permissible—indeed, it is a duty—to mislead them, compromise them and, if necessary, have them perish." This is what Bakunin said about Nechayev's program. In *The Devils*, after Shigalyov's speech, during "our meeting," there is a discussion of the theoretics promulgated by Verkhovensky to cut off "one hundred million heads" and "leap over the trench."

Natalie Herzen's intuition was right in warning against Nechayevism as she did, and Dostoevsky was justified in saying that, while he made no effort to depict the actual Nechayev in his fictional Verkhovensky, he had looked deep into the killer of Ivanov. Albert Camus devotes a few pages to Nechayev in *The Rebel.* He quotes Nechayev's remark that henceforth politics will be religion and religion politics and sees in him a cruel monk of revolution who dreams of founding an order of assassins for the glory and the ultimate triumph of the adored divinity. Camus also makes two extremely penetrating observations. Thanks to Nechayev, for the first time revolution is explicitly separated from love and friendship and itself becomes more important than the people it wants to save. Today's masters of revolution are descended in a direct line from Nechayev.

Soon after 1917 the Bolsheviks tried to make him their true precursor, but then an embarrassed silence followed, as if a poker player had needlessly showed his cards too soon. So many bonds of kinship and so much effort to appropriate his heritage! Before 1917, the cruel monk of revolution as precursor of the professional revolutionary; and later, an order of assassins for the glory of the revolution as the model of a party elite; a consolidated group of ten chosen people as the embryo of the Politburo; the murder of Ivanov as the prototype of the Moscow trials; the theory of cutting off one hundred million heads and leaping the trench (in the uncut version of Dostoevsky's novel) as a prefiguration of the purges and the bloodshed of collectivization. What comes to mind when reading of revolution explicitly separate from love and friendship, of revolution itself being more important than the people it wants to save, is Natalie Herzen's seemingly naive but actually prophetic and intelligent comment about the marvelously constructed machine that, instead of producing cheap bread for the people, manufactures a paste to poison everyone. This machine is our day's *La Chose,* the name Sartre gave to the Soviet system.

It may be no exaggeration to see a mysterious sign of history in the fact that the year of Herzen's death and the peak of Nechayev's success was the same year as Lenin's birth. Today the new Russian revolutionaries are facing an examination of their consciences and their traditions that is far more complicated and intricate than people think and they themselves suppose. Dubbing Jesus "the first revolutionary agitator" brought Nechayev one advantage: total revolutionary Jesuitry. That was the start of an age that still continues (not just in Russia), an age that legitimizes itself openly or secretly with the slogan Dostoevsky coined for it: "If God does not exist, then everything is permissible." Moral law can be substituted for God, for those who do not believe in Him.

1 9 7 1

Stockholm, March 13 [A disappointed communist]

He is in his fifties and has been a communist since early youth. We rambled for a good three hours around a deserted Stockholm, and at ten we dropped into an empty café near my hotel. Conversation? No, I listened almost in silence. Did he deliver a monologue? Not exactly that. More than a monologue, it was a kind of raving jumble, with the laws of chronology suspended by his burning need to tell all and to tell it at once. It reminded me of the beginning of Camus' story "The Renegade," which, of course, I did not remember exactly. (Noted later: "What a jumble! What a jumble! I must tidy up my mind. Since they cut out my tongue, another tongue, it seems, has been wagging somewhere in my skull, something has been talking, or someone, that suddenly falls silent and then it all begins again—oh, I hear too many things I never utter, what a jumble, and if I open my mouth it's like pebbles rattling together.")

Jails in Poland before the war, work in the party, internment in Bereza, the war, Russia, the labor camps, service in the Red Army,

Albert Camus, "The Renegade," in *Exile and the Kingdom*, Hamish Hamilton, 1958, tr. Justin O'Brien.

the camps again, return to Poland, a sense of defeat, "no one whose hand I could shake, no one to whom I could tell the truth," flight to the West, back to Poland, and now this departure: "what am I doing here living on the charity of the King of Sweden, me a communist? I don't care to live, I have lost the taste for living." I had been told that he was capable of sitting motionless for days on end, staring at the wall. He was one of those bit-part players who make their appearance on the stage of "history freed from its chains," as Jerzy Stempowski liked to put it. There is a character who makes a fleeting appearance in *Doctor Zhivago*, the cattle healer Kubarikha, and rants deliriously about "historic" events. In an essay on Pasternak, Nicola Chiaromonte rightly notes that this turmoil in a cloud of dust is sometimes the only authentic thing we know about the "quickened tempo of history."

Naples, April 8 [Thomas Mann and the struscio in Naples]

The *struscio* is a Spanish custom that has been preserved and is strictly observed in Naples. It comes from the verb *strusciare*, "to drag the feet." The city's main street, the former Via Toledo, is closed to wheeled traffic for three hours at sundown on Maundy Thursday. Then you can walk where you like, even down the middle of the street, *strusciando*, that is to say, dragging your feet. This custom makes it possible calmly to visit the churches where on Maundy Thursday symbolic sepulchers of the Lord are arranged and decorated with white flowers and lighted candles.

I was late for this year's *struscio*: the first notes of a children's choir singing *"Signore sei tu il mio pastore"* were just coming from the city's largest church, and the lambs being led down Via Toledo were put to flight by the onslaught of drivers who had lost patience during the long wait and were making an infernal row with their horns. What was there to do? Seek refuge in a movie house. *Death in Venice* was showing nearby.

Except for the splendid *Buddenbrooks*, I never felt the special veneration for Thomas Mann that made my classmates at school and university read *The Magic Mountain* with red ears and eyes clouded with welling tears. Mine was an instinctive reserve, but it was confirmed by further reading at a later age. I was repelled by that particular air of Mann's as mandarin of things aesthetic, "high priest of art," not a trace of which can be found in writers who are truly great and wise. What Silone said about the conversation he had with Mann when he was an émigré in Switzerland might seem trivial, but it is extremely significant. They wondered if there was a touchstone for assessing different political systems. Silone: "Without a doubt: just find out what place is allotted to the opposition." Mann: "No, a more exalted test is the place allotted to art and artists." Silone remarked that "the reason for Mann's indulgent or tolerant attitude towards Soviet totalitarianism was that the astronomical number of Goethe's works published in the USSR kept him from seeing the shadow of the labor camps. He reasoned like a member of an elite caste." It is no surprise that there has been, and still is, no end of "Mannists" in the "intellectual circles" of the West and the East.

The mandarin of things aesthetic found his ideal cinematographic translator in Luchine Visconti. It is not very meaningful to say that the Technicolor *Death in Venice* is kitsch; after all, many illustrious works of literature have come to a bad end in the hands of the Tenth Muse. The point is that Visconti has faithfully brought out, polished, and burnished all the kitsch that hitherto passed unnoticed in Mann's rather nice-looking tale. This once excellent director, who deserves a whipping for the nonchalance with which he "grafted" Stavrogin's confession onto his recent melodrama about the Krupp family, is now preparing his swan song, Proust's *Recherche*.

May 5 [Naples—the plague]

There is a painting in the Naples historical museum in the Charterhouse of San Martino, *Episodes of the Plague of May 1656 in Largo Marcatello*, the work of Micco Spadaro (Domenico Gargiulo). He was not a remarkable painter, to tell the truth, but he was sensitive and, most important, an eyewitness to the 1656 plague in Naples. Many good things can be said about the precision and the concise concreteness of the written chronicles, but they cannot compete with visual evidence in rendering that concentrated and at the same time elusive atmosphere of dread, the nightmarish tone that escapes words or, even more often, is captured in words only to give off a hollow echo. So it is worth keeping sight of Spadaro's picture whenever reading the annals and histories of a time when Naples was dying.

In Spadaro's picture Largo Marcatello, the modern Piazza Dante, looks like an enormous dried-up well. The painter achieved this effect by setting the city's domes, buildings, and towers high against the sky beyond the bare walls of the square. The walls of the square are truly bare, with hardly a building in sight, and this heightens the sense of being surrounded on all sides. From a distance the picture bears a striking resemblance to the illustrations of the inferno in old editions of Dante. Bodies churning around a dark abyss, little bodies, insignificant, tormented, and damned: a dark net groaning with its freight of death.

Closer approach to the picture brings the actual subject back to mind: episodes of the plague in Naples in May 1656 seen in different parts of the city and then brought together in the single Largo Marcatello scene. Easy as it is to single out each episode and look at it separately, what keeps coming back is a vision of a pulpy mass that absorbs and suffocates, and this is certainly what most concerned the artist. If you take a long look at the picture, a moment comes when it is as if a trapdoor had suddenly sprung open and you touch the bottom of a world built on the desperate nothingness of life. There are corpses heaped against the walls, on wagons, on abandoned stretchers, on the bare earth. Among them are human ghosts, only half alive themselves, dragging others who have just died by their arms or legs. One man has a handkerchief tied over his nose and mouth as he carries a small coffin. Another man is on his knees reaching up his arms and transfixed in a cry not of supplication but of malediction. Two bodies are clasped in a last embrace. A child is suckling at the breast of a dead woman. And again, without so much as turning your head, there is that formless mass, whose sole expression is the absence of any expression at all. Unfettered by the dictates of reality, Orcagna painted his *Triumph of Death* differently. His was a warning; this is a sentence.

The heart of the picture is in the exact center of Largo Marcatello. I do not know what Spadaro looked like, but I could swear he depicted himself in the figure of the young man in dark clothes with eyes blinded as if worn away by tears. He is holding a tipped pitcher, and next to him a man is bending over to drink water from the pitcher. It is a symbolic epitome of thirst, but thirst for what?

The chronicles vary in regard to the number of people who died of the plague, between three and four hundred thousand out of about half a million inhabitants of what was then one of the largest cities in Europe. It is commonly believed that the cause of the epidemic was "poisonous powders" sown by "enemies of Naples," and not necessarily foreigners, at that. Guilty parties were seen everywhere: if someone happened to throw garbage into the street or brush dust off his clothes, that was sufficient for the mob mercilessly to lynch the "sower." To tell the truth, the chronicles give a picture of two plagues: one real and the other psychological. The more ineffectual the struggle against the former was, the more dreadful the devastations of the latter became. Services were celebrated in the churches, there were increasing numbers of supplicants in procession, and patrols of the viceroy's guards rattled their swords night and day, but nothing could stop the slow death of human and divine law. "Since they were to die in any case," one chronicler noted, "they leapt at each other's throats."

I happened on the story of a twenty-five-year-old ragman, Agostino Lanzuolo, in the annals of a religious confraternity. On May 29 guards arrested him as one of a "fierce mob" that had torn to pieces an old peddler woman suspected of *seminazione delle polveri velenose*. The next morning he was taken to Market Square, where the gallows stood. He refused confession, he would not kneel at the altar, and he pushed aside the crucifix that the confraternity's chaplain held out to him. His behavior was haughty, he hurried the hangman, and over and over again with "devilish obstinacy" he said: *"Voglio morire, andiamo presto alla morte."* The chaplain asked that the execution be delayed and ran to get help from other members of his confraternity. Four of them came. They pleaded with him, prayed for him, and wept; they even lit a fire "to make the torments of hell more vivid to him," but to no effect. As evening approached and the execution could be delayed no longer, an official gave the signal. Agostino laughed out loud, boldly climbed the steps to the gallows, and as soon as his hands were untied, he grabbed the noose and "put it around his neck himself." Suddenly something happened that the friars' account calls "a visible intervention of Heaven": Agostino looked around the silent crowd in Market

Square and stared with such concentration and "such suffering in his blanched face" that everyone around him froze. And he asked for confession. Time was running out, so he confessed rapidly, "weeping abundantly, however, and beating his breast numerous times." People in the crowd also wept and beat their breasts, and as soon as the man was hanged, they hailed him with cries of *"Gaudio universale."*

It is curious that the account in the annals of the confraternity ends with this sentence: "And it was as if the city itself were splayed on the cross, thirsting even more for truth than for deliverance from the pestilence, and a vessel with water was raised to its hard parched lips."

May 11 [Gogol in Rome]

A well-documented book about Solzhenitsyn by Giovanni Grazzini has just appeared in Italy. It was reviewed today by Eugenio Montale.

The distinguished poet asked himself if Solzhenitsyn was right not to use the Nobel prize as an escape hatch out of Russia. And Montale's answer was yes: "I do not see the stuff of the émigré and great cosmopolite in Solzhenitsyn. I cannot imagine him at a writing table in Via Sistina." The allusion, of course, is to the house at 126 Via Sistina (the former Strada Felice). There is a large plaque at the height of the first floor, with a low-relief bust above and a laurel crown below, and an inscription in Russian: "Nikolai Vasilevich Gogol lived here in the years 1838–1842. Here he wrote *Dead Souls*."

It really was a Strada Felice, a happy street, for Gogol. Volumes have been written about how well he felt in Rome, the state of constant euphoria in which he lived, how every day he found something new and admirable during his Roman strolls, how much he loved the Italians and "that particular silvery reflection that often appears in the sky and clouds," with what delight he ate in the old hostelries of the Hare and Falcon, and how he spent hours on end at the Caffè Greco (he wrote notes to the painter Ivanov, who was in Rome at the time and with whom he struck up a friendship, and he would address them in Italian: *"Al Signor Alessandro Ivanov, Pittore russo celeberrimo, Roma, Via Condotti, Caffè Greco"*). Nor are the traces of that happy period less numerous in his letters. "If there exists a country in the world in which suffering, sorrow, death and one's own impotence are forgotten, that place is Rome: what would become of me elsewhere?" "Italy is mine! No one can take it away from me. I was born here. Russia, St. Petersburg, snow, scoundrels, teaching, the theater: that was all a dream. I woke up anew in my homeland." "It is not possible for beautiful souls to live in Russia, only pigs can keep their heads above water there." "I am gay. My soul is luminous. I am working and I try with all my strength to bring my book speedily to an end. Life, life, a little bit more of life!" Every afternoon, in the shade of drawn shutters, Pavel Annenkov took Gogol's dictation and made a clean copy of a new chapter of *Dead Souls*, and when he was unable or unwilling to hide his admiration, he exclaimed: "I consider this chapter a work of genius, Nikolai Vasilevich!" Then Gogol would answer in a soft, barely perceptible little voice: "Believe me, Pavel Vasilevich, the others are just as good." And immediately afterward, excited and beaming, he would drag his copyist out for a walk to quiet the proud beating of his heart.

And yet? And yet there was another Gogol as well, described in the following words by Daria (Olsufeva) Borghese in her book *Gogol a Roma*: "Sleeplessness had already begun to torture him then. He often spent the entire night sitting on a small sofa afraid of fainting or, worse yet, of experiencing the dreadful sensation of lethargy that occasionally overwhelmed him. At dawn he pulled back the top sheet on the bed so that Nanna, the Cellis' maid, would not notice the strange manner in which Signor Niccolò would pass his nights."

Signor Niccolò!

Marina del Cantone, July 5
[Zulik, or the soul of animals]

Our little dog licked and barked me awake very early this morning. Someone abandoned him in our courtyard a few weeks ago; he was emaciated, small as a ball of yarn, all full of lice and covered with sores. A week later he had already gripped onto life with all the fierceness of his half-breed hunting blood.

I fed him and took him to the rocks. The rising sun warmed the surface of the rocks, and he settled himself comfortably in one of the hollows. In the distance, in the direction of Capri, the morning mist was still peeling away, but in the inlet of Cantone the sea, smooth and clean as a sheet of tinfoil, washed the shingle beach with a regular silent movement. The tardy night fishermen were hauling their nets off the boats, shaking out more algae and branches than fish. The sea here has been polluted for years, and the destruction is being completed by illegal fishers who use homemade bombs and mines. An orchid of smoke spouted from the little cloister on the peak of San Costanzo.

He had fallen asleep stretched out on the rock with his head between his paws, but he soon rolled over on his back. He was dreaming something and waving his paws in the air, as if in a gesture of self-defense, and every now and then he emitted a sound that was neither a cough nor a bark. There was a time when the dreams of animals were considered decisive proof that they had souls, but the matter was neither simple nor unchallenged. In the late nineteenth century a Lord Russell (perhaps the philosopher's father) went to see the Pope to induce him to try to mitigate the cruelty of Italians to animals. The heir to the tradition of Saint Francis seems to have replied that "animals do not have souls." And it was then that the argument about the dreams of animals was advanced. The outcome can be judged by anyone who has seen dead dogs by the dozen on Italian roads or heard about the beastly cat hunts in Trastevere and the incredible massacre of birds on the first day of hunting season in Italy. Two recent news items for people who doubt that animals have souls: Some savage shot an arrow at a stork in Vienna's Prater, and for several days the stricken bird went back and forth, leadenly flapping its weakened wings, to bring food to its little ones in the nest. And in Marsa Matruh, Syria, a Bedouin's horse committed suicide after its master's death. During the Bedouin's illness the horse stood guard by his tent and refused to eat. And as soon as the burial was over, the horse rushed to the top of a steep hill and jumped into the ravine. Dreams are dreams, but suicide!

During the war, in the Iraqi desert, a newborn puppy was brought into the zone where our battery was lodged, probably a waif from the nearby Arab village. We did not know how to feed it, and then I had the idea of poking a hole in a condom, turning it into a nursing bottle, and filling it with diluted condensed milk. And once the puppy was weaned and on its way to conscious life, I was the one who gave him the name of Zulik. He was a delightful little dog, our battery mascot, and all the soldiers pampered him. In Egypt we were forbidden to take him with us on the ship that was going to Italy: he ran up and down the pier frantically as we sailed out of the port. A couple of months later he turned up in the front line of our battery at Monte Cassino. I was assigned to Rome after the Italian campaign; from then on Zulik's one father was Sergeant P, who seems to have taken him back to Poland in the end. I kept only two photographs as memorials of the war: Zulik on the hood of a jeep and General Sosnowski decorating me in Ancona. I lost both of them in some tavern brawl: there was a lot of drinking in Rome in those days.

Naples, August 8 [Bubko the crook]

I do not know whence Bubko suddenly appeared after thirty years or more. There is a trick to what opens the rusty valves of memory: what forced this valve may have been the strong pressure of reading *Sleep Tight, Dear Comrade* [a novel about the Moscow underworld].

In the summer of 1940 we were rotting in a small cell of the Grodno prison waiting only to be deported. There were not many of us (considering how crowded the prisons were on the other side of the Bug River at the time), and we knew so much about each other we could have burst, so constantly had we bored each other with the same chatter about our interrogation and our former life. So for hours at a time we would sit on our bunks, motionless and silent, and stare at the patch of blue outside the bars.

Late one afternoon the cell door opened and a new companion was thrown in. The stock phrase "like a caged animal" fitted him like a glove. He was well built and tall despite a slight stoop, and his wicked predatory eyes were mere slits in his enormous shaven head. He rampaged up and down the narrow aisle between the bunks, hurled his whole body against the door and the wall under the window, and howled with rage as he kicked the toilet bowl. He finally calmed down and threw himself on the bunk where we had made room for him, but he tossed often during the night and bellowed even in his sleep.

The next day he greedily wolfed his chunk of bread and washed it down with hot water, and then he spoke up. His name was Bubko, he was (and he stressed it proudly) a star of the Grodno underworld, and at various times he had done ten years in prison in prewar Poland. He might have done time again under the Russkies, but now there was the firing squad for thieves as well. He had gone to Bialystok on a job the week before, returned home earlier than expected, and found his mistress in bed with a lieutenant in the NKVD. He slaughtered the lieutenant, beat up the woman, and then hightailed it to the Bug River with the intention of escaping to Warsaw. They tripped him up right at the border. There was no way to deny it, they had heaps of evidence, and he signed everything at the first inquest. They seemed to have the firing squad every Saturday late at night. And today was Thursday.

That disclosure gave him relief; after mess at midday he burrowed into a corner of the cell and sat there dozing until evening roll call. That night he slept like a log. Friday he joined us in gazing into the blue beyond the bars, but every now and then he lowered his eyes and looked us over carefully, me especially and my officer boots. That night he woke me up; we were sleeping next to each other. He raved deliriously in a chaotically galloping whisper, the gist being that the story of the faithless mistress was all an invention to throw those stupid Russians off the track, it was "as a Pole" that he had killed the lieutenant. There was also something about an "organization," and over and over again he said, "Tell them about it after the war." I did not challenge what he said: he simply needed help dying, someone to accept his nonsense unquestioningly as if it were true.

The key grated in the lock late Saturday night, and immediately a shout rang out: "The letter B!" Bubko immediately responded with his name and sprang from the bunk. I was the only one he said farewell to as he left the cell. He was calm, and something like a knowing smile crossed his cruel bloated face. The next minute we heard a roar from the corridor, snatches of curses, and the muffled sounds of a struggle.

Maisons-Laffitte, September 25 [Venice is a dream]

There is an exhibition of eighteenth-century Venetian painting at the Orangerie museum with the motto "To save Venice." It is an exquisitely arranged portrait of the city along several parallel lines. Canaletto and Guardi: the elegance of the architecture, the play of stone and water, form and nature; the elder Tiepolo: the frenzy of Carnival, faces that look like masks, and masks that look like faces, and the theater of Goldoni; the younger Tiepolo and Longhi: dress and gesture, but also the recurrent motif of costume as a mirror, on the borderline of derisive masquerade and rigid convention; Piranesi: putrefaction, mold, underground prisons, scaffolding with no one on it and vaults supporting nothing.

What is Venice? Ask a Venetian this question, and nine times out of ten, he will reply that it is *un miracolo, un prodigio.* For me, since the week I spent in Venice one winter, it is a dream rather than a miracle.

We arrived on a December evening. The fog was thick; the steamer from the station to the Accademia moved as slowly as a turtle, constantly sounding its horn and anxiously raking its beacon over the canal. It was only thanks to a passerby with a powerful flashlight that we managed to get from the Accademia to our hotel. The hotel on the Zattere, the house where Ruskin wintered in 1849 writing or drafting *The Stones of Venice*, was almost empty. The fog did not lessen, and the weather reports were that it was going to last quite a while. By day we ventured out for short walks, groping blindly through a pudding of white. In the evenings we visited the bibliophile T., who lived next door to the hotel and whose principal object of interest and research at the time was Frederick Rolfe (Baron Corvo), who had fallen in love with Venice and its young gondoliers and died in some Venetian garret in indescribable squalor as he worked on the manuscript of *The Desire and Pursuit of the Whole*. At night the silence was occasionally broken by the horns of ships going up the Giudecca canal. Yes, it was a dream, exciting and ephemeral, with a premonition of something dazzling to come which (as in a dream) cannot be fully experienced but which certainly exists: the desire and pursuit. At midday the banks of fog happened to thin for a moment, and we caught sight of fragments of the city as if it were a theater set glimpsed through the slit of a curtain carelessly drawn aside. The morning of our departure, the weather unexpectedly turned fine, and Venice finally appeared whole and clear in a bright gilt-greenish aura. There was a touch of strange regret in this awakening from the dream of Venice.

If Venice is not saved (which is something quite likely in Italy), Europe will fall ill from "psychological poisoning," which is how psychiatrists describe the condition of people who do not suffer from insomnia but have lost the ability to dream.

Naples, October 25 [Gorky's untimely considerations]

When I was gathering material to write a political "mystery story" about the "seven deaths of Maxim Gorky," I obviously could not help but happen on evidence of the bitter conflict between Gorky and Lenin right after the revolution. But those were minutiae, mere scraps, in comparison with a book recently published in Russian in Paris. The title is *Nesvoevremennye mysli* ("*Untimely Considerations*"), and the book is a complete collection of the articles Gorky published in the St. Petersburg paper, *Novaja Zizn*, which he edited from 1917 to 1918. In the period in which Gorky would improvise his articles on the spur of the moment, his considerations were "untimely" in the sense that they could not influence the course of events. Of course they must have irritated Lenin the way flies bother a lion, and hence *Novaja Zizn*, after two warning suspensions, was finally shut down on July 16, 1918, at the personal order of the leader. Ultimately it was much ado about nothing, all the more so that Gorky took a safer line in the twenties, calmed down and saw reason, and allotted Lenin no mean place in the Russian pantheon, between Peter the Great and Leo Tolstoy. Another Tolstoy, Alexei, subsequently dismissed his great ancestor and took his courtier pen in hand to reserve the place next to Peter the Great for Stalin alone.

Those thoughts, "untimely" in the tumult of revolution, have singular resonance today. I must take note of some of them *pro memoria*. "Lenin, Trotsky, and their acolytes are already infected with the putrid poison of power, witness their shameful attitude towards freedom of speech." "Blind fanatics and adventurers bereft of conscience are rushing at breakneck speed along the would-be road to social revolution —actually it is the road to anarchy and the ruin of the proletariat and the revolution alike." Events should have opened the eyes of the proletariat "to the absolute impracticability of Lenin's promises, to the full extent of his lunacy, and to his Nechayev-Bakunin kind of anarchy." "The working class cannot fail to understand that Lenin is simply conducting a certain experiment on their flesh and their blood; he is trying to drive the revolutionary mood of the proletariat to its ultimate extremes and see what happens." "What is the difference between the attitude of Lenin to freedom of speech and that of such people as Stolypin and Plehve? Doesn't Leninist rule throw in prison anyone who thinks differently, just like the rule of the Romanovs did?" "The rational exponents of democracy must decide if they wish to march alongside conspirators and anarchists of the Nechayev type."

Lenin used Nechayev's methods to introduce the socialist system in Russia: "full steam through the mire." Lenin, Trotsky, and all the others evidently shared Nechayev's conviction that "the easiest way to seduce a Russian is to give him the right to act dishonorably." "Lenin is undoubtedly a man of exceptional strength, a gifted man, with all the attributes of a real 'leader' at his disposal, including a complete lack of any moral sense . . . and a pitiless, totally lordly attitude to the life of the masses." "Nothing bothers Lenin, a slave to dogma, nor his cronies, his slaves. . . . For him the working class is what ore is to the metal worker. Is it possible with conditions as they are to fuse a socialist state from this ore? Probably not, but why not try anyway? What does Lenin risk if the experiment fails? He works like a chemist in a laboratory, the difference being that the chemist works on lifeless matter, while Lenin is works on living matter. Alert workers who follow Lenin must understand that a pitiless experiment is being carried out on the Russian working class, and it will annihilate the best forces of the workers and long delay the normal evolution of the Russian revolution." "No, in this outburst of zoological instincts I do not see any clearly expressed elements of social revolution. This is a typically Russian uprising without socialists and without any socialist psychology."

What I found particularly surprising was Gorky's obsessive refrain about "Nechayevism." About a year ago I wrote apropos of an extract from the diary of Natalie Herzen: "It may be no exaggeration to see a mysterious sign of history in the fact that the year of Herzen's death and the peak of Nechayev's success was the same year as Lenin's birth." I was not yet familiar with the *Untimely Considerations*.

November 10 [Bukharin in Paris]

In his memoirs Jozef Berger tells something he heard in late 1937, when he was in the Solovki labor camp in Siberia, from Aleksander Aichenvald, one of Bukharin's acolytes. Shortly before his trial, Nikolai Bukharin was interrogated face-to-face with Aichenvald for five hours, after which the two men were allowed to say their farewells without witnesses. At the time Bukharin was writing the last book of his life in his prison cell. "What is it about?" his disciple asked. "About the nature of man," the master replied. He went on to say that "we should stop thinking about ideology, about economics, and about politics; we should devote all our strength to understanding the meaning and purpose of life." Aichenvald could not believe his ears.

If he had known the subject of the conversations Bukharin had with the Menshevik Boris Nikolaevsky outside Russia in 1936, he would not have been so surprised by the idea of the one-time "darling of Ilyich and the party" behind bars engaged in spiritual exercises so clearly incompatible with Marxism. A selection of Nikolaevsky's writings, *Power and the Soviet Elite*, was published some years ago in America. The book hinges on the famous "Letter of an Old Bolshevik," formerly attributed to Bukharin but actually written by Nikolaevsky on the basis of his conversations with Bukharin. (I remember that it was the first thing I read after graduating from high school in Kielce, when I was recovering from my flirtation with communism.) But today Nikolaevsky's direct account of those conversations seems much more interesting than the letter.

Bukharin went to Paris in February 1936 at the head of a delegation that was to negotiate the purchase of the Marx and Engels archives, which Nikolaevsky had taken from Berlin at the request of the German social democrats. Negotiations went on for two months and got nowhere despite a handsome offer from Moscow. But the "legal"—nay, "official"—cover offered by the proposed transaction made it possible for Bukharin and Nikolaevsky often to meet privately. It is likely that Nikolaevsky took notes after every meeting.

Bukharin was tired, exhausted; he longed for a rest. It was suggested that he become an émigré and found an opposition paper. "I couldn't live outside Russia. All of us have become used to the strain of life in Russia," he answered. One day, half serious and half facetious, he suggested they both go to see Trotsky in Oslo: "We have had our clashes, but I will never cease to admire him and respect him." Bukharin avoided direct comment about the situation in the USSR, either because he did not trust his interlocutor one hundred per cent or because (and this is Nikolaevsky's hypothesis) he feared the conclusions he would inevitably have been forced to reach by too open an exchange of ideas.

Did he know, or even suspect, what was in store for him? There would seem to be evidence that he did, since he described his relations with Stalin as "exceptionally bad." There would seem to be evidence that he did not, since he spoke of the new Soviet constitution with unfeigned euphoria: "I wrote the whole thing with this very pen. Yes, the whole thing, only Radek helped out a bit. I came to Paris because I had finished the job. They are printing the text now. From now on there will be more room for the people, they can no longer be ignored." In any case, euphoric or not, he kept coming back obsessively to two points: the need to found a second party and the extreme urgency of purifying the work of the revolution through "proletarian humanism."

Without a second party, how can the Soviet regime distinguish itself from Naziism? It does not have to be a party contrary to the new order: suffice that it advocate "change and reform." It might be drawn from the intelligentsia so as not to disrupt the unity of the working class. As to "proletarian humanism," Bukharin himself had seen sufficient horrors during forced collectivization—horrors that could not even be compared to the pitiless but ineluctable cruelty of civil war—to look to the future with the utmost concern. The very psyche of the communists had been contaminated and mutilated: instead of going mad, after the experience of collectivization, they became professional bureaucrats, partisans of terror as the natural method of government, slaves of obedience to any order from above, of obedience considered as the supreme virtue. "They are no longer humans, they are gears in a terrible machine." That is where the most serious danger is hidden, that is why the coming of "proletarian humanism" is so important and imperative to prevent the Soviet Union from turning into a "a regime with an iron boot."

He was so fervent, and constantly repeated the same things with such desperate obstinacy, that Nikolaevsky interrupted him at one point: "Nikolai Ivanovich, what you are suggesting is a return to the Ten Commandments. That's not new." Bukharin thought about it: "Do you believe that Moses' commandments are outdated and anachronistic?" Nikolaevsky: "I am not saying they are outdated and anachronistic. All I am saying is that they have existed for five thousand years. Are we going to discover that the Ten Commandments are a new truth? Is that the point we have reached?" Bukharin made no answer. It was only in a Moscow prison cell that Aichenvald finally heard the answer, between the lines of Bukharin's confession on the threshold of his last agony.

People who remember the "Letter of an Old Bolshevik" from before the war should consider it a postscript. It is all the more valuable because we can never read Bukharin's last book on the "nature of man": the Soviet Union may buy the archives of the fathers of Marxism, of course, but it neither sells nor opens the archives of its faithless and harshly punished children.

Rome, December 2 [Ignazio Silone]

Silone has aged, it is an effort to get up from his chair, and there is enormous fatigue in his face. But his mind is clear and sharp; more than that, it is as if it had been enriched by the slow distillation of his thought. Almost forty years separate *Fontamara* from the *Adventure of a Poor Christian*: a long road through time and experience, yet barely perceptible because of the care with which he has carved out what *conta davvero,* what "really counts." It is like stone that is sculpted day by day by a stream of running water and indifferent to the gurgle of novelty, fashion, ideological rhetoric, political demagogy, and intellectual coquetry that the stream carries away. "I identify myself in what Hofmannsthal says: writers are people for whom writing comes harder than for anyone else. . . . Were it not for the laws of the publishing market, I would write, polish, complete and correct the same book over and over again." And this is exactly what Silone does, despite the long list of titles "by the same author." The *cafoni* of Abruzzi under fascist rule in *Fontamara* would be perfectly at home with the language and way of thinking of the thirteenth-century

Abruzzi hermit Fra Pietro da Morrone, who for a few months was Pope Celestine V, in the *Adventure of a Poor Christian*. What Camus admired in Silone, and in Ortega y Gasset, was the capacity to be at the same time "both European and incredibly rooted in his native land." After breaking with the Church, Silone was *un povero cristiano;* after breaking with communism, he was *un povero socialista.* "That is it exactly: I am a Christian without a church and a socialist without a party." What does really count? An image of man in which "it is human souls that are immortal and not institutions, not kingdoms, not armies, not churches and not nations." Hence his sense of affinity with Simone Weil and the sudden gleam in his eye when he talks about her main precept: "We must always be ready to change sides, like justice, the eternal fugitive from the camp of the victors."

During our visit today, I was reminded that once, in a despondent moment, I had muttered some bitter words about my sorrows as an exile. He looked at me in near astonishment: "I was an exile in Switzerland for many years, now I am an exile in Italy." On that occasion too the conversation turned to the "eternal fugitive." Anyone who is deeply convinced that he is saying something important is not ashamed to say the same thing more than once. The secret is the gravity of the words, and what gives words their gravity is unceasing (religious?) vigilance.

Naples, December 13 [Stavrogin's suicide]

Last summer in Zurich I went to the exhibition of masterpieces from the Dresden Gallery. In front of Claude Lorraine's *Acis and Galatea* I could not for the life of me remember on what occasion it is mentioned in Dostoevsky. I kept asking my friends, and no one could remember. Was I imagining things, had I mixed things up? No. It is just that the chapter "At Tikhon's" with Stavrogin's confession is not included in most editions of *The Devils*, since Mikhail Katkov decided that *Russkij Vestnik* ["*The Russian Messenger*," where it was first serialized] should have every regard for its readers, whether they were genteel or not. I obtained that chapter a long time ago in a separate little volume, but I simply overlooked it when leafing through my volumes of Dostoevsky. After the story with the little girl, Stavrogin, who is in a shabby little German hotel, dreams of Claude's picture and identifies it with the vision of humankind's golden age. And just as he is awakening from that idyllic dream, Ivan the tsarevitch manqué sees "a tiny point." He associates it at once with the "tiny red spider" he saw on a geranium leaf in his Petersburg room that afternoon when the minutes seemed like hours, a stone's throw from the garret room where the eleven-year-old Matryosha hanged herself. The Golden Age and the little red spider: Dostoevsky did not disdain symbolic shortcuts in setting "cursed problems." But he has to be judged by the fierce and stubborn way he dug into those problems. He was a genius at it.

There are a host of interpretations of Stavrogin's suicide, all of which ultimately come down to his absolute irremediable solitude. Completely cut off, he poisons himself with his hatred of people and the world. "I never loved anyone and I do not know how to love." He has experimented on himself and on others to convince himself that there is no way out, or rather, that there are only "stupid" and illusory ways out. In the confession he gives Tikhon to read, there is a statement of what rankles every suicide: "I was so bored I could have hanged myself, and if I did not, it is because I still continued to hope, as I have done all my life." Hope? Kierkegaard would have said *that kind* of hope offers despair its most welcome nest. The sickness unto death (or the devil: the names do not matter) is the impossibility of making any breach in the wall other than scorn and hate. Kafka said that man is incapable of living without trust in something indestructible inside himself, although he is usually not conscious of this indestructible "nucleus": one form of this lack of consciousness is faith in God. But what if one consciously rejects both God and this indestructible "self"? The only card left to play is the card of solitude, pride. To laugh aloud in defiance so that everyone can hear. Tikhon understands him full well but commits an error. He warns Stavrogin that the world may respond to that laughter with laughter of its own. Stavrogin grows pale, and Tikhon realizes too late that he has played a risky game; now he knows for sure that Stavrogin will take his own life to *avoid* publishing his confession. "Damned psychologist!" Stavrogin shouts, and leaves the monastery cell without a backward glance.

What was torment for Stavrogin was the chief benefit of solitude for Simone Weil: "the possibility of supreme attention." Stavrogin used this possibility to twist a noose around his own neck because, unlike the author of *La Connaissance surnaturelle*, he was not acquainted with any knowledge other than "natural" knowledge, nor did he wish to be. Kirilov considered it his "duty" to bear "witness to disbelief" with his suicide: he died as the first man in the history of the world to deny the invention of a God; that is to say, ultimately he was accusing someone or something for his death. Stavrogin decided against public confession and, before hanging himself, he scrawled on a piece of paper: "Accuse no one; I alone!" I, that means alone. There is no other character in Dostoevsky's work who is led so consistently step by step to zero point. If an "I" exists, it is only a ceaseless confirmation of one's solitude; and if it is only this, then what is it in us that is indestructible? Stavrogin drew his own conclusions. Dostoevsky needed those conclusions so that his discussion of the existence of God could start from zero point.

December 22 [Chekhov's funeral]

On June 8, 1904, Chekhov and Olga Knipper arrived in Badenweiler after a brief stop in Berlin. Chekhov felt better, and so he wrote in letters to his sister and friends, warmly praising his new doctor, Dr. Schwoerer. He was planning a trip to Italy. Suddenly he was gripped by anxiety, and they had to change hotels at once. He wanted to have a balcony. He spent hours on end on the balcony watching the comings and goings in front of the post office across the way. Sometimes his wife took him out for a carriage ride through the neighboring woods. Late in June he had a three-day crisis. He suddenly improved on the afternoon of July 1. That night Chekhov woke up after midnight. He felt he was suffocating and asked for a doctor (something that had never happened before). When Dr. Schwoerer appeared, Chekhov looked at him and whispered: *"Tod?"* Ice was placed over his heart, and oxygen was sent for. "It's not worth the trouble, I will die before they bring the oxygen." He asked for a glass of champagne. He took a few sips and then fell back on the pillows, talking deliriously: "Has the sailor left?" Had the distant echo of the Russo-Japanese war perhaps intruded on his agitated thoughts during his death agony? He came back to himself and said in a very quiet voice: "I am dying," and in an even softer voice he told Dr. Schwoerer: *"Ich sterbe.''* He fell back on the pillows again. He died at dawn, and it was reported that at that moment a large moth circled the lamp, loudly beating its wings.

The corpse was placed in a zinc casket tagged "fresh oysters" and transported to Moscow by freight car. Another train arrived at the Moscow station at the same time, with the corpse of General Keller, who had been killed in the war. There was a bit of confusion, and some of the people who had come for Chekhov's funeral followed Keller's hearse and were surprised that a military band was accompanying the writer to the cemetery. When the misunderstanding was cleared up, it was impossible to keep from chuckling. Gorky reported that "there were no more than one hundred people behind Chekhov's casket. I still remember two Moscow lawyers with brand-new shoes and gaudy ties: they might have been on their way to a wedding. One was expanding on the intelligence of dogs, and the other was extolling the beauty of his dacha. A woman in a mauve dress and carrying a lace parasol kept turning to a little old man at her side and saying: 'He was so darling, so intelligent!' The old man gave a skeptical cough. It was a hot and dusty day. At the head of the procession a corpulent police officer advanced majestically on a fat white horse. It was all terribly vulgar, it offended the memory of that great and sensitive artist."

It was simply Chekhov's last story, "The Artist's Death and Funeral." Gorky played the role of the sworn enthusiast but poor and not very insightful reader of Chekhov.

1 9 7 2

Maisons-Laffitte, January 5 [The suicide of
Marina Tsvetaeva]

Doctor Zhivago has been criticized for its excessive use of coincidence,
of human destinies intersecting on a such a vast scene with a nonchalance that offends the "sense of reality." But often what strikes us as
merely a gratuitous play of the fortuitous and the accidental is actually
the secret language of a tragedy slowly and inexorably unfolding.

It is clear from Tsvetaeva's letters that when she was an émigrée
she longed to meet Pasternak. Altogether unexpectedly they met in
Paris in 1935. Tsvetaeva later called it a "non-meeting." Pasternak
was scared, his mind was elsewhere, and he did not even say good-
bye before boarding his flight to Moscow. "He just went out for cig-
arettes and disappeared." Before he disappeared, Tsvetaeva had time
to ask him what he thought about her idea of returning to Moscow
with her family. He replied evasively, neither encouraging nor dis-
couraging. Perhaps she did not understand that in those days even
this "non-answer" was an answer.

Tsvetaeva returned to Russia in 1939. We know nothing about

her last moments, I wrote in my journal. But we do know something, says J., referring to a conversation he had with Konstantin Paustovsky in Paris. After the outbreak of the Russo-German war, Tsvetaeva and her son were evacuated to the Tatar Republic, to the little town of Yelabuga on the Kuma River. Before leaving Moscow she needed some string to tie up her shabby suitcase and got it from Pasternak. She felt lost in Yelabuga. In vain she appealed for help or a job: her husband had disappeared into prison, her daughter was also behind bars, and she was in constant anxiety for her son. She might have found safety by moving to Kazan, where the majority of evacuated writers had been sent. Paustovsky failed to get her request approved at the meeting of the Kazan writers' organization, and years later he spoke of it with a note of pain and almost guilt in his voice. She bolted the door while her son and landlady were out and hanged herself.

That is all. And the words of Pasternak's poem on her tomb: "There is unutterable reproof in the silence of your detachment."

January 18 [Nicola Chiaromonte]

R. telephoned from Rome: Nicola Chiaromonte has died. His second heart attack after more than ten years. He was not even home but at the radio station, where he was recording a discussion program. It is too little to say that I have lost a good and loyal friend. We did not see each other very often in recent times, but it was enough to know that someone like him was at hand, a magnificent person. It will be difficult in Italy without him, difficult and empty. Besides the pain, a sense of personal threat.

January 19

I met Nicola in 1956, when he and Silone founded *Tempo Presente*. He did not like to talk about himself, but I had already heard a great deal about him from others. In the early 1930s he decided to leave Italy. In the anti-fascist émigré circle in Paris he came into contact with the man he was always to consider his master. This master was

Andrea Caffi, born in St. Petersburg to an Italian father and a Russian mother, jailed in Moscow as a Menshevik soon after the revolution, a solitary and erudite wanderer with little inclination to write, in the style of Stempowski. Nicola learned a respect for libertarian socialism from him, an aversion for the arrogance of power and the state, and such an exalted concept of friendship that it suggested the rules of a sect or a religious community. He fought in Spain in Malraux's squadron. After the defeat of the Republicans he went back to France. Before long he had to flee, pursued by the Germans. In Algeria he found a kindred soul in Albert Camus. He went to America in 1941 and spent six years there, teaching and writing for *politics* and *Partisan Review*. Again he could write and be published: it had been a rather long time since his articles appeared in the Rosselli brothers' *Giustizia e Libertà* in Paris.

Every new conversation, every new essay, every incidental note on politics and drama review showed me a writer who was unusual for Italy, a land of traditional literati, masters of the clever and fatuous scrawl at the service of the latest intellectual fashion. The kind of writing in which a sentence is not just the vehicle of free and lucid thinking but also of ceaseless moral tension, writing in which the words are alive with the whole being of the person who utters them as his long-meditated and suffered truth: that is the kind of writing that has always captivated me. And that was how Nicola wrote. He never let himself be caught in the trammels of "great systems" and "general interpretations," he mistrusted "dialectical games," which mutilated life, and "ideological shadows," which obscured reality. He scorned psychologism and historicism, for what interested him was man in the concrete faced with concrete events, man capable of ethical judgment à la Tolstoy and at the same time aware of something impenetrable beyond him. How could this measured "humanism" have evoked wide response in a world enchanted by the rhetoric of false "universal" ideologies, in a climate of hypocrisy half-mixed with fanaticism, in a "consumer civilization" of arid hearts and sterile minds? Nicola became ever more acutely aware of his isolation. The title he gave his last book was *Credere e non credere* (What should one believe in, and what not?) "Ours is not an age of faith, nor is it an age of disbelief. It is an age of bad faith, of beliefs which are clung to . . . in the absence of genuine convictions." What is the cure for *bad faith,* this terrible ailment of our time? He desperately sought a remedy. An atheist or at least agnostic, he once admitted: "It is just as hard not to believe in God as it is to believe in Him."

It must have been April that he paid a visit to Maisons-Laffitte: he had long wanted to see how we lived and worked at *Kultura*. I went back to the station with him, and as he was getting on the train he suddenly leaned over and whispered: "I envy you." Coming from Nicola, a pessimist who was convinced that only in Eastern Europe was the struggle still alive for the value of human existence, the remark had a very definite overtone.

Naples, June 4 [La Tour's night scenes]

Andrzej Ciolkosz once argued at length that the replacement of candles and oil lamps by electricity inflicted a mortal blow on the novel. As usual, this charming and brilliant young man's reasoning was seemingly facetious, with that contrary grin of his, but actually terribly serious. The light of a candle or an oil lamp cast a different, enigmatic dimension on the way in which a novelist looked at people; it sited the understanding of human destiny on the fragile border between the seen and the unseen, between the graspable and the ungraspable. The incandescent bulb dispelled the dark and created a flat and shallow illusion of clarity.

The Georges de La Tour exhibition at the Orangerie, which I managed to see before leaving Paris, brought home to me the discernment of Andrzej's remark. There is something similar in painting as well. La Tour, or the discovery of an unrecognized genius after three centuries. What a wonderful and intelligent painter! Caravaggio comes to mind, of course: it is clear that the master from Lorraine owes much to Caravaggio's realism, but the affinity is in technique rather than in vision. The *tableaux nocturnes,* pictures painted at night, by the light of a candle (mostly) or an oil lamp, are a miracle for the clarity (sometimes an almost abstract clarity) of nocturnal reflection on "all our diurnal doings." To elicit the mysterious ambiguity of objects and human faces in daylight, the light has to be filtered through the thick and often colored glass panes of the houses of Delft. Vermeer set most of the scenes in his canvases near the window: a woman weighing pearls, a woman playing a lute, a girl reading a letter, a woman with a jug, a servant pouring milk, a woman at a spinet, a woman drinking wine, a music lesson, a geographer, an astronomer, letter-writing, a laughing girl in the company of a soldier, a coquette. The faces express motionless, concentrated, and yet elusive "likenesses of the soul": that is all we know about others; we know even *less* about ourselves. The effect that Vermeer entrusted to daylight streaming as it were through stained glass, La Tour obtained with a candle's flame flickering in the penumbra of the night. *The Dice Players* is dazzling, the *Woman Picking Fleas* is enthralling. Years ago I hung two reproductions in my room, one next to the other: Rembrandt's *Bathsheba* and a Modigliani nude in the same pose. I always see the Rembrandt differently, with new eyes; the Modigliani has turned into an arabesque, charming though it may be.

There may be a grain of truth in Pierre Schneider's claim that the profundity of La Tour's nocturnes is partly due to history. In 1632 Lorraine, despoiled by invading armies, trampled and crushed into a smoldering wasteland, bloodied by soldier steel, and prostrated by epidemics, was a cursed land, a heap of corpses and burned ruins. For almost ten years (as a contemporary chronicler testified) "no one feared death any more, because it had become so familiar that there was nothing else one could possibly encounter except death." La Tour too encountered it every night, shut up with his models and his meditations in the space that a tremulous candle won from the darkness.

September 3 [Religion without God]

My wife, Lidia, is still busy deciphering and transcribing Antonio Labriola's letters to Croce; today I looked over her shoulder, and my eye was caught by this sentence in a letter of 1887: "This is the problem: to have *religion* without God; which may verge on the absurd, but that does not make it any the less true."

Four years after Marx's death, this eminent Italian Marxist who corresponded with Engels wanted "to have a *religion* without God." The italics were his. So Salvador de Madariaga may be right after all in saying that for his followers Marx was something like a scientific biblical prophet without God (or rather with History in place of God).

It "may verge on the absurd, but that does not make it any the less true." It was "true" in a sense: most of the prophecies did not come true, and yet the specifically Marxist religious conviction long survived, until the moment when, under the weight of evidence, there was nothing left but a choice between an act of "apostasy" and an act of capitulation. "Apostasy" was generally attenuated by illusions of "revisionist" heresy. Capitulation to the sole form of all institutionalized religions, with or without God, capitulation to the inflexible and arbitrary structures of power over man. Man (we are told) longs for certainty and will never cease yearning for it. But authentic religion, like authentic freedom, means ceaseless questioning, more even, the ceaseless doubting of living souls. Certainty exists only among the ranks of the disciplined, the servile and deceptive certainty of dead souls.

December 1 [Kafka and Felice Bauer]

Kafka's *Letters to Felice Bauer* have been the publishing event in Italy for a while now. I do not think that this large tome, the story of an abortive engagement, shows the reader an "unknown Kafka." It is monotonous and boring to read, for the very reason that the themes of Kafka's novels, stories, and diaries constantly recur in the letters but watered down and muddied. It took many years before his letters to Milena Jasienska were recognized as an independent work.

The five tortured years of his engagement to Felice Bauer (broken off at a certain point and then resumed) have generated a host of controversial interpretations. For psychoanalysts, the subtext of the letters is Kafka's impotence, but even they have been outdone by investigating magistrates in their hatchet job on texts and subtexts. There is a more reasonable observation at the opposite extreme, that Kafka was victim and poet of a dual obsession: a yearning for "normal" life and a dread of any form of dependency or domination of one person by another. In one letter he speaks of himself as "a basement tenant" whom Felice is vainly trying to lure into the light of day. To tell the truth, it is not worth the effort to read this enormous volume because anything it may add is already there in the few lines of his "Little Fable."

"Alas," said the mouse, "the world is growing smaller every day. At the beginning it was so big that I was afraid, I kept running and running, and I was glad when at last I saw walls far away to the right and left, but these long walls have narrowed so quickly that I am in the last chamber already, and there in the corner stands the trap I must run into." "You only need to change your direction," said the cat, and ate it up.*

There was something of gnomic genius in Kafka's self-knowledge.

December 24 [Esther mute with love]

"One winter, when I was a child," W. recounted, "a girl from the nearby town started coming to our pond. Esther was small and ugly, she wore a poor threadbare coat, with a little wizened face under a mop of shaggy hair. But her eyes, what wonderful eyes she had, deep and sad! The first time she appeared was Christmas Eve in the afternoon. She stood outside our house without uttering a word in response to our invitation to come in, and then she tripped off toward the embankment taking cautious little steps in the snow. My older brother ran after her, but too late, she had disappeared among the trees. After that she appeared almost every day, she would sit on the embankment, venture into the meadow, and probably wander all night long around the pond, indifferent to the icy cold and never knocking at any door. It was said she suffered from the 'black melancholy.' Her family had stopped worrying about her, they simply provided food and a warm place next to the stove when she came home. We gradually became accustomed to her presence, or rather to her absence, because it is hard to find another definition for the way she stared hours on end at the frozen surface of the pond. No one asked anything of her, and she bothered no one. Only the peasants occasionally made a surreptitious sign of the cross when they saw her. When spring came she found a regular spot where the meadow abutted on the embankment, by a dense clump of reeds and rushes surrounded by an expanse of water lilies in rather shallow water that had a muddy and treacherous bed.

* Translated by Willa and Edwin Muir, in Franz Kafka, *The Complete Stories*, New York: Schocken Books, 1971.

Early one morning in the middle of summer, a shepherd on the hill across the river saw Esther step into the water fully dressed with her arms outstretched. She slowly moved away from the bank and then suddenly sank like a shot, as the mud gave way and pulled her under. The shepherd gave the alarm, people came running, but it was noontime before they fished her out with hooks. It may seem funny, after all I was only a child, but I will never forget the expression of serenity and perhaps happiness on her pale wan face."

"In a word, a provincial Ophelia," I said.

"You're mistaken. Many years later I often spoke about her with the people of the village. Nothing had ever happened in her life to suggest a 'concrete cause for tragedy' or confirm 'a mild form of madness.' Her peculiar vow of silence was labeled 'black melancholy.' She was silent, she never said a word; now I suspect that it was an almost superstitious fear of the faculty of speech. Isn't naming something like stealing it? Trappists and poets understand something about it. If she had a religious soul, and I think she did, she did not believe that 'in the beginning was the Word.' If she had been a painter! But, who knows, maybe painting is also to some degree a way of stealing the world."

"You rule out suicide. . . ."

"A person kills himself for revenge, for anger, for hatred, for everything that we stick in the bag of despair, not out of love. According to me her silence was the sign of a religious love for the world. That summer day she made a natural gesture of immersing herself in the work of creation with no foreboding that she might drown."

"Aren't you letting yourself be carried away by words? Aren't you using words yourself to steal something from that poor drowned girl that we know nothing about?"

"Very likely. But even so, the theft implicitly enhances my praise for her eternal silence."

December 26 [Atheism and religion]

W. continued his automobile journey (to Sicily) and gave me a lift as far as Dragonea. The walls were impregnated with moisture, and the firewood was damp, so it took a great deal of time to get a fire started.

Everything was silent in the vicinity, the fields and the road were deserted, and when the sun went down it was rare to see light in the windows of the evanescent houses. It was impossible to spend the night in Dragonea: I took the last train from Salerno back to Naples. I carried away with me the smell of rotting leaves and damp bark, a whiff of something familiar far away, and the lesson that I find total solitude increasingly hard to bear.

On the train Simone Weil's question kept running through my mind, I do not remember where she wrote it: "How was it that I received orders from God when I was a child, when I was an atheist?" She must have asked herself in a moment of distraction. She knew full well that serious atheism is the refusal to accept religion as a source of consolation. People who consciously reject consolation, thus purified go unconsciously to meet religion. They may never find it, but that was not Simone Weil's case.

December 28 [Platonov's Chevengur]

Andrei Platonov wrote *Chevengur* in the late 1920s. More than forty years after the appearance of the novel and twenty after the death of its author, *Chevengur* has finally been published in Paris with an introduction by Michael Heller. Gorky, who had an infallible nose and a perfect ear for these things, may now be cited as a good prophet: the "lyrico-satirical" *Chevengur*, with its "anarchist" subtext, never had the least chance of passing through the eye of the censor's needle. Stalin had dismissed Platonov's story "Profit" with a single word in the margin: scum. That "scum" now ranks among the most interesting postrevolutionary Russian writers. Heller calls *Chevengur* a "philosophical novel" and its protagonists "knights errant of ideas." Quite right, but there are places where I had an urge to present Platonov's unprecedented enterprise somewhat differently. It is a morality play about the revolution, marvelously mounted in a strictly realistic and occasionally even brutal narrative. Russia at the time of Kronstadt, waist-deep in hardship and dripping with blood, and in the heart of this Russia is the county seat of Chevengur, "Sun City," the capital of "pure Communism" grafted onto corpses, the seat of abstract madness, which keeps exhausted men on their feet in pursuit of "the end of history and of everything." As in morality plays, the action seems to unfold on two levels: below, human adversity whirls; above, the dream of human happiness staggers gropingly in a fog. In Platonov the two levels are perfectly attuned, they are so precisely matched that the whole often has the tone of a dramatic poem. What welds the two levels together? The author's sorrowfully ironic smile. "The end of history and of everything" will not be achieved, the popular dream of palingenesis will not be fulfilled. His reflections on life taught Platonov to value "love of what is near" more than "love of what is afar." By 1928 or 1929 he had no illusions whatsoever and already realized that the "knights errant of ideas" would have to grow into insensitive and cruel apparatchiks, madly intoxicated specialists in using an iron fist. But the smile, while it is ever more sorrowful, endures till the last page of the novel.

I see that smile too in the photograph of Platonov in the front of the French edition of *Chevengur*. It is a sweet, benevolent, slightly uncertain smile on a pained plebeian face. Later it would disappear altogether. In 1938 Platonov's fifteen-year-old only son was arrested on charges of "plotting against the Soviet Union." Two years later the father succeeded in entreating Stalin for the boy's release from a forced labor camp in Norilsk only to watch him die of galloping tuberculosis. Platonov started drinking, and his friends found him a job as watchman at the Gorky Literary Institute. Under the Soviet regime, that was not the worst job for a serious writer, and in the moments when he was not drunk or on duty as a watchman, he could take advantage of the institute's rich library. He had contracted tuberculosis from his son and died in 1951.

December 29 [A communist dreamer]

Platonov's smile bothered me all day long as it burrowed into my memory in search of its counterpart. At last. Marcin C., one of the forty of us in the same prison cell in Vitebsk, had a smile like that. He was a young worker from a family that had lived in Lodz for generations, a communist, self-taught and extremely intelligent, who shortly after the defeat of September 1939 reached the "homeland of the world proletariat." He ended up in the same prison camp I did,

Kargopol, but he was sent to the worst section, the Second Alekseevka. After the Poles were amnestied, he passed through Yercevo central, and I accompanied him from the transit prison to the guard station. All that was left of his smile was a twitch in the sharp emaciated features, like the scar left by a poorly healed wound. I never heard of Marcin again after the kiss we silently exchanged outside the sentry box. Did he join Anders' army? Was he recruited by Berling's? Did he settle in some Russian Chevengur that had come back to its senses? I cannot tell why, but the third possibility seemed the most likely. In Russia in those days, there were cases of burned-out communists who inflicted irrevocable humiliation on themselves as punishment for the old dream.

1 9 7 3

Naples, April 15 [*Kafka's law*]

Here is Kafka's parable "Before the Law": Before the Law stands a doorkeeper, and a man approaches him and asks for admittance. The doorkeeper replies that he cannot grant admission at the moment. And later? That remains to be seen, but not at the moment. The postulant decides to wait. He waits a month, a year, two years, three, sometimes he pleads with the guardian, sometimes he tries to corrupt him with gifts but all in vain. The years go by, he watches the doorkeeper constantly, and he curses his fate. He grows old, his eyes bother him, he can no longer tell if darkness has engulfed the world or if his eyes simply deceive him. Yet he can see a light constantly gleaming inside the gateway of the Law. When he is on the verge of dying and almost deaf, he motions to the doorkeeper to come near; he no longer has the strength to stand up. He has long since formulated an important question, and he must ask it. "You are insatiable," the doorkeeper grumbles, but he comes over and puts his ear to the man's mouth and hears a whisper: "Everyone strives to reach the Law, so how does it happen that for all these many years no one but myself has ever begged for admittance?" The guardian roars his reply: "No one else could ever be admitted here, since this gate was made only for you. I am going to shut it as soon as you die."

This is Kafka's parable updated: Before the Law stands a door-keeper. He waits a month, a year, two years, three, no one comes. The years go by, he watches the road constantly, he reviles his fate. He grows old, his eyes bother him, he can no longer tell if darkness has engulfed the world or if his eyes simply deceive him. At the same time the light inside the gateway of the Law slowly dims. One day, when he is near death and almost deaf, he feels someone put a hand on his shoulder. "Are you still alive?" a voice echoes in the darkness. "I am still alive, and I am waiting to grant you admittance to the Law. This gate was made only for you." The stranger leans over him and raises his voice: "You are insatiable. This door no longer serves any purpose, it was made to give you something to guard. I am going to shut it as soon as you die and give the key to your successor." The doorkeeper is amazed: "If nobody is ever going to ask for admittance to the Law, why should my successor have to stand here and wait?" The stranger shrugs his shoulder and snickers softly, so softly that the dying doorkeeper, luckily for him, does not hear the snicker.

Maisons-Laffitte, May 7 [Stendhal and egotism]

"Egotism, provided it is sincere, provides a tool for painting the human heart." So said Stendhal in *Souvenirs d'égotisme*. He was deceiving himself and being coy with his future readers, amazed by the speed of his pen in Civitavecchia. What he called "sincerity" was imagination with an autobiographical drive: the *Souvenirs* are not so much the rough draft of what was meant to be a memoir as the skeleton of an unintended novel about himself. It has been rightly said that Stendhal was a man sick with nerves who cured himself by telling stories. Nerves, nerves: he wanted to be someone other than the man he saw reflected in the mirror, he preferred to recompose his feelings and experiences after the fact. Diaries and memoirs born of egotism may be enchanting (as the *Souvenirs*), but no "sincerity" should be expected from them: they exploit looser formal constraints in order to "follow the dream" freely. Or else (this is the case of Gombrowicz) they are a struggle for the self in which the distance from the dilemma of false-

hood or sincerity means "smuggling out the dull taste of my impris-
oned ego." Samuel Pepys was sincere in his double-locked diary
written in cipher. When his sight began to fail and he was forced to
shift from cipher to dictation, he decided to restrict his entries to
matters that could be exposed to the whole world. In the third volume
of Jan Lechon's diary, he quotes an essay of mine on Pepys and concludes that "analysis and especially self-analysis leads to sterility." No,
that is not so: Pepys drew a wonderful secret self-portrait. The sterility
of diaries and memoirs comes from a mania for bookkeeping, which
is precisely Lechon's case.

And what about diaries that are not egotistic? They arise from the
chronicler's need to establish some distance from the world and are
an attempt to find a sheltered spot in the chaos of the world.

May 25 [Mann/dictatorship in the service of man]

Mann's letter to the Union of Soviet Writers is dated April 5, 1937.
He had been invited to contribute to a symposium volume in com-
memoration of the twentieth anniversary of the foundation of the
USSR. The letter begins with coquettish evasiveness: "Honored gentlemen, what a daring risk you ask me to run. To display one's communist sympathies in Europe today, what am I saying, even merely
socialist sympathies, means exposing oneself to martyrdom and persecution, unleashing a hate campaign of which you, esteemed gentlemen, have no idea at all." This nonsense (the situation was the exact
reverse: in those years the fashion of sympathizing with communism
was all the rage among "the leading spirits of Europe") is seasoned
with that ceremonious-rancid rhetorical sauce typical of Mann. No,
God forbid, he does not want a communist dictatorship for the
German people after the fall of Hitler's dictatorship, but in the name
of intellectual honesty he must acknowledge there are dictatorships
and dictatorships. "In my heart of hearts I can distinguish between
them. I can well imagine a dictatorship in the service of man and the
future, in the service of truth and justice, instead of a dictatorship of
falsehood and crime." The honorable gentlemen in Moscow certainly
blushed with pride on reading this passage from Mann's apostolic
letter, since the context made it clear which category *their* dictatorship

belonged to. And there was an even more lavish helping of honey waiting for them: "That the Russian Revolution has and continues to do great things for the cultural elevation of the Russian people is by now an accepted fact, and it may very well be that one day its work of profound human reform will be judged not inferior to that of the French Revolution. . . . No idea today is fresher, more vigorous, or richer in content than the idea of freedom. But the freedom that must reign is a conscious freedom, fully aware of its own dignity and based on a manly humanism ready to fight: that robust social democracy delineated by the young Soviet constitution, a democracy which, I hope, the Russian people and all the other peoples will achieve."

Writers, distinguished writers, literary eminences, golden pens . . . the cloud of incense probably helped to get Mann's books published in Russia. An international congress of the Pen Club was held in Frankfurt in 1959 or 1960, and the agenda included consideration of the possibility of suspending the Budapest section until the Hungarian writers arrested after the insurrection were freed from prison. It was known in advance that Moravia would be the new president of the organization, so much depended on him. I arrived in Frankfurt the day before the conference opened, and that evening I stopped in a beer hall near the hotel. As chance would have it, Moravia walked into the beer hall half an hour later and sat down at my table. "Something quite incredible" had happened to him. In Rome the day before, the cultural attaché of the Soviet Embassy had telephoned to invite him to dinner to share "the good news": Moscow had decided to give its *nihil obstat* to the translation of novels and stories of his that the Soviet censors had previously banned because of the "particular Soviet puritanism." "What do you think that might mean?" Moravia elbowed me and winked archly. He answered his own question during the last day of the Frankfurt congress, when he tipped the scales of the discussion on the side of "non-interference in Hungarian domestic affairs."

It is a question of taste, of course, but, were I forced to choose, I would prefer Moravia's sly wink to Mann's solemn hypocrisy.

Naples, November 3 [Job]

After allowing Satan to reduce Job to the state of a worm crushed against the ground and deprive him of everything except his life, God pronounces two discourses. In the first he celebrates his own wisdom, the proof of which is the work of creation. In the second he shows that his own omnipotence is demonstrated by his dominion over the forces of evil. The purpose of the two speeches is to grind the worm farther into the ground, before he is restored to human form in recompense for his humility and acceptance of his fate. Several questions torment the upright man of Uz. Was it necessary that the Creator speak with the voice of undeserved scourging and affliction of a sinner without sin? Are such terrible punishments necessary to make man understand what his place is with respect to the Omnipotent? Is not this omnipotence tarnished by its abuse? Is not the image of goodness stained if it chastises and rages against him as if he were wicked? Does not power then become abuse, strength become violence, judgment become caprice, and eternal law become eternal suspicion? Vain questions! After God's first speech, Job confesses: "I am vile" and "I will lay mine hand upon my mouth." After the second speech, he admits: "Wherefore I abhor myself, and repent in dust and ashes." Head bowed, he accepts the religion of fear. From that moment his human condition will be marked by a single sentiment: fear unconnected with his conscience, dread rooted even in purity and righteousness. The Lord that Job sees in the height of heaven is a Lord blinded by his own omnipotence, who demands that man seek justice even in His amorality, since in His divine omniscience he does not know what human suffering is. Perhaps this is how one should understand Job's reference: "I have heard of thee by the hearing of the ear: but now mine eye seeth thee." In other words: now I understand who you are, the only possibility you offer us is to tremble before you and fear for our very lives.

The Book of Job is a parable of total faith in which *horror religiosus* entails a theological suspension of morality. The epilogue is Job's "rehabilitation" (to use a contemporary term). God has treated Job as a sinner; absolving him of sin and doubling his possessions as recompense for having borne the heavy test without rebelling proclaims the principle of innocence, which is always problematic and always conditional.

The essence is that God in his omniscience does not know what human suffering is. Christianity arose from people's yearning for a suffering God. And from a yearning for God's fellowship in human suffering. Job did not obtain a satisfactory response to his solitude in suffering and to the indifferent silence of Heaven. His successors, thanks to the Son of God nailed on the cross, have emerged from solitude notwithstanding the indifferent silence of the world.

November 28 [Marina Tsvetaeva's last months]

A few, very few new details about Marina Tsvetaeva's return to Russia and her suicide. In 1937 her husband, Sergei Efron, returned to Russia by way of Spain, and that same year their daughter went back. The edition of Tsvetaeva's poetry that appeared five years ago in French has a short autobiographical note in which she says: "In the spring of 1937 I renewed my Soviet passport." After taking that step she probably distanced herself from the Russian colony, although she continued to publish in émigré papers. In the autumn of 1938 she and her son moved from the *banlieue* to Paris to a shabby little hotel near the Montparnasse station. They lived in poverty if not in misery. Was she postponing their return until they had news from Russia, or were they making difficulties for her? Finally in 1939 the two of them boarded a ship bound for Poland at Le Havre; they reached Moscow June 12 by train from Warsaw. Efron and the daughter were still free; they were arrested in August. Tsvetaeva was surrounded by a vacuum, people avoided her, they would not even talk of publishing her poems, she supported herself and her son by translating Georgian and Belorussian Jewish poets. How terribly alone and outcast she was! She wrote to a friend: "Zenia, my dearest, I thank you. Yours is the first letter I have had in four months, and this is the first time in four months that I sit down to write a letter." At the same time she was afraid, she was constantly afraid. An entry in her "little notebook" in September 1940: "They all think I am brave. I know no one more fearful than me. I am afraid of everything. . . . No one sees—no one knows—that for (almost) a year I have been looking for chandelier hooks, but there are none, there is electric light everywhere." They described her on the day she was evacuated from Moscow to Yelabuga: "At the station Tsvetaeva did nothing but glance all around in alarm, looked for her son, though he did not move a step away from her; there was a bewildered expression on her face." She reached Yelabuga on August 18, 1941. She liked the little house of a retired couple the minute she crossed the threshold, perhaps because she finally glimpsed the longed-for hook. Ten days later, a Sunday, the little house emptied in the early morning; the landlady and Tsvetaeva's son went to *voskresnik* [voluntary Sunday work], the landlord and his grandson went fishing. She probably hanged herself as soon as they left. Her son joined the army and died shortly afterward. Sergei Efron died in prison or was shot by a firing squad. Only the daughter was spared. Years afterward the exact location of the poet's grave in Yelabuga could not be established, so a small metal cross was set up under a pine tree with the following inscription: "In this part of the cemetery is buried Marina Ivanovna Tsvetaeva 1892–1941."

In 1940 someone organized a secret meeting for Tsvetaeva and Akhmatova in Moscow, at the apartment of a mutual acquaintance. After a long private conversation, they looked troubled when they came out of the room; we shall probably never know what they said to each other. Tsvetaeva decided to leave first, and when they parted, Akhmatova made the sign of the cross over her. They met once again, by chance, on a Moscow street. In Paris, before she died, Akhmatova recalled: "There were two men who followed us step by step, I always wondered whom they were tailing, her or me."

Small postscripts to the great books of Nadezhda Mandelstam.

December 3 [A soulless world (Russell and Conrad)]

Bertrand Russell was in love with Joseph Conrad: it shows in the essay in *Portraits from Memory*. When they met he was overwhelmed by an emotion "as intense as passionate love and . . . all-embracing." Russell rarely strikes such a tone in his writing. And his summing up: Conrad's "intense and passionate nobility shines in my memory like a star seen from the bottom of a well. I wish I could make his light shine for others as it shone for me."

I remember my visit to Russell at Richmond in the summer of 1951. I went to thank him for his preface to *A World Apart*. He was rather caustic and coolly attentive in conversation, his voice grating and his bearing stiff as a stuffed bird, but he changed completely at the sound of the word "Conrad." It was as if his dried feathers came to life and stood up, as if his vocal cords became softer and sweeter. "He was a great writer and a great man; he had a noble soul." He bowed his head and repeated several times, more to himself than to me, "A noble soul." I said that Conrad was gradually being forgotten. "That is because we live in a soulless world. And we may not be able to get out of it." At the time he was gripped by *1984,* and he shifted from Conrad to Orwell. "He is accused of exaggeration, they suggest that these are the ravings of a man who was mortally ill. He too had a noble soul; he saw the threat of our soulless world earlier and better than anyone else." And after a moment of thought: "Some people seek salvation in religion. Religion is the fruit of fear, and fear kills the soul. Conrad and Orwell, they had courage, courage first of all, even in despair."

Today we would be astonished by this insistent appeal to the "soul" in the mouth of a rationalist philosopher; twenty years ago it was considered an ordinary relic of a convention that did not proscribe the interchangeable use of the two terms "soul" and "mind." In a certain sense this was actually the case with Russell: he could well admire Conrad's "noble mind" and wring his hands over "our mindless world." But it was different with the rationalist Orwell. There is a startling short piece of 1940 in his collected works. It begins with the recollection of "a cruel trick." One day at breakfast he had cut in half a wasp that was sucking a drop of jam on his plate. The wasp was totally absorbed by its banquet and continued to suck without thinking of anything else. Only when it tried to fly away did it realize that something dreadful had happened. So it is with contemporary man: he has not "noticed" that his soul has been "cut away." This was inevitable since religious faith in its traditional form had collapsed. What has taken its place? Orwell protests against wrenching out of context Marx's famous remark about religion being the "opium of the people." Orwell quotes the full text: "Religion is the sigh of the soul in a soulless world. Religion is the opium of the people." And then he adds this comment: "What is he saying except that man does not live by bread alone, that hatred is not enough, that a world worth living in cannot be founded on "realism" and machine guns? If he had foreseen how great his intellectual influence would be, perhaps he would have said it more often and more loudly."

Winston Smith in *1984* marks the end of the pilgrimage of modern man with his amputated soul. The title of the short 1940 article is "Notes on the Way." Midway into the 1970s the situation appears like this: on the one hand, man has replaced his lost faith in the immortality of the soul with a skin-deep faith in the immortality of the body (thanks to the constant progress of science); on the other hand, he keenly feels the fragility of a rational and scientific world in which fear and violence reign without the complicity of religion.*

December 28 [Alienation]

In conversation and in the press, the apocalypse has ousted alienation without a by-your-leave. Eliot is back in fashion and the last strophe of the "Hollow Men" is frequently quoted:

> This is the way the world ends
> This is the way the world ends
> This is the way the world ends
> Not with a bang but a whimper.

The differences in opinion in discussions about the apocalypse come down to one question: will the world really end with Eliot's whimper, or will we (or our children) hear a grand finale with a bang? A metallic bang is more effective (especially since it can be accompanied by beating a fist on the table) than an asthmatic whimper; nevertheless, Eliot's prophecy seems much more realistic. A whimper here, a whimper there, then a chorus of general wailing, and the whole business is over. Yet sudden shouts at the moment of death cannot be totally ruled out, so there might also be a bang.

While alienation, under the pressure of the apocalypse, is taking

* "Notes on the Way," April 6, 1940, in *Time and Tide*: in *The Collected Essays, Journalism and Letters of George Orwell*, II, London: Secker & Warburg, 1968.

its leave of current ab-usage, I should like to give it a farewell page in my journal. In 1964 the American literary critic Gerald Sykes published a thick anthology, *Alienation*: I received the two volumes as one of the (living) authors crammed into the alienation bag. Alienated man: alienated from what or from whom? From God? From nature? From society? From himself? Sykes is not very helpful in his introduction to the anthology: Most people do not understand what alienation means, he says. When they run into the word, they look embarrassed, worried, or scared. For a few, it has already become a stereotype overloaded with tendentious associations. It would seem that a heavy tome on alienation ought to begin with a definition. No, he continues, it is better to treat alienation as a mystery which in due time will be revealed to experience. Among the hundred or so texts the anthologist selected, there are two that offer this experience in an extraordinary way, whether one knows what alienation means or not, and whether or not it is necessary to resort to the word to name the mystery: Gogol's "The Overcoat" and Melville's "Bartleby the Scrivener."

Gogol wrote "The Overcoat" in 1841, Melville wrote his tale around 1856. Bashmachkin and Bartleby are so strikingly related that surely one day a bright Ph.D. candidate will be tempted to compare them closely in a learned dissertation loaded with footnotes. Bashmachkin is a scrivener incapable of anything else but copying. Bartleby is a scrivener who dismisses any other instructions from his employer with the brief and categorical "I should prefer not to." Both of them are infinitely alone in a big city: Bashmachkin in St. Petersburg, Bartleby in New York (the subtitle of Melville's tale is "A Story of Wall Street"). The only living thing in Bashmachkin's life is his new overcoat. (Jozef Wittlin recalls that in the Tuwim's theatrical adaptation of Gogol's story before the war, the hero took the overcoat into the drawing room during the party and seated it on the chair next to him). Bartleby does not have even this companionship; as soon as he finishes his work as a scrivener he spends hours at his window staring at the wall across the street. They are dead in life. In Wittlin's beatiful essay "The Tragic Gogol," he calls Bashmachkin "a dead soul" and goes on to say that "his soul came to life only after his death." For Vladimir Nabokov the live Bashmachkin is his ghost haunting the streets of St. Petersburg at night. Bartleby comes to life a bit when he refuses to continue copying and, like a stubborn and immovable ghost of himself, haunts the office. In the end he dies like a dog, huddled by a wall. It turns out that, before he became a scrivener, he worked in the Dead Letter Office in Washington. "Dead letters! does it not sound like dead men?" Melville ends his tale with the exclamation "Ah Bartleby! Ah humanity!" The same exclamation would suit Bashmachkin's story as well.

What we usually describe with the fuzzy all-embracing word "alienation" was in the genius tales of Gogol and Melville a presentiment of the coming absolute solitude in large human agglomerations. Why then does alienation let itself be driven out, since solitude is increasing rather than diminishing? What happens with solitude is what happens with the sun and with death in the famous maxim of La Rochefoucauld: *Le soleil ni la mort ne se peuvent regarder fixement.* In times of relentlessly growing solitude, a vision of apocalypse is the last sensation we can share as a community.

1 9 7 4

Naples, April 5 [Gombrowicz]

I absolutely cannot remember either when or with whom Witold
Gombrowicz bet that he could write a novel in installments for the
popular press and that "plebeian" readers would like it. What I remember is that the master's young devotees, who were tolerated with
condescension and honored with pharmaceutical doses of conversation
in his court at the Zodiak Café, were given the task of verifying the
second part of the wager, when the novel began to appear in the
Warsaw paper *Dobry wieczor-Kurier Czerwony*. Now that *The Bewitched*
has been included in the volume *Various Writings* of his complete
works, it is easier to establish an approximate date. If the novel started
to appear in installments on June 4, 1939, then my report on the
preliminary sampling must have been laid at the master's feet at the
Zodiak Café about the middle of June. At the time I was living in
Zelazna Street, a "plebeian" neighborhood indeed; and I see from the
editor's notes that *The Bewitched* was also published in the *Ekspress
Poranny*, the Kielce and Radom paper, so it is not out of the question
that my report included information about my home town by way of
frosting on the cake. In any case the scales tipped decidedly in Gom-

browicz's favor. Yes, yes, it all fits: the master must have been thoroughly satisfied, for after an evening at the Zodiak he invited me for a walk along the avenues, and that walk (just before I left on vacation) I shall never forget. Sitting on a bench, Gombrowicz suddenly dropped the manner of the "great director" and "great scorner": his face sharpened in a spasm of panic, and he offered me a grim picture of the earthquake that was about to shake Europe. His thoughts fled to South America, "where at least one can graze bulls in peace."

The Bewitched has stood the test of time much better than might have been expected. The novel is written with verve and an imagination marked at times by a fine sense of the comic, and the natural flow of the narrative makes it readable without a trace of any artifice to make it "accessible" and "popular." There is also a sense of another level for the aficionados who had induced Gombrowicz to wager in the first place: a delicate pastiche of thriller and Gothic novel à la Ann Radcliffe with pearls of the philosophy of "Ferdydurkism" scattered throughout an inexpensive paperbound edition.

Dragonea, August 11 [Pavese and the business of life]

I tried to explain to C., the Piedmontese woman poet, once an acquaintance and still an enthusiastic admirer of Cesare Pavese, why I do not like his diary *Il mestiere di vivere*.

"In general I do not like diaries that are too personal. They almost always force the author to play the game in such a way that the future reader gradually, step by step, gets the upper hand. Does this make me look all right? And this? Should I groan aloud? Should I muffle the sigh? Will it be grasped? Should I commit myself more deeply? If 'a' is said, does 'b' have to follow? What impression do I make in that situation? There is a part of man, as there should be, which no one, except for God, has the possibility or the right to enter. Paradoxically a good diary, or in any case one that is worth reading, is one in which the author only rarely pokes his antennae out of the shell—and then draws them back at once. When he crawls all the way out of the shell, he is completely defenseless and uttered by others. The utmost sincerity in literature is conceivable only with the license of third-person narrative or a conventional first person. In a diary this is equivalent to accepting a prompter or believing an actor sincere. This is why I assign diaries special status on the periphery of literature. The only exception is when the diary consciously and from the outset accepts the rules of the game and plays them as the theme. Then it turns into a duel between the writer and the others: against distortion from outside and on behalf of one's own 'nakedness' or 'authenticity,' which in any case is never fully displayed: one, because it is only dimly known and two, because it fears being named. This was not the case with Pavese. His diary is literary in the most dangerous sense of the word: in the sense that he is bound to his 'persona,' which is put on public view, and his life is dominated by literature. Pavese was a victim of this domination, and he paid for it with his life. The title of his diary is deceptive and misleading and expresses a longing rather than a reality. It is not 'the business of living' but 'the business of writing.' "

I knew that I was overdoing it, that I was provocatively "overstating" the case, but there was a grain of very real truth. I am irritated by the Pavese myth in Italy, a country of incorrigible literati and the cult of fine writing, the *bella pagina,* the beautiful page. I sniff ambiguity, sterile anxious writers feeding on someone else's tragedy, trying on the brave bloodstained feathers of a man who ultimately did not waver in his desperate attempt to get free of the snares that trapped him.

We were walking along the path in the direction of Molina, the heat was scorching, on the horizon the valley was ringed with fires. C. listened in silence, or perhaps she was not listening at all, because she simply recalled in a plaintive little voice that "it was August when it happened."

Yes, August 1950. The forty-two-year-old Pavese was at the peak of success: praised, feted, awarded prizes, translated, and dubbed the "restorer" of Italian literature. A volume of poems, several collections of well-wrought stories, and an enormous effort to familiarize Italy with American literature (his translation of *Moby Dick* is a masterpiece). Life was writing, sailing an ocean of paper in pursuit of the white whale. And then came that sultry August day in a deserted Turin, when the air was motionless, the paper Captain Ahab's spyglass was sucked into the empty whiteness on the horizon. He rented a room in the Albergo Roma across from Porta Nuova, drank down a horse's dose of sleeping pills with a glass of water, and stretched out comfortably on the bed without undressing. On the night table they found his little volume of poems *Dialoghi con Leucò* with an inscription on the title page: "I forgive everyone and ask everyone to forgive me. All right? Don't gossip too much." A few days earlier he had said farewell to his diary with words that his admirers today still repeat as if it were a password: *"Tutto fa schifo . . . Non scriverò più."* ("Everything stinks . . . I will no longer write.") With a curse and the declaration that "I will no longer write" is how the "business called living" ends.

A letter survives that was sent to friends a week before his suicide: "I am like Laocoön. I adorn myself artistically with garlands of snakes and ask for admiration, but every now and then, I realize the state I am in and I shake off the snakes, I tear them away and they writhe and bite. The game has been going on for twenty years. I begin to have enough of it."

Poor C. will probably never understand it, this rebellion of a life in the grip of greedy overbearing literature. For her it would be a sign of cruelty to conclude a quarter century later that Pavese's death in the Turin hotel will outlive his books, including the diary.

1 9 7 5

April 20–25 [A brief tour of Umbria]

There is a place on the road to Todi where it is worth stopping to bid Orvieto a distant farewell. On the hilltop across the valley the profile of the town is outlined against the morning mist. The quivering pink air alternately sharpens it and then smudges it against the sky. A bell-ringing drove of sheep moves down the valley, and horses graze on a green strip of meadow alongside a trail. A line of trees marks the course of a stream, and stalks of fleecy smoke quiver above the scattered farmhouses. There is something unreal about everything, something somnolent and slow-motioned, and that is how all of Umbria will remain impressed in my memory. It is a hedged-off region, a land where time dawdles, halts, and then idly resumes its course. Except for Perugia and the pilgrim-tourists' Assisi, the towns are dormant. Todi: the wonderful piazza with the staircase leading up to the cathedral, farther up San Fortunato with the tomb of Jacopone, and on the slope little streets like pathways carved in stone. Medieval Gubbio and medieval Spello: also with stone corridors for streets. Bettona is ringed by walls that were originally Etruscan and then medieval, and everywhere scatterbrained pigeons that are not easily frightened in the fissures between the large blocks of stone. Even in Orvieto, early on weekday mornings or at dusk, old people on benches seem to cock their ear for bygone voices as they stare motionlessly at the Duomo's organlike façade.

Aside from impressions that were repeated or merely freshened by yet another visit, I owe this brief trip to Umbria some new impressions and corrections. The way you look at things—well, the order in which you look at things—may be fundamental. This time in the San Brizio Chapel in Orvieto I began with the famous "self-portrait as signature" in the corner of one of the frescoes: Luca Signorelli and Beato Angelico. Previously I had barely glanced at this painted monogram; this time it was long before I could tear my eyes away. It was a bit as if Luca had wanted to alert us: observe the author carefully; you will appreciate his work more. The self-portrait has a sense of weight and earthiness, especially the outstretched leg planted on the ground with enormous strength. When you move immediately to the *Deposition* (as I did), the muscular body of Christ with his mortally weary peasant face, bare even of the expression of dull pain that Antonello painted, evokes an obvious association with Piero's *Madonna del parto* in the country cemetery at Monterchi, a robust pregnant peasant woman with a stern face.

In Assisi too, sequence had its role. On previous visits I had always started my tour of the Basilica with Giotto in the upper church; so the darkness of the lower church and the light of Giotto, which lingered under my eyelids, made me less sensitive. But if you stop first in the lower church in front of the Saint Francis painted by Cimabue and then go to the upper church, you are shocked by disbelief to see how iconographically theatrical Giotto's frescoes are. Heresy? Certainly, but after Cimabue, it is hard to imagine the Saint of Assisi any other way. He is a startling combination of emaciated insignificance and tranquil might.

In Perugia there is a small Camaldolese oratory, San Severo, that the custodian who lives next door opens only on request. He opens it and hands you an information leaflet, and then, thoroughly pleased with himself, he recites word for word what some museum curator has written for the leaflet. That the row of six saints in the upper part of the wall was done by the twenty-two-year-old Raphael, Perugino's disciple, on his return, in 1505, from Florence, where the prodigious youth from Urbino had been able to contemplate the painting of Michelangelo and Leonardo; that he did not finish the fresco; that only in 1521, one year after Raphael's death, the nearly eighty-year-old Perugino in his stead filled the lower part of the wall with six more saints; and that visitors are invited to note the sad contrast between the young disciple's period of luminous vigor and the tired old master's period of decline. In Perugino's far more beautiful fresco, the curator failed to hear the sound of a "unique chord."

Naples, May 7 [The suppressed rage of Russia]

Early in February 1942, on my way from the labor camp near Archangel to the army in Central Asia, I happened on a small town outside Vologda. I was traveling on luck, at each stage hard put to gain a place on trains jammed with people and even harder put to get something to eat. Experience had taught me that, if you waited in silence next to a bread line, someone might break a piece off his loaf and quickly thrust it in your hand. Early in the morning, in that small town outside Vologda, a long line had indeed formed in front of the bakery in the market square, where the little Orthodox church had just been reopened after being boarded up for years. It was bitter cold, and in my prison camp rags and cord shoes I could count only on the first customers. They paid no attention to me. I had already decided to go back to the warm station waiting room, when a young soldier with an amputated leg came into the square on crutches. He asked permission to buy bread without waiting in line. No one answered him, they all looked the other way. Then he shouted: "I fought for the homeland!" That was greeted with scornful grumbling. We walked back to the station together without exchanging a word.

I have recounted the episode outside Vologda many times, as occasion arose, as a grain of proof of the fragility behind Soviet lines during the victorious advance of the Germans. This grain of proof still carries a grain of weight, but now another feature of my recollection strikes me, a feature that is probably still true to some degree today and tomorrow: we know so little about what lurks beneath the surface in Russia, how dissimulated and deep-driven is the blind, savage, black rage of the people. Amalrik did not exaggerate when he spoke of the atrocities of an eventual future revolution. The rage ferments, turns poisonous, and sometimes explodes over a bottle of vodka (since there is no other outlet). There is a drunken train, in a dramatic vein, in Maksimov's novel *Quarantine*. There is a drunken train, in a comic vein, in Yerofiejev's splendid "poem" *Moscow on the Vokda*. The *Psychiatric Guide for Dissidents* of Semen Gluzman and Vladimir Bukovski makes it clear what the proper Soviet man should be: colorless, smell-less, tasteless.

July 10 [The man who won't divulge his address]

One item of a report sent from Poland keeps troubling me. It is about the repatriation of Poles from the USSR in the years 1957–1958 under terms agreed by Gomulka and Khrushchev. Unlike the earlier repatriation of the years 1944–1955, this one also covered prisoners and deportees. The local Soviet authorities clearly sabotaged it; therefore, according to the authors of the report, "only a small percentage of Poles have returned to Poland, about fifty thousand people, counting free men, prisoners, and deportees; the others have remained forever, because now only individuals can by some miracle return. Five years ago X. came back from the camp, after being arrested in 1939, when he was twenty. He is the shadow of a man, his spine bent in two, his silent lips sealed, he is an invalid and deranged, and he will not tell anyone his address. All that is left are the handsome features of his face."

A Polish Solzhenitsyn, if we had one, could write a novel about the man who "won't divulge his address."

1 9 7 6

January 18 [Chiaromonte and Camus]

Nicola Chiaromonte died four years ago today. The first two volumes of his selected works are about to be published. M. has finished editing the third volume and let me look through it.

There is a beautiful obituary of Camus from 1960. Nicola met him in April 1941 in Algiers, when he fled from occupied France. At the time Camus was a local celebrity in Oran, the mentor of a group of young journalists, writers, and actors. They warmly welcomed the Italian émigré, but Chiaromonte was so absorbed by the thought that "we had arrived at humanity's zero hour," so alone among the remains of the accoutrements of the past, that their friendship remained superficial. Only later did he understand how far the thoughts of the taciturn Camus went in the same direction—later, after the war, when he went to the port of New York to welcome the author of *The Stranger*, *The Myth of Sisyphus*, and *Caligula*. He saved his notes on Camus' talk at Columbia University, and one excerpt is enough to imagine with what satisfaction he must have taken down the words of the friend with whom he had been reunited: "Now that Hitler has gone, we know a certain number of things. The first is that the poison which impregnated Hitlerism has not been eliminated; it is present in each of us. Whoever today speaks of human existence in terms of power, efficiency, and 'historical tasks' spreads it. He is an actual or potential assassin. For if the problem of man is reduced to any kind of 'historical task,' he is nothing but the raw material of history, and one can do anything one pleases with him. Another thing we have learned is that we cannot accept any optimistic conception of existence, any happy ending whatsoever. But, if we believe that optimism is silly, we also know that pessimism about the action of man among his fellows is cowardly. We opposed terror because it forces us to choose between murdering and being murdered; and it makes communication impossible. This is why we reject any ideology that claims control over all of human life."

What linked him with Camus' thought was just this hatred of the "global" claims of any ideology, his belief in the inviolable secret closed in the heart of every man, in the transcendence of man over history (hence his admiration of Tolstoy), and in a truth that no social imperatives can obliterate. He did not like Kafka, but often and willingly he made reference to his reflection that man cannot live without persistent trust in something indestructible inside himself, even if all his life he remains unaware of this indestructible "nucleus" within him, and one form of this constant unawareness is faith in God. Nicola, like Camus, wanted to replace God with full consciousness. Once, after reading *The Plague*, I spoke of Camus' "lay sanctity." Sometimes Nicola approached the threshold of a lay mysticism (his essay *"I confini dell'anima"* in the third volume of his selected works). He was a humanist who refused to choose between God and man as slave to the "laws" of history.

But this choice still exists; indeed, it becomes harsher day by day, deepening the isolation of thinkers like Camus and Nicola. One of the tributary streams of Nazism was the nihilism of Ernst Junger, who proclaimed that the "new type of man" would be a "synthesis of high organizational capacity and total color blindness to human values, of belief without an object of belief and discipline without any justification." He identified the "new type of man" in the soldier and in the modern industrial worker, since both were the incarnation of "a higher degree of abstraction." In 1939 Junger backed off from Nazism in the novel *On the Marble Cliffs*, which includes a song with a bitter finale: "Since no one can bring us any help, we turn in our great need to God." Communist nihilism evokes a similar reaction from some of those who have been devastated by it. Especially in the East. As for the West, in the acute stage of disorder and confusion of all the tongues, the only thing that can be said is that the ground is shrinking fast on which the myth of Sisyphus was reborn after the defeat of Nazism, the myth of the man who rebels against the superior meaning of history as well as against supernatural grace.*

April 8 [Hofmannsthal and literary silence]

Dear friend, it cannot be simple coincidence. The day I left Maisons-Laffitte, when I was saying good-bye to Jozef Czapski in his small picture-crammed room, he suddenly took a worn little book off the shelf. It was Hugo von Hofmannsthal's *Letter of Lord Chandos*. "I have been reading it often lately," he said. Today I received your note from Krakow with the concluding passage of the *Letter* and your remark in the same spirit as Czapski's admission. And again today, while I was looking at the latest arrivals in the bookstore, I found the *Letter* with an introduction by Claudio Magris, an intelligent Italian scholar of German. So Hofmannsthal's text, written on the threshold of this century (1901), has rather unexpectedly come back to life. As soon as it was published it created something of a sensation, and then it gathered a layer of dust. What is the meaning of this revival? And is it really so unexpected?

A young English aristocrat, a highly esteemed writer, announces in the *Letter* sent to Francis Bacon in 1603 that he has decided to put away his pen forever and "completely abandon literary activity." The fragment you cite in your note reads: "[never] shall I write [another] book whether in English or in Latin . . . because the language in which I might be able not only to write but to think is neither Latin nor English, neither Italian nor Spanish, but a language none of whose words is known to me, a language in which inanimate things speak to me and wherein I may one day have to justify myself before an unknown judge."

Let us consider briefly the premises for this decision. Lord Chandos

---

* Nicola Chiaromonte, *The Worm of Consciousness*, New York: Harcourt Brace Jovanovich, 1976.

realizes that the distance from which he observes human beings and their actions has been frightfully reduced, and now he sees the surrounding world as close up as he had once looked at his little finger through a magnifying glass, like a vast field full of holes and furrows. He is no longer able to grasp things with the "simplifying eye of habit." "Everything disintegrated into parts, those parts again into parts; no longer would anything let itself be encompassed by one idea." One by one, words floated around him and turned into eyes. These eyes obstinately stared at him. And he stared back, but this made his head spin. They were like whirlpools, reeling around incessantly, sucking him down and submerging him, and beyond the words he fell into the void. It is not this way with the whirlpools of inanimate objects. They also carry one away, but, unlike the whirlpools of language, they do not lead to the void. On the contrary, in a certain sense they allow recognition of the self and give breathing space in the deepest recesses of a placated world. And then comes the conclusion which you evidently consider your own: a farewell to literature and an attempt to establish a secret alliance with reality without the mediation of words.

Mockery would be easy: this literary manifesto of silence and the rejection of the mediating functions of language had to be expressed in words, after all. It was not by silence that Lord Chandos informed the illustrious Bacon of his renunciation but by a masterpiece of epistolary eloquence; and Hofmannsthal's writing did not come to an end with the publication of the *Letter*.

It did not come to an end, and yet the *Letter* was something more than the personal testimony of a poet's crisis. It put literature back at zero point, it inaugurated the twentieth century with a question about its raison d'être (and of art in general, if we consider Hofmannsthal's pet formula of the "indecency of the brush stroke"). Magris goes farther and traces a line that runs from the zero point of the *Letter* to Kafka's "Conversation with the Drunk Man," in which things are no longer where they used to be and cannot be expressed in language, and to Musil's *Young Törless*, with its talk of a "second life of things, secret and elusive," of "a life that is not expressed in words and yet still is my life"; for Musil it is indeed "this second or third or fourth reality," hidden behind the facade or under the surface that paralyzes the possibility of speech. I would venture even farther than Magris. Ultimately what was Joyce's *Ulysses* if not an effort to adapt language to the disintegration of things into ever smaller parts? But here we are entering areas which, as I once wrote in my journal, border on the self-destruction of literature, self-destruction in an act of sublime, cosmic gibbering. As to Hofmannsthal's *Letter*, it can be summarized as a renunciation dictated by the discovery of "how little, how terribly little can be said with words!"

Seventy-five years after the publication of the *Letter* we are at the opposite extreme. Not a paralysis of the possibilities of speech, but rather their elephantiasis. We are infested and eaten away by words; the mad idea is gaining ground that "words can exhaust all, absolutely all of reality." With the result, exquisitely formulated by Gombrowicz, that "the wiser, the stupider." The revival of Hofmannsthal's text, a writer's vow of silence, is an instinctive reaction of fear that ought to have been expected. Ours is an age that has lost its center. Literature (since that is what we are talking about) began with a declaration of asceticism of the word only to become, after many turns and experiments, dissipation of the word. Hofmannsthal's Lord Chandos broke his pen because it seemed impotent in the face of reality seen from too close up and the mystery that was hidden too deep behind it; he chose to "flow into" in the world with his lips sealed. Thousands of contemporary pens briskly cudgel us with reality as if there were no longer any mystery to it. To regain the center between reality and mystery, and to give literature back its weight and its dignity, there has to be a wish and a will to write, despite everything, in a language every word of which tries to answer questions that are put to us every day by an unknown judge. Do you think it is too late? Yours, G.*

Naples, November 3 [Inner experiences]

It is very late, the city has finally quieted down, outside my window the leaves on the bushes and trees glisten after the rain, and the sky is shaking off its frayed clouds.

I have been reading recently found excerpts of Lev Chestov's diary: "Inner experiences, even the simplest, are either so sacred that nature

---

* "The Letter of Lord Chandos" tr. Tania and James Stern, in Hugo von Hofmannsthal, *Selected Prose*, London: Routledge & Kegan Paul, 1952.

itself guards them jealously or so paltry that it is not worth revealing them to others." Sacred or paltry, in both cases they are allergic to the written page. But they have a form of their own, on the order of a disorderly fragmented confession whispered in thought. These admissions, like the shreds of dream after waking, are not lodged in articulate language. So what are they? A semi-devotional stammer aimed in darkness at a single invisible and silent listener: in periods when it is intense, a diary remains untouched.

November 28 [Chiaromonte on Malraux]

The most penetrating essay on André Malraux was written by Nicola Chiaromonte, "Malraux and the Demon of Action." There is a passage about Malraux's "epic dream," an idea that also emerges from his conversation with James Burnham in 1946: "the liberal hero" who combines willpower and determination with a sense of man's nobility and respect for the values of culture. To Malraux, the incarnation of the "liberal hero" was Colonel T. E. Lawrence, a soldier, an ascetic of action, and an intellectual. But while Malraux admired Lawrence, he saw De Gaulle after him. You have to trust in the liberal will of the "man sent by providence"; indeed, who else can bridge the gap between history and man, between contemporary man's formlessness and the task of renewing "the structure and vigor" of Western civilization? Man is incapable of saving himself; he needs redemption or a redeemer. According to Chiaromonte, Malraux ultimately declared for the side of Gaullism for the same reason he had used in defense of communism: there was no other *power* capable of doing what had to be done, *il faut parier.*

Two or three years ago, I saw an interview with Malraux on French television. He was walking with a journalist through the park, his topcoat unbuttoned. He stopped once in a while to catch his breath, tossed off highly elaborate phrases, and raised his arms and dropped them at once in a weary monotonous movement. He looked like an injured bird sweeping its wings on the ground and vainly trying to take to the air again. His panting monologue was a display of high rhetoric as cold and empty as if it came from a cemetery haunted by the ghosts of action.

1 9 7 7

Naples, November 26 [Vulgarity and pain]

Some years ago Elémire Zolla, a very intelligent Italian critic, wrote an essay *"Volgarità e dolore"* [Vulgarity and Pain]. All I remember is the splendid title—no, remember is not enough, it comes to mind constantly. The contrast of vulgarity and pain holds everything there is to say about the nature of our crisis. Pain, the basis of human awareness, is being supplanted by vulgarity. When I say "vulgarity" I do not at all mean (for example) the orgy of "indecency" that has pervaded literature and the mass media, annihilating once "customary" restraints and revealing man's "animal" nature. "Indecency" is not necessarily vulgar; it becomes so only in its "pure" form, when it exists as an end in itself. Henry Miller is "obscene," yet his vision of man has a substratum of pain. Vulgarity consists in wrenching man from his existential condition, in a diabolic effort to convince him that "he is what he is," that "he comes down to a couple of elementary instincts," that "he deserves to be free from the damned problems of life and death," that "he ought finally to triumph over everything that cramps and limits him." It is like the taste that the word "permissive" leaves in the mouth: canceling and banning all pain. Gide is vulgar in his diary when he shrugs at Pascal's "lamentations." How much wiser Hebbel was, according to Gide, with his "witty" aphorism: "What is the best thing a mouse can do when he is caught in a trap? Eat the cheese on the hook." Programmatically vulgar (to take a typical example of current "cultural" production) is the film about Nietzsche I saw yesterday: *Beyond Good and Evil*, or self-affirmation through copulation. A vulgar man, a one-dimensional man: stripped of any "problem," cut off from the past and holding off the future, insensitive to mystery, indifferent to mediation.

The idea of mediation, of bridges between human misery and divine perfection, was invented by the Greeks. We have preserved those bridges just to look at them, whether we are believers or not. These two remarks come from the notes of Simone Weil. They are followed, seemingly unexpected, by one of the few Orphic fragments that have survived, a text of extraordinary beauty: "You will find a spring by the dwelling of the dead, to the left. Next to it stands a white cypress. Do not approach that spring, do not go near it. You will find another spring that pours from the lake of Memory, cool water gushes out of it. There are guards in front of it. Address these words to them: I am daughter of the Earth and the star-covered Sky, and I descend from the Sky; and that you know; I burn and die of thirst; let me drink quickly of the cool water that gushes from the lake of Memory. And they will allow you to drink from the sacred spring." Memory is a bridge of mediation, memory as experience of pain and the mystery of the ephemeral, it is the life-giving water of the sacred spring by the dwelling of the dead. So another definition of vulgar man might be this: a man without pain, without memory, floating in the stream of life from who knows whence to who knows where and who knows why. Or, if one prefers Hebbel's "witty" metaphor, the mouse totally absorbed in gnawing at the cheese in the trap.

1 9 7 8

Naples, January 17 [The Katyn grave]

Soon after moving to Naples, late in 1955, I decided to see Professor
Vincenzo Mario Palmieri, director of the Institute of Forensic Medicine at the University of Naples and one of the twelve signatories of
the International Medical Commission at Katyn (where the bodies of
4,500 slain Polish officers were discovered in 1943). Father C., a friend
of mine who also taught at the university and knew Palmieri, tried
to arrange a meeting. The reply was a polite refusal. The professor
"fully appreciated" my interest, "nevertheless he preferred not to dig
up the Katyn grave again in conversation, he did not want to call up
painful ghosts of the past." At the time I translated the refusal in
political terms (Palmieri had been the Christian Democratic mayor of
Naples for a while, and he had probably learned diplomatic prudence
in dealing with the local, exceptionally aggressive communist left),
but it was sweetened by my charming Barnabite friend, who, in a
typically ecclesiastical gesture, spread his arms and lifted his glance
to heaven.

Years passed, and I forgot all about Palmieri, or I may unconsciously have thought he must be dead. And then a few days ago, his

name suddenly cropped up during dinner at the home of Dr. S, who operated on me a year ago. "Palmieri? Yes, yes, he is still alive, he is very old, he retired years ago, but he is alive and still even works a bit." The next day S. telephoned him and called me at once with an invitation for this morning: "He would so like to see you, he would so like to talk with you."

It has been raining since this morning, letting up only briefly, and the biting wind was so gusty that it all but flew me to the old university quarter hanging from my ballooning umbrella like the pensioner in Bruno Schulz's story. I dashed rapidly through the maze of backstreets, panting, soaked through, and excited, although well aware that when I reached my destination I would not hear anything new. At a certain point All Souls' Day 1952 emerged from the meanders of my memory: it was a cold rainy day like today—though it was morning it seemed like nightfall—and I was on my way from Munich to Dachau. My life is empty and lonely in Naples with an emptiness and loneliness that can be understood only by someone who has emigrated to an irremediably foreign city. This morning I had the feeling that I was going to a Polish cemetery, a feeling like the lump in the throat I always get at the sight of the abbey of Monte Cassino from the highway to Rome. And Palmieri? Why did he so want to see me? Why did he so want to talk to me about what he experienced thirty-five years ago? Mysteries of old age? Mysteries of eyes suddenly welling with tears and a violent need to lock everything up in words uttered aloud to someone who *sente l'argomento,* "feels the subject"? Or awareness that he was one of the last, if not the very last, of the commission of twelve?

The Department of Forensic Medicine is housed in what was once a convent, neglected and near ruin, like all of tattered old Naples, with a weed-infested garden that has become a semi-garbage dump. Palmieri has kept his old office, although he rarely appears, and even more rarely is he bothered by his successors. At eighty years old, he still has the library and files to straighten out.

My interrogatives proved to be the fruit of an overexcited imagination. He spoke in a colorless matter-of-fact voice, with only a slight trace of emotion, as if he were simply taking advantage of an unexpected occasion late in life to summarize and file away a matter that was unparalleled in his fifty-year career in criminal medicine. He took down from a shelf a large box stuffed with hundreds of photographs and laid them before me. Here was a Polish cemetery illustrated in the heart of old Naples. I ran my eyes over them, kept arranging new piles of photographs on the table, and caught only fragments of his account.

"A stench, a terrible stench that I will never forget. That made it hard to do our work, even though the corpses had been well preserved in the dry earth; and even identity cards survived in the uniform pockets, as well as letters, newspaper clippings, family photographs. Look at these photos, heads in a block of earth, they look like bas-relief ovals on the facade of some excavated temple . . .

"There was no doubt about it, not one of the twelve of us had any doubts, there wasn't a single reservation. What decided the matter was when Professor Orsos from Budapest dissected a skull: he found a substance on its inner wall that only starts to form three years after death. The stand of birch trees planted over the trench was also three years old. We stayed up till three in the morning to write the report, because even the slightest revision and nuance had to have the approval of all the signatories. The report was irrefutable. Professor Markov from Sofia and Professor Hajek from Prague had no compunction at all about signing it, but their subsequent retraction is nothing to be surprised at. I might have retracted myself if Naples had been liberated by the Soviet army. . . .

"No, there was not the slightest pressure on the part of the Germans, only we had a liaison officer *ex officio* to help us, Professor Buhtz from the University of Breslau, who, by the way, was later executed in connection with the Stauffenberg plot. It seems that a lot of books have come out about Katyn, I have not read them: what can they add to what I know personally? . . .

"The crime was committed by the Soviets, there are no two ways about it. One day the Russians will have to admit it. Is it true that Khrushchev suggested they do so? Nothing would be easier than putting all the blame on Stalin and asking the Poles for forgiveness. To this day I am still haunted by an image of Polish officers on their knees, their hands tied, kicked into the trench with a bullet in the back of the head. . . .

"Right after the war, in liberated Naples, I was given a hard time of it for having been part of the commission. Literally day after day

Mario Alicata, who had been a promising fascist activist as an under-graduate, attacked and insulted me in *L'Unità* [the Italian communist party newspaper]. He demanded that the university fire me. It got to the point that even Adolfo Omodeo, an upright person, whom Croce had backed as the new president of the university, advised me to resign my chair voluntarily, for fear of demonstrations on the part of the communists and insults on the part of students. I did not let myself be intimidated, somehow I held out. . . . Our meeting, *caro amico,* is the end of a long story."

January 29 [Caligula in Moscow]

An article appeared in 1953 by Boris Suvarin, written jointly with Valentinov-Volski, "Caligula in Moscow, the Pathological Case of Sta-lin." On the basis of confidential statements by senior Soviet functionaries (probably obtained by Valentinov-Volski, an old friend of Lenin), Suvarin analyzed Stalin's "paranoid psychosis," the diagnosis advanced in 1937 by two Kremlin doctors, who were shot the follow-ing year at the despot's orders.

But who was Caligula? Folk legend has it that when the son of Germanicus and successor of Tiberius was still a child, he lost his parents and two older brothers through Tiberius' fault. Caligula fell seriously ill shortly after ascending the throne. As soon as he recovered, the "Caligulan" merry-go-round began of treason trials, atrocities, and despotic caprices. He decreed the death of the prefect of the Pretorian guards to whose support he owed his throne. He broadcast his claim to divinity and ordered monuments erected to himself during his life-time. When his beloved sister Drusilla died, she received the title of divine, the first time a Roman woman was so honored. Her widower died at Caligula's wishes. Caligula himself died at the hand of con-spirators. Many attributed his crimes and follies to the psychological consequences of his illness. In other words, they suspected that the life-and-death struggle on his bed of pain had inoculated him with a form of madness. Historians are skeptical about some of the evidence of his madness and relegate to fable the anecdote that Caligula made his horse consul.

His adoration of the goddess-to-be was not in the nature of Platonic love between family members: Drusilla was sister and lover to her brother. This historic fact is the literary hinge on which Camus' *Caligula* turns. In his introduction to the American edition of the play, Camus speaks of a world that, "on the death of . . . his sister and mistress," became "poisoned with scorn and horror" for Caligula and says that the trauma led the emperor to reject "friendship and love, common human solidarity, good and evil."

It would be malfeasance—for so many reasons!—to stretch the literary resemblance between Stalin and Caligula too far, but it would be infeasible totally to ignore the role that Nadezhda Alliluleva's suicide in November 1932 played in the life of the Moscow despot. We know very little about it. Even taking Svetlana Stalin's account in her *Twenty Letters* with a grain of salt, there is still the episode cited in Isaac Deutscher's biography, which probably came from reliable sources: after the death of his second wife, for the first and only time Stalin submitted his resignation from the post of secretary general; of course, the resignation was rejected. And now I have by chance found another item, slight but rather significant.

Aleksander Gladkov's book *Meetings with Pasternak* has just been published in English. What most interested me was the long introduction by Max Hayward. The British Russianist dug up a hitherto unnoticed article written by Korjakov in 1958. Hayward says it seems certain that the pathological side of Stalin's nature was deepened by tragedy in his private life, Nadezhda's suicide. The rabid paranoia that took possession of him in 1937, and then again in the postwar years, may have had its roots right there. In 1932 "the cult of personality" was already in full bloom, so the announcement of Nadezhda's death (false, the cause of death was attributed to peritonitis) elicited an avalanche of stereotyped condolences. The letter from the Writers' Union, printed on the front page of *Literaturnaia Gazeta*, was also a stereotype. Pasternak did not sign it, but he added his own declaration of condolences with this tenor: "I share the sentiments of my comrades. The day before [before the news of Alliluleva's death was announced] I had been thinking deeply and intensely of Stalin; it was the first time I had done so as a poet. The next morning I read the news. I was overwhelmed, as if I had been there, living by his side and had seen it." According to Korjakov these words must have aroused the superstitious feeling in Stalin that Pasternak, as a poet, possessed the magical gift of second sight. Moreover, Korjakov believed that this conviction led Stalin to spare Pasternak and take him under his wing during the years of the purges.

Two years later, in 1934, Stalin telephoned Pasternak. Today we know exactly how the telephone conversation went, from the accounts of Anna Akhmatova and Nadezhda Mandelstam. Stalin informed Pasternak that his and Akhmatova's intercession on behalf of Osip Mandelstam (through the mediation of Bukharin) had been successful. Once the Mandelstam question was settled, Pasternak went on to say that he would like to see Stalin and talk with him privately. "About what?" Stalin asked. "About life and death," Pasternak replied. Stalin hung up.

April 26 [Terrorism = madness + despair (Conrad's Secret Agent)]

In Conrad's *Secret Agent* the driving force of terrorism is the coupling of "madness and despair." When the embassy official Vladimir initiates Verloc in his plan for blowing up the Greenwich Observatory, he settles for madness. There are two essential observations in his tirade: "A bomb outrage to have any influence on public opinion . . . must be purely destructive. It must be that, and only that. . . . You anarchists should make it clear that you are perfectly determined to make a clean sweep of the whole social creation." And afterward, the key of terrorism inspired by a foreign state: "madness alone is truly terrifying, inasmuch as you cannot placate it either by threats, persuasion, or bribes."

But Verloc is a secret agent, a terrorist in the pay of an embassy; he has no sense of despair, he need only accomplish his mission as spreader of madness. The figure of the Professor (of dynamitology) is the one that gives the best idea of Verloc's comrades, the real terrorists. In the epilogue to the novel we see the Professor after he has talked with Ossipon over a tankard of beer. He leaves the beer hall. He walks straight ahead, "averting his eyes from the odious multitude. He had no future, he disdained it. He was a force. His thoughts caressed the images of ruin and destruction. He walked frail, insignificant, shabby, miserable—and terrible in the simplicity of his idea of calling madness and despair to the regeneration of the world. Nobody looked at him. He passed on unsuspected and deadly like a pest in the street full of people."

Forty days after the kidnapping of Aldo Moro by Red Brigade terrorists, the only word that comes to mind to describe the prevailing atmosphere in Italy is "pest." I felt it as soon as I returned from France, early in April, when Moro had already spent more than two weeks "behind the bars of the people's prison." The atmosphere has become heavier day by day, and every day here now means rushing from the latest editions of the newspapers to the latest bulletins on the radio and television. What are the components of this pestilential atmosphere? Unsubstantiated suspicion blindly aimed in all directions. Nerves on the verge of panic. Constant fear of being taken unawares. Creeping paralysis from helplessness. Immediate acceptance of the wildest rumors and conjectures. Disturbance of the sense of balance, if not actual illness of the inner ear. Paresis of the bonds of collective life. Sufficient, I think, to suggest at least a laceration of the whole fabric of society. When Pope Paul VI "knelt down" before the Red Brigades and assured them that, despite everything, he "loved" them as a Christian and begged them in the name of this "love" to free their prisoner, the madness of terrorism won a partial victory. All that was lacking to make it complete was the imprisonment of the Pope himself or Moro joining the Red Brigades.

Efforts are now made to trace the genealogy of the Red Brigades and hastily put what elements are available together in some kind of credible likeness. They are the misbegotten children of 1968 confrontation politics. They are the orphans of the Italian communist party, which, it is true, has taken a firm stand on the ground of defending the state and categorically rejects any negotiation with the terrorists, but until yesterday—how many years!—it worked for the erosion of the "bourgeois state" and the dissolution of its organs of self-defense, fomented "revolutionary" gibberish, and heated any slight spark of conflict to demagogic incandescence. They are the by-product of thirty years of Christian Democratic government and corruption. They are the grandchildren, born late, of Lenin, Trotsky, and Stalin. They are the natural consequence of mindlessly jammed universities and increasing unemployment among young people. They are the victims of the mental and moral brutalization of Italian intellectual demons, sustainers of the principle "if God does not exist, then everything is permissible." They are the children of a nation that one hundred years after unification is not very convinced of its unity; and children of a church that after almost two thousand years of Christianity has lately begun, as it were, blushingly to seek forgiveness for still existing.

The list could be extended, for every day the papers offer matter for reflection and feverish "examination of conscience." But while each of these elements contains a (larger or smaller) grain of truth, the picture that emerges is ultimately too diffuse, an identikit without identifying signs. I once referred to Western terrorists as "desperate necrophiles of ideology." At the time I did not remember *The Secret Agent*, which I had read long before, with its formula "madness plus despair." Madness does not require explanation. And despair? In a note of 1946 in his recently published *Journaux de voyage*, Camus remarked, long before the books of Raymond Aron and Daniel Bell appeared: "Remember that our times are the end of any ideology." For thirty years the "revolutionary" West has not wanted to remember this, not for anything will it admit it. Who knows, maybe deep down this is where the seed is hidden, the seed that gave rise to the despair of terrorism.

Dragonea, August 28 [The death of Ignazio Silone]

The urn containing the ashes of Silone, who was cremated in Geneva, were buried yesterday in Pescina dei Marsi, his birthplace in the Abruzzi. He died in Switzerland, where he had spent many years in exile. One day in his apartment in Rome, when I happened to bemoan my fate as an exile, he smiled sadly: "It is no great consolation for you, but I too am an exile in Italy." Shortly before he died, he was asked if he was homesick for his Abruzzi. He shrugged his shoulders: "My Abruzzi can be anywhere."

"I was born May 1, 1900," he often recalled with a half-ironic and half-contented sparkle in his dark, deep eyes. Anyone inclined to seek a symbolic meaning in dates might now add: "And he died the night between August 21 and 22, 1978, almost exactly the tenth anniversary of the invasion of Czechoslovakia." These two dates, which encompass the life and works of one of the most important contemporary writers and one of the very few authentic socialists as well as authentic Christians, also mark an entire epoch: from faith in ideal socialism to the final burial (in the West) of "real" socialism. Silone's thought and experience can be summed up in the observation that "there are no reforms capable of fundamentally changing man with his problems, capable of eliminating the conflict between the individual and the community, between society and the state, capable of mitigating the dissonance between pain and the pursuit of happiness."

It was probably around 1936, in the next-to-last year of gymnasium in Kielce, that I read *Fontamara* and *Bread and Wine* (in Polish, of course). They made an enormous impression. Silone was one of the favorite writers of the Polish left. Even the communists, as yet unaware of the excommunication looming over the "renegade's" head, were captivated by his books. After the war, at the so-called "helm of power," they of course sentenced him to nonexistence. The Polish "October" made it possible to republish *Fontamara* by a fluke. After which he continued not to exist, surely under pressure from Moscow. Recently Jerzy Turowicz made an obviously unsuccessful effort to publish the *Adventure of a Poor Christian*. He was allowed only to publish two of the "renegade's" fairly "innocuous" stories in *Tygodnik Powszechny*.

I remember an episode that Silone told me when we were just becoming acquainted. Edward Ochab made an official visit to Rome after Saragat's visit to Poland. The ambassador of the Polish People's Republic gave a reception in a large Rome hotel for the "cultural world" of the capital.

Silone was invited and after much hesitation finally decided to accept. When it came time for introductions, Ochab's face lit up: "Silone? Oh, what a pleasure, how happy I am to meet you personally! I devoured your books in the prisons of reactionary Poland before the war." To which Silone replied: "I am flattered, Mr. President. But if this is the way things are, couldn't my books be republished in the progressive state of which you are the head, if not for readers in prison at least for readers at liberty?" Ochab turned pale and did not answer. This was total Silone: indifferent to the "rules of the game" when truth was at issue, caustic yet wonderfully human, resolute and calm. The same Silone who, in Moscow in 1927, was the only one to oppose

Stalin at the meeting of the Comintern and refused to condemn Trotsky's "counter-revolutionary" document "sight unseen."

I met Silone late in 1955 at the same time I met Nicola Chiaromonte. They asked me to write for the monthly *Tempo Presente*, which they had just founded. It is not unusual nowadays to read and hear *Tempo Presente* acclaimed as the liveliest, most stimulating, and most independent Italian periodical of the postwar years. But at the time, in an atmosphere of intellectual conformity, bad faith, misinformation, and moral torpor, the issues of *Tempo Presente* were usually greeted with distaste if not with loathing and gnashing of teeth accompanied by the usual stupid tag "a product of the Cold War." In any case, for me, an émigré Polish writer who had just settled in Italy, the possibility of finding anchorage in that natural port was a gift of fortune.

Both Silone and Chiaromonte soon became friends of *Kultura*. Silone's "Choice of Comrades" was published by *Kultura*, and a beautiful short text of his is printed on the back cover of all the volumes in the series "Archives of Revolution."

Silone's excommunication in Russia took effect immediately after Togliatti's last conversation with the "renegade" (in Switzerland in the early 1930s), so he is less well known there than in Poland. The situation has changed somewhat, because a Russian edition of *The Adventure of a Poor Christian* was published abroad a few years ago. I had evidence of this when the review *Kontinent* was founded. Vladimir Maksimov asked me to persuade Silone to be part of the international editorial board and added that Solzhenitsyn and Sakharov were very keen. It took two minutes for "my work of persuasion." Silone admired free Russian, Polish, Hungarian, Czech, and Yugoslav writers and intellectuals. "I greatly admire Solzhenitsyn," he said in his last interview a month before his death, in answer to a question about Solzhenitsyn's speech at Harvard, "even if I do not always agree with him. It is not true that spiritual strength today survives only in the East."

Once again, as after Nicola's death, Rome has become smaller for me; I will no longer be going to that small street in the vicinity of Piazza Bologna. The dual exile (Battaglia in my story "The Unyielding Prince" has many of his features) has gone back forever to his native Abruzzi.

Naples, November 10 [Nietzsche in Turin]

Nietzsche went to Turin April 5, 1888, at the advice of a friend who had recommended the capital of Piemonte as something half-way between Nice and Sils-Maria, the philosopher's two favorite places. He rented a room on the sixth floor of a building off Piazza Carlo Alberto, in the home of Davide Fino, a well-to-do news-stand owner. And indeed Turin won his heart: "Here is a city in which you can still breathe the good air of the eighteenth century." The clear dry air, the portico-shaded streets, the patisseries and their exquisite cakes and ices, the frequent concerts, the prom-enades along the Po and in the enormous Michelotti Park across the river, and the rich polyglot Loescher bookshop. Peace and quiet, all his ailments miraculously disappeared, not a day was wasted, and he worked feverishly. He quickly made friends with his land-lord, a piano was available in the apartment, and sometimes he played four hands with the charming young Miss Fino. The piles of written pages continued to grow. Away from the world, as if in hiding, gone to ground, filling sheets with violent strokes of the pen in a little room with a view of the beautiful square, or plunging into Turin life, which revived him like curative waters, it was easier to pass sentence on the world. Not a one of the passers-by he met on the street, the occasional ramblers along the river and in the park, or customers at the neighboring tables of red-plush-lined cafés could have suspected that the all-but-unknown *pro-fessore tedesco* had almost finished planting the dynamite and was now unrolling the fuse. Sometimes this idea elicited from him a short guttural laugh, so foreign to him that he would unwittingly turn to look behind him. No, no, he was alone, and strong in his solitude.

On May 12 he suddenly made the following entry in his notebook: "Motif for a picture. A cart driver. Winter landscape. The cart driver, a hideously cynical expression on his face, pisses on his horse. The poor creature, its hide galled and bruised, turns its head—gratefully, very gratefully." Had he dreamt that picture? Or had he actually seen it? We do not know. We know only that it plunged him into a state of fretfulness for several days and prevented him from concentrating on his explosive work. There were moments in those days when he looked at his manuscript with anxiety.

The anxiety passed and then the Piemonte summer arrived, premature and sultry. Again he struck his pen on paper, thickening the underlining of particular words, but he gasped for breath and dried his perspiration with a large handkerchief. He fled to Sils-Maria at the beginning of June, after assuring his landlord that he would return to Turin in September.

"I have been in the depths since I left Turin. Constant headaches, constant vomiting." In the letters from Sils-Maria he complained incessantly of "deep nervous exhaustion" and being drained of his vital force. He struggled vainly against "the saddest thoughts" but with no loss of clarity in assessing his "own situation." He was alone and weak in his loneliness. He spoke of a hereditary taint: "My father died from total loss of vital force."

He went back to Turin on September 20. And at once: "Marvelous clear air, autumn colors, a delicious sense of bliss." He wrote rapidly, almost breathlessly; he did not tear himself away from his desk except to sleep at most five hours. On September 30 the explosive work was ready. He gave it the title *Der Antichrist—Fluch auf das Christentum*. But "the curse of Christianity" in the title was not enough for him, and he added "The Law Against Christianity" in seven paragraphs signed by the Antichrist. "Promulgated on the day of salvation, the first day of year one (September 30, 1888, by the false chronology)." He prefaced the seven paragraphs with the quintessence of the decree: "War to the death against infirmity: the infirmity is Christianity."

His "bliss" in Turin fostered his delectation of the finished manuscript. He riffled through it often, each time more satisfied with himself. He half closed his eyes and in imagination he watched the flame that streaked lightning-quick along the fuse. What an explosion, what an explosion! He seemed to hear the deafening blast already. He considered certain passages in the work at length. For example, in the "Law":

Sixth paragraph. "Sacred" history shall be called by the name it deserves: damned history; the words "God," "Savior," "Redeemer," and "Holy" shall be used as insults, as marks of infamy.

And this passage in the same text:

Christianity was not "national," it was not racially conditioned: it addressed every sort of life's disinherited and found its allies everywhere. One of Christianity's foundations is the rancune *of the sick, an instinct directed against the healthy,* against *health itself. Anything that is well done, proud, and bold, especially anything that is beautiful, offends Christian eyes and ears. Once again I recall Paul's priceless words: "The* weak *things of the world, the* foolish *things of the world, the* base *and* despised *things of the world hath God chosen." "This* was the formula, *in hoc signo* decadence con- quered." "God on the cross, do they still not understand the monstrous world of thoughts hidden in this symbol." "All that suffers, all that is nailed to the cross is divine. . . . We are all nailed to the cross, hence we are all divine. . . . We alone are divine. . . . Christianity conquered, and a* much nobler *mentality perished because of it, to this very day Christianity has been mankind's greatest misfortune."*

Splendid, splendid! Even he was surprised by the energy and precision of his blows. Now he roamed around Turin euphoric, as if he were drunk; he would stop for no reason at all and say out loud: Antichrist. He was introducing himself to the throngs still unaware of his new name, drowning it out sometimes with his raucous laugh. Again that laugh sounded alien; it seemed to come from someone else's throat. The illusion lasted only a moment, it passed at once, but it left a trace of apprehension, the way a man immersed in thought on a dark still night is startled by the sight of his own shadow.

Autumn in Piemonte, mild and mellow; by day the city was beneath a golden-gray bell jar; in the velvet of the evening the white globes of the gas lamps glimmered. People chatted under the porticos, carriages rolled by, and orchestra music was heard. He stopped working regularly in this period, he ambled around Turin at a leisurely pace until his legs felt heavy, and he constantly changed cafés and eating places. He went to Loescher's almost every day. But the books he bought he glanced at absentmindedly and impatiently, and they ended up on a growing pile in one corner of the room.

In mid-November the cataracts of heaven opened. It poured, the weather was foul, even the fog was sooty, and by early afternoon it was already twilight. He left the house only to eat his meals in a nearby trattoria, he locked himself in his room, he avoided the landlord and his family. Euphoria was supplanted by such grievous apathy that he feared a possible relapse into illness. Yet he did not consider leaving Turin. Since it was in Turin that his work had taken on its final form, since, on the first day of Year One, it was there he had given the signal of salvation and set the seal on the annihilation of Christianity with the signature of the Antichrist, Turin had in a certain sense become the capital of the future universal kingdom for him. But before it could be established on the rubble of the old blown-up world, some elementary matters had to be settled for those few, *the happy few*, who deserved to be admitted to the secret. One of them was Georg Brandes. And it was to Brandes that on December 10 he drafted a letter:

Dear friend, I believe it indispensable to inform you of a couple of things of unprecedented importance: give me your word of honor that it will remain between us. . . . I am preparing an event that it is extremely likely will split history in two, to the point that we will witness the birth of a new chronology: starting from 1888 as Year One. Everything that is now on the crest of the wave, the Triple Alliance, the social question, will shift completely to a position of antagonism between individuals: we will have wars the likes of which have never been seen, but not between nations, not between classes: everything has shattered and dissolved—I am the most dangerous dynamite in the world.

As to translations of the *Antichrist*, he anticipated "a million copies in every language as *first* printing." He went on to say:

Since this is a demolition blow *against Christianity, it is obvious that the only international power that has an instinctive interest in annihilating Christianity are the* Jews. *. . . So we must make sure we influence all the centers of decision that this race has in Europe and in America: not to mention the resources, that such a movement needs great amounts of capital. . . . The result is that dynamite will blow to bits any organization of the army, any constitution: since the enemies having nothing with which to oppose it, they will be unprepared for war. The officers will be on our side, faithful to their instincts: that it is something* disreputable, craven, *and* filthy *to be Christians. . . . As to the German kaiser, I know how to deal with that sort of idiots. . . . My book is like a volcano, none of the literature of the past can give any idea of what I have said in it, or of the paths by which the deepest secrets of human nature leapt on to its pages with terrifying clarity. There is something simply* *superhuman in the voice with which I pronounce the death sentence. . . . When you finally read the law against Christianity, which closes the book and is signed "Antichrist," I fear that even your legs may tremble.*

This letter, though it was never copied out clean or sent, put him in somewhat better humor. Not for long. For days on end a light snow fell and melted on the black streets; it was damp with the melancholy of a winter that was not really winter. Before Christmas, frost gripped the city in a vise of ice. He had informed the landlord well in advance that he did not want to be disturbed in any way during the holidays. He intended to dedicate himself at last, during the holidays, to the pile of books that lay in the corner of the room.

He knew Dostoevsky and admired him. He had read *Crime and Punishment* before, but now reading the novel purchased at Loescher's was a shock. First he read it straight through. Then, lying on the bed, he went back to the beginning and read chapter five a countless number of times. Again and again and again . . . "When people are in a bad state of health, their dreams are often remarkable for their extraordinary distinctness and vividness as well as for their great verisimilitude. . . . Raskolnikov dreamed a dreadful dream." The seven-year-old Rodion witnesses an awful scene: a peasant beats a poor nag to death for not being able to pull his overloaded cart. With a shout the little boy "cleared his way through the crowd to the mare, embraced her lifeless bloodstained muzzle and kissed her, he kissed her on the eyes, on the lips . . ." Raskolnikov awakens "in a sweat, his hair wet with perspiration, gasping for breath . . . Good God! . . . is it possible that I will really take a hatchet, hit her on the head with it, and crack her skull?"

Nietzsche too woke up wet with perspiration, unsure what time of day or night it was, unable to reconstruct and remember his dreams one moment after awakening. He did not know if they were a replica of Raskolnikov's dream or if they were fragments of his own imaginings and illusions. He knew only that the same words—suffering, love, good, evil—may just as easily be living flesh or empty sound. What he heard was not the wished-for boom of the explosion, but rather the faint boring rustle of paper. He felt a pain swelling in his head as if it were seeping in drop by drop through a small opening in his temple.

In those days he all but ceased to exist for his landlords, who had to listen at his door to make sure he was in. On January 3, 1889, a heavy snow fell in Turin. There had been no sound from the tenant's room all morning. Davide Fino went out after lunch. As soon as he turned the corner, he saw two policemen in the distance helping someone along and flanked by a crowd of curious people. He had a foreboding and quickened his pace. Yes, the man was Nietzsche. They had found him in Via Po, his arms clasped around the neck of a horse, and they could hardly pull him off. According to eyewitnesses, he had approached the horse hitched to a cart, thrown his arms around its neck, and pressed his face to its muzzle. Fino persuaded the policemen to turn the man over to him.

He was taken to Basel on January 8. In the meantime he lay in bed in his Turin room writing illegible notes. He signed them Caesar, Dionysus, and Lord of the World. And also the Crucified. The day of departure he put up resistance; he did not want to be separated from his "beloved" landlord. He was pacified with the gift of Signor Fino's nightcap. And he wore that nightcap to the Turin train station, looking like a runaway circus clown. For fear of a scandal at the station in Basel, they talked him into believing he was a prince traveling incognito and that he must pass in silence through the crowd from the train to the carriage.

In March he was committed to a hospital for the mentally ill in Jena. His medical history was charted day by day for a whole year, until March 1890, and it is excruciating in its monotony: he ate his own excrement, he drank his own urine, he rubbed his excrement on himself, he broke the windowpane . . .

He was taken from Jena to Naumburg, his home town, where he vegetated for seven years before his mother's eyes. When she died, his sister, Elisabeth Forster, took him with her to Weimar. He died there in August 1900 without ever regaining consciousness, "in a state of total physical and mental decay." Except for one moment before he died, when he turned to a visitor for whom an exception had been made, he pointed his finger at himself and under his drooping mustache murmured in Italian: *un povero cristo.*

This rather unphilosophic little story about a philosopher is based on facts and documents (Nietzsche's May notebook entry and the rough copy of his letter to Brandes in December were only recently deciphered). I wrote it after reading a book by the Italian Germanist Anacleto Verrecchia, *The Catastrophe of Nietzsche in Turin*. Could I explain why I consider this "catastrophe" so significant? I very much doubt it, and in any case the whole sense of my little tale is what is not said, the blank spaces, in the abeyance of words, in the fact that the *i*'s are not dotted, no comment is hazarded, and internal dissonances are not smoothed over.

Of course the narrative and descriptive framework is mine. And two elements are invented. There is no evidence that Nietzsche reread *Crime and Punishment* in Turin before his final attack of dementia, although it is known that Dostoevsky fascinated him. I also invented the dying Antichrist who refers to himself as *un povero cristo.* Probably no other language in the world, aside from Italian, has such an expression for rendering human prostration. The name of Christ in this case is written with a small letter.

Late November [Anti-Semitism]

"Antisemitism in Britain," an article by Orwell in 1945 in the *Contemporary Jewish Record.* His conclusions are given in four points. One, there is more anti-Semitism in England than is thought or admitted; and the war has accentuated it. Two, anti-Semitism does not at present lead to open persecution, but it makes people callous to the sufferings of Jews in other countries. Three, the only effect of Hitler's atrocities is that now people tend to conceal their anti-Semitic feelings. Four, anti-Semitism is quite irrational and will not yield to argument.

Some years ago in Paris, in a small cinema in the Latin Quarter, I saw Max Ophuls' more-than-four-hour-long film *Le chagrin et la pitié* (efforts to show it in the major cinemas and on television all failed). It was a detailed, largely documentary account of daily life in Clermont Ferrand under the Vichy government. It was quite appalling. With no particular pressure on the part of the Germans, the French *homme moyen,* of his own free will, gladly wallowed in the anti-Semitism decreed by Pétain's *équipe:* he followed traces, sniffed out, and denounced. The postwar version that the Germans had imposed the anti-Semitic policy on the Vichy government was a fiction, as Hannah Arendt pointed out in *The Origins of Totalitarianism* on the basis of her research in French archives. For a spectator from Eastern Europe, Ophuls' film evokes a single consideration: if Hitler's *Endlösung* had been carried out in France with the same methods and with the same terror used in Eastern Europe, French participation in the operation would have warmed Himmler's heart. As for what might have happened in Britain, had it been occupied by the Germans, only the imagination of the author of *1984* would have been equal to such a theme.

What is most striking in the four conclusions of Orwell's article is the statement that the war (with the holocaust in progress) *accentuated* British anti-Semitism, while it made the British *callous* to the sufferings of Jews in other countries. It would seem that it should have been just the opposite. But the psychology of irrational phenomena, which are refractory to any argument, functions in a way of its own. Likewise in Poland, war and the mass extermination of the Jews had the effect of increasing anti-Semitism in certain sectors of society, and the poisonous exhalations of this process still foul the air over the graveyard of three million victims. One fact is worth stressing, however, that is generally passed over in shameful silence in the West: the fact that during the war the poison of "mystic racism" spread *almost everywhere* in Europe. But in the meantime it is its Polish variation that has been singled out after the war as the "original" and "classic" form of anti-Semitism par excellence. It will take very little for Germans themselves in the near future to give a meaningful wink of the eye and allude to Polish anti-Semitism, since its ghosts are now being evoked in France in regard to . . . the affair of the native-born Nazi Darquier, either to replace or exorcise the ghosts of its own anti-Semitism.

1 9 7 9

Naples, January 15 [Shalamov and Kolyma]

Two matching extermination areas are treated in tandem, Auschwitz and Kolyma, most recently in Robert Conquest's book *Kolyma, the Arctic Death Camps*. It was a miracle that after nearly twenty years of imprisonment Varlam Shalamov came out of Kolyma, a writer before whom all the gulag literati, Solzhenitsyn included, must bow their heads. A volume of more than one hundred *Kolyma Tales*, published in Russian thanks to the efforts and with the introduction of Michael Heller, probably contains everything Shalamov wrote about the camps.

I should like to take note here of one feature of Shalamov's tales. Never, in his picture of the hell of Kolyma, does he do more than give a brief, dry, almost colorless account of the monstrosities of Kolyma, of the pit of human existence; he shuns any temptation to match his style and language to the cruel facts he reports. He uses the conventional matter-of-fact language of the chronicler or summarizer rather than that of a fiction writer. He eschews the exclamatory and the dramatic heightening of words, even where the subject itself might seem to call for it. He speaks in a voice that is calm and balanced, as if it were slightly softened by a touch of sad reflectiveness. In short,

I sense his instinctive or conscious fear of the snares of the "brutal" literature of the shocking, in the name of fidelity to his own memory. This fidelity is so pure and absolute and, at the same time, so deeply rooted in the reality of the world of Kolyma, that it endows Shalamov's tales with the splendor of art. A strange unexpected splendor in the depths of endless night.

In the three-page tale "Prosthetic Appliances," some prisoners are being put in isolation, all of them invalids except the author. They are forbidden to take anything with them that is not authorized by regulations, so their prostheses are "confiscated": a steel brace, a wooden leg, an artificial hand, a hearing trumpet, and a glass eye. Shalamov's turn comes; he is standing naked in front of the isolation guard. "We collect body parts here," the guard snickers under his breath. "And what have you got to hand over? Your soul?" "No," I said. "I won't give you my soul."

Perhaps the whole meaning of the *Kolyma Tales* is here. Will you hand over the "prothesis" of your soul or not? In another story, Shalamov remarks: "The camp was a great test for man's moral strength, for ordinary human morality, and ninety-nine per cent of the people did not endure this test." He also speaks of the *religiozniks:* "I never saw anyone in the camps with more dignity than the believers; depravity invaded everyone's soul, only the believers resisted." Shalamov was not one of them, which shows that the word "only" is an overstatement. But it is only a seeming overstatement, because in the Soviet "concentration camp world" attachment to the "prosthesis" of the soul was equivalent to faith or, in any case, a predisposition to faith. The name of God was not taken in vain, and prayers that atheists, agnostics, and the indifferent invented for themselves to recite inwardly were the whisper of defenseless but tenacious humanity. When that tenacity failed, something happened before the final capitulation that psychology calls "stupor": a dull absent stare at a fixed point; this certainly had something to do with a vague delayed awareness that man is too weak to seek support only in himself.

Is it possible to live without hope? Dostoevsky asks the question in *Memories from the House of the Dead.* There is a distant echo in my *World Apart.* Heller quotes two remarks about hope, one from Shalamov in Kolyma and the other from Tadeusz Borowski in Auschwitz. Shalamov: "Hope is always a shackle for a prisoner. Hope is always slavery. The man with hope will change his behavior for anything, he acts wickedly more often than the man without hope." Borowski: "Never in the history of mankind was hope stronger, and never did it bring such wickedness as it did in this war, in this camp. We were not taught to reject hope, therefore we die in gas chambers." It is impossible to live without hope, but in the labor camps living with hope meant depriving oneself of the miserable remains of participation in one's own destiny, were it only the capacity for hopeless rebellion or suicide. The hope of the *religiozniks* was different, however; it soared above consideration of days, months, and years, and attained a freedom to which the tormentors had no access.

Things change and lose much of their urgency. With the passage of time Solzhenitsyn's three volumes will be consulted like an encyclopedic guidebook to the gulags, and Shalamov's hundred tales will be examined as if they were under glass in a display case like a hundred petrified flakes of "prison civilization" with the clear imprint of words and faded rust-colored stains. And a future historian of Russia will say that its "prison civilization," erected after the victory of the "socialist revolution," played a major role in stimulating Russia's "renaissance of religion."

July 17 [Stories of spies and immaculate ideology]

Fitzroy Maclean went into the diplomatic corps in the thirties. Early in his career at the British Embassy in Moscow, he was an observer at Bukharin's trial. During the war he distinguished himself in the air squadron in the western Sahara. In 1943, after promotion to the rank of brigade commander, he parachuted into Yugoslavia, where he directed the British military mission at Michailovich's headquarters. Later he received orders to move to Tito's headquarters. He had doubts about the wisdom of this move and decided to express them openly to the prime minister. Churchill called him back to order and reason and asked if by any chance he intended to settle in Yugoslavia after the war. Indeed, he did not move to Yugoslavia after the war but stayed in England, where he was elected to Parliament for the Conservative party. Twice he was undersecretary of war, in the Churchill and Eden governments. In his free time, he wrote his memoirs. In the first volume, *Eastern Approaches*, he devoted a fine chapter to Bukharin's trial. I translated that chapter into Polish, with the author's permission, of course. While I was translating it, we exchanged letters in connection with the person of Dr. Levin, who was accused at the trial of having caused Gorky's death.

Now Sir Fitzroy Maclean, no longer M.P., has written *Take Nine Spies*, a book about famous spies from Mata Hari to Colonel Oleg Penkovsky. The weakest figure in Maclean's gallery is Azef, the most interesting is Kim Philby. At least it is for me, since I have been interested from the moment the bomb exploded, that is, since January 1963, when Philby suddenly disappeared from Beirut to surface soon afterward in Moscow, with a triumphant smile on his mouth and a glint of pride in his eyes.

It is clear that I took an interest in him as another type of communist. Philby did not spy for money. He was, and still is, unreservedly a communist, faithful to the "course" he chose. He has been since 1934, and not since the civil war in Spain, where, after a period of probation, he was finally recruited by Soviet intelligence. (This recruitment and the need for an immediate "cover" may explain an odd and long-obscure episode, namely, his decoration by General Franco in person with a medal of merit for the "objectiveness" of his correspondence for the *Times*.) Until recently it was believed that he was a typical product of leftist fever at Cambridge in the period between the two wars, just more tenacious and obstinate in his revolutionary choice and fervor than the majority of his colleagues and contemporaries, who in the course of time cooled and fell away. Trevor Roper and Graham Greene take him as example of the blinding force of an almost religious feeling, a modern version of the *sacrifice of the mind* of the sixteenth-century Jesuits. While not dismissing these interpretations, Maclean offers a more convincing portrait. Philby was not all that interested in social revolution, nor in the ideal of a classless society. On the contrary. He was firmly convinced of the inevitable world supremacy of Russia and decided to back the Russian horse. His own account of his recruitment by Soviet intelligence betrays the fundamental reason: "You don't look a gift horse in the mouth when you are offered a chance to enter an elite force." From an empire about to be pensioned off to an empire in expansion. Philby did indeed intend to settle in Russia one day. And he achieved his intention. The "elite force" there has a long-standing specific gravity.

Apropos the history of the group of American radicals of Trotskyite inspiration. Philip Rahv, one of the most distinguished American literary critics, died six years ago. A volume of his selected essays was published last year to honor his memory. He said good-bye to communism at the time of the Moscow trials (though he continued to admire the "Old Man," Trotsky). And he had a final argument with his friends during the war.

Why? Mary McCarthy explains the crucial motive in her introduction to the book: she says that he broke with his former colleagues such as Dwight Macdonald and Clement Greenberg over the question whether American radicals should back the war against Hitler or not. McCarthy says that they all thought not. In a long, deeply pondered essay, Rahv argued that they should. She remembers the last sentence, with which she did not agree at the time but which remained impressed and droned in her head: "In a certain sense this is our war."

I have no wish to go into the matter of how much of the imbecility of wartime American radicals (of Trotskyite inspiration) has survived in postwar American radicals. What interests me is the underlying "ideological purity." In the perspective of a great worldwide cleansing, the war with Hitler was not "our" war, because what it was cleansing was not the essential dirt. The scum had to clear first before hands destined for higher aims could be dipped into the laundry basin. Higher aims, the authentic pulse of history, the new man and the new masses, a world radically purified. . . .

The myth of a radically purified world was not a monopoly of revolution "on the left." The permanent communist "purge," with different variations, inclinations, and intensity, had its counterpart "on the right."

The SS physician, university professor, and doctor of medicine and philosophy Johann Paul Kremer made an entry on September 5, 1942, in the diary he kept at Birkenau: "Today at noon special action in the women's camp: the most horrible of horrors. Hauptsturmführer Heinz

Thilo, the garrison doctor, was right when he told me this was the *anus mundi.*"

Professor Antoni Kepinski begins his book *The Rhythm of Life* with a chapter entitled *"Anus Mundi"* (Wieslaw Kielar gave the same title to his memoirs of Auschwitz) and quotes Kremer's remark about the "rectum of the world." "This racy definition," he comments, "as one may imagine, expressed the disgust and horror that the concentration camp aroused in any observer, but it also justified the existence of the camp by the need to purify the world. . . . Hitler's idea was that the extermination camps, beyond the immediate political and economic objective, consisting in the cheapest and most efficient way of destroying the enemy, had a deeper sense, which was to purify the German race of everything that did not correspond to the Germanic ideal of the superman."

Kepinski took the motto at the beginning of the chapter from Pascal's *Pensées*: "What chimera then is man? What a singularity, what a monster, what chaos, what a subject of contradictions, what a marvel! Judge of all things, stupid worm of the earth, repository of the true, cesspool of uncertainty and error, glory and shame of the universe."

November 24 [A climate of treason]

Sir (ex-Sir as of last week) Anthony Blunt, eminent art historian, honorary citizen of Naples because of his frequent visits and studies of the Neapolitan baroque, and art adviser to the Queen, has turned out to be "the fourth man" in the Philby-Maclean-Burgess spy affair. By his own admission, he spied on behalf of the Soviets throughout the war, while working in various units of British intelligence. He probably continued to be part of the quartet (or quintet: a search is on for a "fifth man") for some time after the war as well. In 1964, the year after Kim Philby's flight to Moscow, the knight, his back to the wall, was forced to admit his guilt and strike a deal: immunity in exchange for full confession and cooperation. The immunity automatically included his prestigious function at the royal palace. The queen was ostensibly kept in the dark about everything and continued to avail herself of the services of her art consultant. And she would have done so until his well-earned retirement or death had it not been for the publication of Andrew Boyle's exposé *The Climate of Treason*.

The climate of treason goes back to Cambridge in the thirties. The young Blunt became a communist, or at least a Marxist, in the name of "antifascism." At that time he scouted university talent (in the art of espionage) for future employment by the Soviet agent in London. All that he and the talents he discovered among his university companions had to do was ready themselves for tasks to come. Blunt was ripe to assume these tasks in 1940, at the time of the pact between Stalin and Hitler. Did that alliance not raise any doubts in his "antifascist" conscience? Not in the least: on the part of Russia it was a tactical necessity to gain time. When was it, then, that he began to feel uncomfortable about being a Soviet spy? After the war, with the influx and "cumulative" effect of information about the USSR. Before the war and even during its first phase, until June 1941, there was evidently no possibility of forming an opinion about the "bastion and bedrock of antifascism." And June 1941 heightened his sense of duty as a spy.

Orwell knew what he was talking about when he wrote that British intellectuals who were communists or communist sympathizers felt more patriotism to the USSR than to their own country in those years. "Let us stop this nonsense," he urged, "about defending freedom against fascism."

During a conversation about the *Climate of Treason*, Blunt regaled a friend with this subtle and allusive tale. "The Florentine army was fighting the papal army, and Benvenuto Cellini was on the Florentine side. During a pause in the battle, a voice called out from the papal lines: 'Benvenuto, the Pope wants you to work for him.' Cellini dropped his weapons, joined the papal forces, and became the Pope's goldsmith. When he finished his work he went back to Florence, where he was welcomed with all honors and with joy because he was a great artist." This note of elitist pride—eminent people are not obliged to respect the laws, principles, and loyalties of ordinary people—is also sounded in Alan Moorehead's book *The Traitors, the Double Life of Fuchs, Pontecorvo and Nunn May*, published in 1952.

1 9 8 0

Naples, February 14 [Shostakovich]

The great-grandfather was deported to Russia for taking part in the Polish insurrection of November 1830 and the grandfather for taking part in the insurrection of January 1863; the father was Russianized and the son a famed Russian composer. The premise of Dimitri Shostakovich's "spoken memoirs" is contained in a remark he borrowed from Chekhov and applied to himself: "In my life I have written everything except denunciations." According to Shostakovich, it was probably customary for Soviet composers to write denunciations on music paper and for musicologists to do so on ordinary paper. He thinks that anyone who composed "everything except denunciations" (hence propagandistic rubbish to order, to save his skin and to pursue serious work) has the right to think he survived the Stalinist terror with dignity. Shostakovich's memoirs are not as interesting as might have been expected from the publisher's resounding announcements. It is not easy to write something important or new about this subject after the memoirs of Nadezhda Mandelstam. Moreover, the "spoken memoir" form is not conducive to reflection; it invites swaggering and haphazard thinking.

One passage from Shostakovich's *Testimony* struck me. He says it is sad and regrettable to speak of it, but he must if he is to tell the truth. And the truth is that the war proved to be a blessing. The war brought much suffering and tears. But it was even worse before the war, because everyone was alone with his own agony. Before the war there probably was not a family in Leningrad that had not lost someone, a father, a brother, or if it was not a relative at least a close friend. There was no one who did not have a dear one to mourn, but it had to be done in silence, under cover, so that no one could see. People were afraid of each other, sorrow crushed and suffocated them. Was it possible, before the war, to compose a work that sounded like a requiem without arousing suspicion? No. Suddenly the war made it possible to cry in public, openly, people stopped being frightened of their own tears. "Akhmatova wrote her Requiem, and mine is two symphonies, the Seventh and the Eighth."

There is something quite similar in the epilogue of *Doctor Zhivago*: "And when the war broke out, its real horrors, its real dangers, its menace of real death, were a blessing compared with the inhuman power of the lie, a relief because it broke the spell of the dead letter . . . the war came as a breath of fresh air, an omen of deliverance, a purifying storm."

I still clearly recall the time of my trekking from the labor camps to the army in early 1942, when "the inhuman power of the lie" (synonymous with "ideology" for Pasternak) was cracking and people were becoming different, more authentic—for better and for worse. A regime under which war could be a "blessing," a return to human law and the dimensions of reality.*

Naples, November 24 [Earthquakes]

Last night, seven thirty-five. I was washing my hands in the bathroom; the sound of running water was joined by another, stony sound. The wall ballooned, and a swelling appeared on the ceiling. I swayed slightly and remembered my attack of vertigo in August, so at first I thought this was a replay. Suddenly I was pervaded, or rather transfixed,

*Pasternak, *Doctor Zhivago*, tr. Max Hayward and Manya Harari, London: Collins and Harvill Press, 1958.

by a feeling I could not describe. No, it was not fear; I am well acquainted with fear; fear entails awareness of a concrete source of danger, plus an awareness that somehow there is a way out. Not now. Now I was beset by something formless, implacable, and omnipresent, something far away outside me but at the same time nearby and inside me.

A shout came from the courtyard, *"Terremoto,"* immediately intensified by a longer *"La terra trema."* It is a frequent shout in these parts; there are many notes on earthquake in my journal. I once spoke of the local "atavism of natural calamities," another time of the "atavistic dread," and again of how the earthquake "undercuts man's primordial, elementary sense of his own existence," because it "eludes the senses," it is the work of "a capricious force, blind, obscure, and unaware of its own power." However true they may be, these are only words, words, words.

We rushed into the courtyard, where the tenants of the building had clustered together. The evening sky in the direction of Mergellina was veiled by a cloud of dust. Sirens wailed, and ships howled in the port. A crowd hurtled down the street toward the sea, toward the public gardens, toward the large squares. It was already common knowledge that a nine-story building at Poggioreale had collapsed like a sand castle on the beach (there was a party on the ninth floor for a baby's baptism). The faces of the people they call *terremotati* always have the same expression. Why try to describe them, when all you need say is: the expression of rubble. Today I saw the same expression on the faces of people on the street and in the squares of Naples (stores, offices, and schools are closed, it is better not to stay indoors, better not to enter the churches—the warning being the crack on the old bell tower of Santa Chiara), and in the television reports from Campania, Basilicata, and Irpinia. Television reporters consider it the utmost in technical efficiency to offer listeners the moans that come from the depths of collapsed buildings. The heads bent over the rubble are indistinguishable from the stones that are being removed. The numbers are reeled off of the dead, injured, and missing; corpses are shown laid out side by side in neat rows; a woman pushes through the piles of stones convulsively clasping a dead baby in her arms. What cannot be said clearly should not be said at all. Instead of words, words, words, one phrase might say more: man reduced to dust by the single blow of an Unknown Hand. That is what arouses a feeling different than fear, impossible to describe, vaguely present even in silence.

1 9 8 1

Naples, January 8 [The death of
Nadezhda Mandelstam (1)]

Even the little that is known about the circumstances of Osip Mandelstam's death is not altogether clear; there are different versions.
One has it that he began to betray signs of psychic disturbance during
his transfer from Moscow to the transit prison in Vladivostok in September 1938 (after his second arrest in May of that year): he suspected
that they wanted to poison him, so he refused his own daily ration
and stole food from other prisoners. This did not stop when he got to
the transit prison (whence prisoners were transferred to Kolyma in the
months when it was possible to navigate as far as Magadan); so he
was thrown out of the barracks. Filthy and smelly, he lay in wait by
the garbage dump and fed on refuse. Once in a while the doctors in
the infirmary gave him something to eat; occasionally readers of his
poems did. There is another, literary version in one of Shalamov's short
Kolyma tales about the death of a poet in the labor camp. A dying
poet lies motionless on his bunk and composes his last poems in his
head. As night falls he dies, but for two days his fellow prisoners in

the barracks keep the death a secret so they can take his food ration. "The dead man lay holding one arm up like a marionette. He died before his death date, no trifling matter for his biographers." It is not certain that this detail was taken into account when December 27, 1938, was established as his date of death.

Nadezhda Mandelstam died December 29, 1980, almost exactly the forty-second anniversary of her husband's death. In the last years of her life she liked to repeat *"Menja nasi cari bojatsja"* ("Our czars are afraid of me") to reassure foreign guests, who were amazed and at the same time concerned for the increasing harshness of her pronouncements about the "prison civilization" of the Soviet system. No, this was not a mixture of coquetry and boldness on the part of an old woman alone. "An old woman who fears nothing and hates force" (her own words) had learned a lesson from the period of persecution and suffering: courage is the sole response to terror. If you count on courage alone, defending even its last remains to the end, you may even instill a drop of fear in the persecutors, who are not accustomed to victims' resistance and are disoriented by such tenaciously rooted human dignity. But no sooner did Nadezhda Mandelstam die than the "czars" shook off that touch of fear. They immediately appropriated her remains, kept the dead woman's friends at a distance, and waited several days before designating a cemetery and a grave site. They sealed her apartment in Moscow, perhaps in the belief that they could finally get their hands on the secret manuscripts of the Mandelstam archive. Fortunately, Nadezhda Mandelstam had made preparations in advance for her departure. In her 1966 will she had entrusted the care of her husband's papers and her own to a "commission of just men," eleven "honest people" listed by name in a special appendix, to prevent the bequest from ending in the hands of "that Assyrian monster which is the Soviet state." Because "it is not the guards who should be the heirs of the galley slave, but those who were chained with him at the oars . . . let the state take the inheritance of those who have sold their souls to it." From which it is fair to conclude that fourteen years later the envoys of the "czars" placed seals on things of little or no worth.

"I always envied Antigone: not the Antigone who led her blind father by the hand, but the Antigone who gave her life for the right to bury her brother. . . . Life must be nice in a small country where they do not gag people who shout to defend their rights, where you can sneak off with a forbidden corpse and where the three of you—Mandelstam, Akhmatova and I—do not have to scour the woods around Petersburg in search of the tomb of a poet who has been shot (Gumilev, Akhmatova's husband, had been executed by the Bolsheviks in 1921). . . . I, a widow who did not bury her husband, pay final homage to a corpse marked only with a tag on its foot by remembering him and mourning; I weep without tears, we all belong to a dry-eyed generation. I always expect them to come and take away these little scraps of paper of mine. If they come, they must also take me. And if they take me, I will stop envying Antigone."

With these words, Nadezhda Mandelstam herself gave the finest description of her two splendid books: *Hope Against Hope* and *Hope Abandoned*, which easily stand comparison with Pasternak's *Doctor Zhivago*, Akhmatova's *Requiem* and *Poem Without a Hero*, Bulgakov's *Master and Margherita*, and Solzhenitsyn's novels and *Gulag Archipelago*. They never managed to steal "the forbidden corpse" from her or to gag the mouth "that shouted to defend its rights." Listening for a knock at the door, she buried the body of her husband and the poet with a "tag on his foot" in those hundreds of "little scraps of paper." She did more: she erected an indestructible monument to him against the background of an age of terror. She erected it with patience, and love and anger transformed her into a great writer. Ten days ago, when she breathed her last on the eve of her ninetieth birthday, who knows if she did not gaze at the birthday candles lit before the portrait of her husband as a young man and murmur to herself: "I did not go off in silence like most of my generation." I think of her with deep emotion and immense admiration. A requiem for the fearless Russian Antigone.

May

Rubble

I

Late one evening early last December, soon after the earthquake, I was on my way home after dining with my friend Captain Mauro P. We parted company outside the restaurant in the center of town.

"I have to report to headquarters at once," he said. "I am leaving for Lucania December 15. Think about my offer. If you decide to come, call me at the hotel the morning of the fourteenth. The village in Lucania is called Tora Alta."

Flakes of snow were falling, and rather heavily at that, but it melted at once on the sidewalk and street and formed a thin film of slush. It lasted only a few minutes, and then a cold rain poured down with hailstones. I stopped in an entryway. The sky brightened over Vomero as if in a glow of flame. I remembered that strange brightness in the night. It had accompanied the earthquake in November and sowed panic among the fleeing people. At the time someone cried out: the sky is on fire!, and the shout was taken up by the crowd.

Two Abruzzi mountaineers in their black capes took refuge next to me in the entry, one with a bagpipe and the other with a fife, an everyday sight in Naples in the Christmas holiday season; and so did a hunchbacked Neapolitan street musician, his barrel organ covered by a shred of dirty cloth. The rain did not stop, indeed it got stronger and lashed the street with slanting streams. The organ grinder turned his handle and cranked out the sounds of one of those Neapolitan songs that mix maudlin, cloying sentimentality with the lurching rhythm of a lively refrain. But it abruptly fell silent, as if the man's hand had been wrenched from the crank. The bagpiper whispered something to his companion. The noise of the downpour now blended with a fife plaint that lasted as long as there was breath in the man's lungs.

When the rain suddenly stopped and cloud glazed the reddish light over the Vomero, we all stepped out of the entryway. I did not have far to go home, by a shortcut through the backstreets. It was nearly midnight, the backstreets were empty and silent, not a living soul, torn garbage bags lay scattered along the walls, and big fat rats skittered among them. It was not like that in the past, probably even the year before, when the approaching holidays were greeted with illuminations and fireworks almost till dawn. For a couple of weeks any mention of our city, any commentary in the papers had been in the style of a funeral oration.

II

I met Captain P. some time ago, a mutual friend from Piedmont introduced us. Mauro was also Piedmontese, his family came from Novara. I do not know what led him to choose a career in the military. He was interested in everything, except what he had to do in the army: philosophy, literature, art; and he had a variety of hobbies, for example, he photographed the Christmas crèches in Italian churches. A confirmed bachelor, he was the kind of person who performed his professional duties conscientiously but with absolute and slightly ironic detachment. He might just as well have been a bank teller or a postal clerk as an officer. You sometimes had the feeling, though, that he wore his military uniform like a monk's habit, that he had chosen the army in place of the cloister.

That December day we had arranged to meet in a church near Piazza Dante, actually in the church basement, where he had permission that evening to photograph the *presepe poliscenico.* From there we were to go to dinner.

The Christmas Crib is a Neapolitan mania, in private and public alike, and it deserves a place of its own in the history of Neapolitan art. Indeed, the San Martino Museum boasts several rooms of remarkably beautiful and imaginative seventeenth- and eighteenth-century crèches. The Church of Santa Chiara has a Nativity scene that goes on display in early December every year in the cloister vestibule, a truly lavish bequest from a Neapolitan patrician of the last century. Other less important churches make do with whatever they have and enhance their Nativity scenes with new additions every year. The tradition of renovating and enriching crèches reigns in private homes too, so starting in November dozens of stalls appear in a few backstreets of the old town selling figurines, huts, moss, tree bark, and suchlike accessories for the *presepe a casa.*

An exhaustive treatise on "crèche-ism" would need a whole separate chapter on its philosophy. What a difference, for example, between the sumptuous crèches and the poor ones! Not just in the sense of the difference of means, the contrast of splendor and poverty, but the distinct image of Arcadia, the different visions of the myth of Arcadia. The *presepe poliscenico* in the church in Piazza Dante was one of the sweetest specimens of bucolic Arcadia. Extremely plain, even paltry means had been used to create a mountain village above the little manger scene in the foreground, and the imagination that went into it was touchingly naive in its power. The composition centered on a water mill with a turning wheel, and in some peculiar way, it gave life to the whole rest of the picture: people in the lanes and in front of their houses, animals in the field, little shops and inns, women at the well, dancers in the little squares, children by a stream; and it linked the earth to the sky, which was pink instead of blue, hung with silver stars and a golden disk of the moon in the center. The crowd of visitors, mostly from the backstreets of the "Spanish Quarter," the hardest hit by the earthquake, were just as moved as the photographer in his army uniform.

Almost as soon as we sat down in the restaurant, he made his offer to me. Tora Alta, a village in upper Lucania, had been almost totally annihilated by the earthquake. It had been decided not to rebuild the village, and the surviving inhabitants were evacuated, some housed in hotels in nearby towns and on the Adriatic coast, and some camping in tents and trailers on a plateau five kilometers from Tora Alta. Not all the bodies of the dead could be dug out, because the walls of the houses threatened to collapse. It would take until Christmas to level the village to the ground. In the meantime a military cordon had been set up around the village to prevent the inhabitants of the nearby encampment from digging up the dead and hunting for the rest of their belongings themselves. Mauro had been posted to relieve the detachment commandant in Tora Alta for ten days. Wouldn't I like to go there with him for those ten days? Something would be found for me to do as well. He had already mentioned the possibility to his superiors, and they had nothing against it.

III

I got home after midnight. The pattern of my life at this time was set to an irrational vigil every night. I made an effort to stay awake in my armchair till dawn, dozing off from time to time, and I was forever looking for books that could help sustain my voluntary wakefulness. I had discovered two things during the preceding weeks. That the night seems to increase the dread of earthquake. And that this fear poses man the ultimate questions with exceptional clarity and force.

I must have vaguely sensed the second thing even earlier, years before, when I wrote the story "The Tower." For how else explain the fact that its solitary hero, the habitual reader of François-Xavier de Maistre's *Le lépreux de la Cité d'Aoste*, has exactly the life story he does? "Not much was known of his past. He was Sicilian by birth, and before he was sent to Turin after the first war he had taught in Sicily, where he lost his entire family—his wife and three children—in the famous Messina earthquake of 1908. It was rumored that he had been retired prematurely because of the scandal arising from an attempt at suicide." For leprosy, which was once considered a "mystical" disease, I sought a counterpoint or perhaps rather a kinship in a wound, a wound that can never be healed, the *terremoto;* in the poisoning, or in the infection, of the soul of a man who has felt the earth quake and seen an abyss open beneath his feet. Both figures in "The Tower," the leper from the city of Aosta and the Sicilian *terremotato,* stood before a glass corroded and darkened by age; and in it each of them made out a reflection he would have preferred never to see.

When in the course of my night's vigil in the armchair I turned back in memory to the period when I conceived and wrote "The Tower," I realized, of course, what the source of my intuition was, whence the need to find such a companion for the soul of the leper of Aosta. In those years I often heard accounts of Croce and the historian Salvemini, who were antithetical in a certain sense yet surely the most distinguished figures in Italian intellectual life in the fascist era. In 1883 the young Croce lost his parents and sister in the earthquake on Ischia. Salvemini lost his wife and all his children in the Messina earthquake of 1908. Somebody, someone who knew both of them well, described the "peculiar sensation" (I remembered that term and the idea that followed from it) that always crept into any extended conversation with them: "It was as if, independently of the topic of conversation, sometimes even in conflict with the subject and mood of the conversation, there always came a brief moment of total absence, when the glance of Croce and Salvemini alike was suddenly suspended in the void."

I mentioned my ceaseless search at that time for books to keep me wakeful during my nightly vigil. On the whole, very little of those readings has remained with me, they were like pills that stimulate the senses and dull them at the same time. And yet, now as I try to give a faithful account from beginning to end of my unsuccessful expedition to Lucania (for "Rubble" is merely a report), I reach for the book that most often kept me company before my departure from Naples, for *Crime and Punishment*, and I find two heavily thumbnailed passages in it. In one it is Raskolnikov who speaks: "I read somewhere of a man who was sentenced to death, and an hour before the execution he says or maybe he just thinks that if he happened to live somewhere on a cliff, or on a rock, or on a ledge so narrow that there was only room for his two feet—and that he was surrounded by an abyss, an ocean, eternal darkness, eternal solitude, and a never-ending tempest —and that he had to stay that way, standing in one square foot of space for a lifetime, a thousand years, or eternity—it would be better to live like that than to die at once! In any case to live, live, live! In any way—anyhow to live! . . . How true that is! God, how true! Man is vile! And anyone who calls him vile because of that is vile himself." In the other passage it is Svidrigaylov: "Eternity always strikes us as an idea that is impossible to comprehend, like something enormous, enormous! But why enormous after all? Just imagine that suddenly instead of all this there will be one little room, something like a country bath house, black with soot and spiderwebs in all the corners, and there you have all eternity."

Mauro telephoned the morning of the thirteenth of December. He had been ordered to leave sooner, he would be ready to come by for me in the early afternoon, that is if I decided to go. Yes, yes, I had more than made up my mind—I was anxious to make that expedition.

IV

We left Naples at sunset in a downpour, and we crept along the *autostrada* to Pompeii and then to Salerno in a column of trucks, vehicles with trailers, medical vans, and platform trucks with building materials.

"Yesterday at headquarters they told me again that they are unable to dig out all the dead in Tora Alta. They tried several times more, but the walls collapse on the diggers. The only thing to do is knock down what is still standing and cover the rubble with lime."

"Like Agadir in Morocco?"

"Like Agadir in Morocco. And here it is even harder."

In Lucania and Irpinia (we heard on the radio) it was still snowing heavily, and there were occasional blizzards in the mountainous region of the earthquake. The radio newsmen on the scene reported a rampant psychosis that the end of the world was at hand. Handwritten leaflets appeared here and there announcing *un evento escatologico,* an eschatological event: the precise details were to be found in the Bible, and it had to be "prepared for with unceasing prayer." The area was swarming with magicians, palmists, fortune-tellers, and preachers. The peasants of Lucania and Irpinia did not know what an "eschatological event" meant, their familiarity with the Bible was usually limited to piously pressing their fingers or lips to its cover, but the words "end of the world" struck a familiar chord in their hearts. The priest in Sottomonte, which was only lightly hit by the November quake, tried in vain to prevent the shepherds from driving their herds up to the high plateau above the village.

It was easy to smile reading that "eschatological" bells were ringing. It was harder to laugh off the reverberations they called forth. The shepherds of Sottomonte fled with their sheep to the snow-covered heights, straight into a trap they took for a promise of salvation. "The whole world won't perish," they replied to the priest who tried to dissuade them. "God would not allow it." A familiar folk strain! Was it so very different from the stare of the wise men suspended in the void?

Beyond Salerno, in a monotonous stifling drizzle, Mauro took the first turn off the main road. He had decided to take the back roads to reach Eboli by late evening. Eboli was made famous by the book *Christ Stopped in Eboli* (according to folk wisdom, Christ did not have the heart to go any farther, to Lucania forsaken by all), and it was the epicenter of the earthquake. That is to say, the point from which the seismic waves spread out, sparing that point in its work of devastation;

the eye of the cyclone, cloaked in white silence. That still silence at the brink of the abyss had plunged the town into stillness. The shutters were bolted in all the houses, faint streaks of light trickled through the slits, few lampposts were on, and the streets were almost totally deserted. The bar in the square was closed. We drank water from a well and walked wordlessly around the square to stretch our legs.

We had maintained silence since we left Naples, interrupting it only for brief factual remarks. I sensed it would continue to be like that. There are different kinds of silence; ours, I think, was an instinctive dread of catching the plague of dramatic rhetoric. People do not realize how insidiously, in certain circumstances, they can be infected by the rhetorical. And how important it is at least to try to shake it off. And to do so in the name of what seems a simple but is actually a perverse rule, that it is on the slippery confines between the banal and the mysterious that we only fleetingly brush against the never wholly grasped nature of things.

We made our way along a bumpy, little-used road and reached Muro Lucano before midnight. There the broad highway to Pescopagano was again choked with a line of trucks and cars, continual bottlenecks stopped traffic, drivers jumped out of their cabins in the darkness, shouted, lit lanterns, insulted each other, and brandished their fists. It was actually snowing, but the air was clear, the black sky was sliced by the crescent moon, and the mountains in the distance were hooded in white. There were two guards at the turnoff to Tora Alta. One of them on motorcycle led us up a gently winding road the few kilometers to the military base. Before going into the tent we were assigned, we stopped for a moment to look at the ruins of Tora Alta farther up the slope. After the snowfall the rubble looked like a hastily abandoned quarry.

V

I got dressed before dawn and silently went out of the tent. The whole camp was still asleep, guarded by sentries under a wooden shelter on the opposite side of the road in front of a row of tents along the flat precipice. The last bit of road to the village, certainly no more than a kilometer, was straight and steep. In the grimy gray of dawn the rubble stood out pale and barely visible, but it was no longer covered by white patches everywhere. It had suddenly warmed up during the night, and the rubble quickly soaked up the melting snow.

I saw the rubble clearly only up above, where patrols blocked access to the village at both ends of the road and from the footpaths up the slope. A patrol had even been stationed on the other side of the village to block the approach from the summit of the heights. The cordon around the village was airtight.

Tora Alta had about one thousand five hundred inhabitants. Some six hundred people perished in the earthquake, and not much more than five hundred had been dug out. There was an improvised cemetery down below, near the village, in a place that had formerly served as a playground for the children. Branches were stuck in the ground all around it, and there was a pile of open coffins nearby in the event other bodies were dug up. The graves were marked by low crosses made of two slats nailed together. Instead of a given name, surname, and date, some of them were marked *uomo non identificato, donna non identificata, bambino non identificato* ("unidentified man," "unidentified woman," "unidentified child").

These were mostly for those who had died in the church, where evening mass was in progress at the moment of the quake: the number of victims in the church was estimated at more than a hundred, less than seventy of whom were dug out. The body of the priest was not found; it was said that he had escaped and run away from Tora Alta. An eight-year-old girl named Concetta was miraculously spared; she was outside playing on the church steps during the service. Her mother, grandmother, and two brothers were killed at home, and her father was dug out alive six days after the earthquake. The soldier who told me all this added that only about four hundred of the survivors refused to leave Tora Alta. A small trailer camp had been set up for them on the plain. Three barracks had also been erected: a school combined with a chapel (a priest came from Muro Lucano to say Mass on Sundays), a field hospital, and a provisions shed.

Now the hatching dawn raked the remains of night from the ruins, and I could observe them closely to my heart's content. They looked ghostlike in the purplish light, and yet the shade of the dead village still lived on. The way the face of someone who has just died, before his features go finally stiff and rigid, still has something of his former expression in a little twist of the mouth or the creases under the eyes, so the mounds of rubble of Tora Alta still obstinately preserved faint vanishing traces of its soul. I use the word reluctantly, but I cannot find a better one. There was a kind of proscenium of shattered stone, smashed beams, and crumbled plaster, and to the right of this frame stood a well that had been spared, its shaft still upright. The church facade dominated center stage, its doors knocked out and empty as far as a mound of brick blocks, tiles, and steel rods that had probably formed when they dug up the dead bodies. The plaster figure of a saint was leaning against the wall on the top step by the opening where the door had been. The villagers must have put it there as the sole undamaged remains of the altar, and since this was a manifest miracle, they probably appealed for another miracle by decking it with beads and rosaries. To the left was a fairly well preserved long narrow lane, its steps totally cleared of rubble all the way up. The buildings seemed less devastated, and a broken sign projected from the window of one of them, *Vino e olio*.

The war accustomed us to the sight of demolished cities, towns, and villages with wastelands of rubble, skeletons of houses, and cemeteries under a tangle of walls and scrap iron. What was it, then, that made this scene so overwhelming? I wish I could say! If I could find a few words to indicate the difference between "human" wars and a blow "out of nowhere"!

As soon as it was light the excavators, bulldozers, and demolition machines came to Tora Alta. They continued the demolition work the earthquake had begun.

VI

What I saw was only part of the picture of the rubble, but I had a full view subsequently. After lunch Mauro decided to take a noncommissioned officer to inspect the progress of the demolition of Tora Alta, and I joined them. A small crowd broken up into little groups stood in a semicircle on the slope at the entrance to the village. They stood anywhere there was room to stand.

"They come every afternoon," the noncom explained. "Five kilometers from that trailer camp of theirs: they take a shortcut across the fields through snow and slush. Men, women, and children. They just stand and look. At sunset some of them go right back to the settlement, others set off for the cemetery. There's nothing to be done about it. We toss them pieces of wood from the rubble to build a fire."

I won't even try to describe them, I have always been shy about my use of words. I shall only say that when I shifted my glance from the shattered village to its surviving inhabitants, I was no longer sure that they had actually survived. They stood motionless, like stone, they seldom spoke, and when they did the words were like shreds torn from lumped throats. Their eyes had a cold numb intensity, as if they were looking at something for the last time: it went beyond the bounds of suffering, to where despair turns to indifference. The children did not cry, they did not shiver with the cold, and they did not fidget their feet in the slush, they only hugged close to the grownups. When it finally began to get dark, the crowd stirred in several places, and they started lighting fires. They bent their outstretched hands over the flames that crept along the ground.

Before the sun set a tall man with a little girl broke away from one of the groups and moved briskly along the newly worn path to the cemetery. We followed after him. They stopped in front of four crosses at some distance from all the others, next to the fence of branches: Calabritto Rosalia, age seventy-nine; Calabritto Maria, age forty-eight; Calabritto Vincenzo, age twenty-two; Calabritto Pietro, age seventeen. The man and the girl stopped awhile, and then the man put his arm around the little girl's shoulder and spoke aloud; he was almost shouting: *"Andiamo, Concetta, andiamo, figlia mia, Dio non c'è"* ("Let's go, Concetta, let us go, my daughter, there is no God"). He drew aside the branch fence, helped the little girl down the embankment, and again put his arm around her. He moved quickly, and the little girl had to run to keep up with him. We lost sight of them beyond a clump of trees on the edge of the field.

"They dug him out after six days," the noncom explained. "He was lying on the narrow ledge of a wall in the cellar of the wine shop, over a deep hole in the ground. He was hanging rather than lying there. If he had moved at all, he would have fallen to the bottom and that probably would have brought down the whole rickety wall. Six days and six nights: it's almost unbelievable! On the sixth day someone heard his feeble cry, *'Salvatemi, salvatemi!'* ('Save me!') They broke through the rubble from the street and made an opening wide enough to crawl into and pushed a folding metal ladder down to the ledge of the wall. Where he found the strength to clamber up the rungs, I don't know. It took him a good hour. They drove him to the field hospital in Pescopagano, and he came back here a few days later. His daughter was the only one to survive; she was playing on the steps of the church, while her father was buying wine at the wine shop. The rest of his family was buried in their house. They haven't dug them out; the house is in the most dangerous part, at the other end of the village at the foot of the hill. When he came back from the hospital, he insisted on setting up those four crosses to one side in the cemetery, as if he wanted the illusion that they were buried or had not lost hope that in spite of everything their bodies would still be dug up."

In the evening we went to the trailer camp. Mauro said they had to find a way to keep the children there during the daily pilgrimage of the adults to the rubble. There was a school barracks but nothing else: the woman teacher died, and the man teacher had preferred evacuation to the Adriatic coast. A young woman looked after the children a bit till lunchtime, and then they went back to their families. They were expecting a volunteer teacher, a woman from Salerno, right after Christmas. Meanwhile, however, the children had to spend the afternoon in the school barracks until the adults came back from Tora Alta. Mauro himself took on the role of temporary teacher. After all, everything here was makeshift and improvised. They expected that once the village had been leveled and covered with lime, it would be easier to persuade the residents of the trailers to evacuate as well.

I woke up the next morning with a high fever. Actually it was Mauro who woke me, alarmed by my raving in my sleep. I spent the whole day alone in the tent dozing, waking, swallowing pills, and dozing off again with the the clang of machinery and the crash of falling wreckage in my ears. When I woke up properly it was dark, the glow of a cigarette in the opposite corner of the tent showed that Mauro had already returned from the settlement. I could feel that the fever had gone down, and I reached for the water bottle. I drank it all down, and I too lit a cigarette. It was Mauro who finally broke the long silence.

"They brought me five boys and seven girls to the school hut, between the ages of eight and ten. Most of the parents simply ignored my orders. They began leaving for Tora Alta at the usual hour. Calabritto took Concetta with him. I realized, of course, there was no question of having regular lessons. I had taken *Fiabe italiane* with me by chance, and it was in my suitcase with some other books. I read fairy tales to them for several hours with breaks. They sat at their desks like deaf-mutes, and there was nothing in the expression on their faces to show that they followed anything other than the movement of my lips. In the breaks they crowded around the chapel door, looking at me sideways. They did not answer my questions."

All that had been missing to make this picture of the rubble truly complete was this evidence that speech too had been destroyed. And, remembering the scene in the cemetery, to ask if the exclamation *"Dio non c'è"* was not something on the order of the dying convulsion of speech crushed under heaps of stone, the infinite weight of the treacherous earth.

VII

The fever shot up again, and violently; there was no sense to lie alone in the tent and burden my host with additional worry. On December 17 I took advantage of a ride to Naples and bid farewell at a distance to Tora Alta. I was stretched out on blankets at the back of the military pickup truck. I counted on sleeping the whole way, largely thanks to the monotonous beating of the raindrops on the tarpaulin roof. But I could not fall asleep. On the contrary, I was pervaded by an unusual lucidity together with a kind of incomprehensible, almost euphoric sensation of pain and relief at the same time. If only I had what the Russians call *shlezny dar,* "the gift of tears"! Why does hope suddenly appear, in the twinkling of an eye, when it is least expected? Why does its shade wear the face of God and not of fate? Why in His mysterious smile is love intertwined with scorn and cruelty? It is better that it all remain a secret. If your lips are unable to utter something that makes your voice ring with conviction, say nothing at all. And pray in silence instead of prattling vainly. Where did I read that or hear it?

At home the fever lasted till Christmas. I do not remember much of this period. All around me reports were nervously exchanged of new tremors in Naples and its environs, dread had returned to the city, and people were spending the night outdoors on the street, in squares and public gardens. Preparations for the holidays went ahead perfunctorily, without enthusiasm, and absentmindedly as if some superstitious fear were being masked. One day I was browsing in Goethe's *Italian Journey* and came upon his account of an expedition to the top of Vesuvius, that "hellish peak which arises in the middle of paradise." After he fled from "that inferno," Goethe noted: "The Neapolitan would be a totally different kind of person, if he did not feel he was caught in a trap between God and Satan." In the late eighteenth century, the "trap" was considered the local curse, and it was visited with anxious curiosity by travelers from other countries, "a totally different kind of people."

Mauro telephoned on the twenty-eighth of December. Tora Alta had finally ceased to exist the previous day. He spoke rapidly, he seemed upset; and he was quick to add that he would tell me the rest in Naples after the New Year. Before I could ask him anything, he hung up or the line was interrupted.

VIII

Despite the mellow New Year, the first sunny day in a long time, the town was fairly deserted. We went down to the sea, which was unruffled and glistening. It was not hard to find an empty bench on the seafront promenade. On the way I thought how right my earlier observation was, that Mauro had chose the army the way he might have chosen the cloister, if the main impulse for becoming a monk was somehow to leave the world behind. Now that the Tora Alta chapter was closed, there was something in the way he moved and in the expression of his face as if he had been burned. There was exasperation in everything he said.

The account he gave was long, rambling, overwrought, and full of digressions, rushing ahead of the story and then quickly running back, so I will reduce it to the bare facts and do so in the manner of a report.

He gave up his "lessons" after two more days of vain effort. Moreover, he was increasingly taken up with his own duties. The demolition work had to be interrupted several times because of heavy blizzards, and since even that did not dissuade the people down below from making their daily appearance at the ruins, the restrictive cordon also had to be reinforced. According to the original plan, it had been decided to drench the flattened rubble with lime the day before Christmas Eve, but that proved unfeasible. The upper part of the village, the most heavily damaged part, was continually postponed on the not unreasonable grounds that at least some of the houses would collapse on their own. Everything stopped on Christmas Day, and the final demolition was to begin the day after. And indeed between Christmas night and the next morning, three houses on the terraced levels of the upper village collapsed. They collapsed so utterly that only a single steel beam slanted up from the ground, like the bare branch of a rotten uprooted pine tree. Just before the crash, two soldiers patrolling the village heard a kind of loud murmur, and one of them saw, or thought he saw, the shadow of a dog scampering off. The next morning the demolition equipment was moved up to the worst damaged area, and it looked as if the last traces of Tora Alta would be gone by the time the sun set over them. But something unexpected happened that afternoon. Someone brought the news that Concetta's father had disappeared. Mauro immediately went down below and found the girl in a neighbor's trailer. She knew nothing, she was sitting curled up in a corner and did not even look up in response to his questions. In the settlement they supposed that Calabritto had gone to his hillside sheep fold for the things he had left there in the autumn, and he would be back. He would be back, but in the winter that kind of expedition takes time. The next morning, when the demolition work was finally completed and the excavators were leveling the mound surmounted by the steel beam, they found Calabritto's corpse, his head crushed by the buried end of the beam.

His funeral took place on the twenty-eighth of December. Tora Alta no longer existed. The body was taken from the settlement chapel to the cemetery, and a grave was dug next to the four empty graves with their crosses. The same forlorn slat cross was set up on his grave: Calabritto Giuseppe, age fifty-three. The priest took Concetta straight from the cemetery to Muro Lucano, and from there she was to be sent to the Convent of the Ursuline Sisters in Potenza.

A chill wind started blowing in from the sea. Traffic along the seafront was heavier now, a jukebox roared from an open-air café in the public gardens behind us, the steamer from Ischia rounded the promontory of Posillipo, and a rocket flared above the castle and burst into a white cluster high against the sun. The adjacent bench was occupied by women, philosophically called *peripatetiche* in these parts, waiting for customers, and some boys hovered among the enormous rocks on the shore with fishing rods. It was as if the city were making a timid and wary attempt to come back to life.

"As I came out of the chapel after Mass, following the crowd behind the corpse, I noticed a curved screen of matting in a corner of the wall separating the chapel from the schoolroom. The screen aroused my curiosity, and I slipped away from the crowd and looked behind it. There was a little manger scene that the children of the settlement must have made. Made, that may be an overstatement. And then, I don't know how . . . Try to imagine a little heap of rubble on the floor and a cardboard box in the middle with tow and mattress stuffing in it and a naked doll with wide-open eyes and pricked all over. The holes in the pink plastic were painted with red slashes and wavy lines, the kind you see on crucifixes in wayside chapels and village churches and in old pictures and sculptures of the Crucifixion. That's all. Nothing else."

IX

What has always impressed me most deeply in the Book of Job is his lamentation in the seventeenth chapter, beginning with the words: "My breath is corrupt, my days are extinct, the graves are ready for me." And the ending, which has been interpreted in various ways: "They change the night into day: the light is short because of darkness. If I wait, the grave is mine house: I have made my bed in the darkness. I have said to corruption, Thou art my father: to the worm, Thou art my mother, and my sister. And where is now my hope? as for my hope, who shall see it? They shall go down to the bars of the pit, when our rest together is in the dust."

Will we rest together in the dust, or will hope turn to dust? Or will it, instead, lie by my side eternally, not abandoning me as I await the end, as in secret it did not abandon me when I writhed in despair, when I cursed the Almighty, when I shouted He does not exist? The only thing we have that is godlike is this: the power of hope, which also expresses—and perhaps all the more violently—the power of despair. When Kafka wrote about the indestructible hard kernel of man, he was thinking about hope, although he did not have the courage to call it by its name. Dostoevsky exclaimed, "You cannot live without hope"; and that is our godlike eternity.

In the days I was finishing my report about rubble, I read the posthumous memoirs of a man sentenced to life imprisonment in Porto Azzurro. There were three other prisoners in the cell with him. A pity he did not describe it in more detail! Might it have been like a sooty country bathhouse with spiders in all the corners? Every afternoon a ray of sunlight would come into the cell under the half-shuttered window. It quivered on the floor, gradually faded, and finally disappeared. They waited for it—day after day, month after month, year after year—"the way a condemned man probably waits for a reply to his appeal for pardon." Later he makes a confession: "Who knows if it wasn't our mutual shame that checked our hidden longing to get down on our knees every afternoon to greet our guest and bid him farewell. He was the only God we had."

I will end my report on rubble with the words Mauro uttered: "That's all. Nothing else."

Naples, November 15 [Isaiah Berlin, Sorel, and cemeteries]

Isaiah Berlin closes his essay on Charles Sorel with the testimony of Daniel Halévy. In 1932, ten years after Sorel's death, the director of the Paris Bibliothèque Nationale went to Daniel Halévy with a "strange story." At a reception he had met the ambassador of fascist Italy, who expressed his regret for the deplorable state of Sorel's tomb and, in the name of his government, offered to erect a monument to the "eminent thinker." A short time later, the Soviet ambassador in Paris turned to him with the same proposal on the part of his government. After listening to the "strange story," Halévy promised to transmit both offers to Sorel's family. He had to wait a long time for a reply. At last he received a curt dry letter of refusal that made it very clear that the condition of Sorel's tomb was a private family matter and was no one else's concern. Halévy heaved a sigh of relief.

Basically there was nothing "strange" about it. In his book *The*

Main Currents of Marxism, Leszek Kolakowski concludes the chapter on Sorel by saying that "the fate of his ideas shows that the extreme forms of radicalism of the right and the left coincide." Even more, he points out that the author of *Reflections on Violence* had "an extremely weak notion of Leninist doctrine, admired Lenin as the herald of the Great Devastation and admired Mussolini for the same reason." So it is natural that the systems created by both "pioneers" suddenly wanted to honor their eminent late "admirer." Nor would it come as a surprise if the simultaneous timing of the two proposals turned out to be "ideological" rivalry in the graveyard, since the Italian ambassador made his appearance as the representative of an "anti-communist" government, and the Soviet ambassador as the representative of an "anti-fascist" government. Yet the episode recounted by Daniel Halévy has an eloquence of its own. And perhaps not just because it offers such a vivid illustration of the deceitful rendition of the "great ideological conflicts" of our century.

The conflict, the real conflict, is one only, between the recognition of man's inherent worth and its denial (whether it be left or right, red, brown or black). The Spanish Civil War passes for the armed practice run of "ideological" confrontation. The rightist George Bernanos' *Les Grands Cimetières sous la lune* appeared in 1938, an indictment of the atrocities of the Francoists. Simone Weil, a leftist participant in the war in Spain, wrote him a letter about the comparable atrocities of the Republicans; what she had found most chilling was the insouciant tone with which her comrades, people she esteemed, told each other about their sanguinary deeds as they chuckled over a glass of wine. She drew the conclusion that, for both sides, anyone who was classified as an enemy automatically, once and for all, became a worthless object, suitable only for death. She was horrorstruck, in this struggle under different ideological banners, by how like each other the combatants were in their anti-humanity.

1 9 8 2

Felice Bauer, Kafka's fiancée, once said she would like to be with him
while he was writing. He replied with a long letter. "Writing means
opening yourself to the utmost. . . . So you can never be sufficiently
alone when you write, there can never be sufficient silence when you
are writing, night is even too little night." He dreamed of a little
closet for himself in the farthest reaches of a vast cellar. He would
have written by the light of an oil lamp, his meals would have been
left outside the cellar door, and he would have gone to get them at
set hours. These would have been his sole promenades through the
vaults of a dark underground corridor. "Who knows the things I
would write there and from what depths I would bring them up!"

This letter of 1913 may be considered the manifesto of "cellar"
literature. It was something totally different from the "ivory tower,"
from the house of the "recluse of Croisset," or Proust's cork-lined
room; it was something akin rather to Dostoevsky's underground. Literature, satiated with the image of a world visible "in all its splendor,"
and ever more mistrustful of it, yearned for its invisible springs and
roots. Today the visible world often deserves the epithet of "Kafka-

esque," so Kafka's disciples, imitators, and admirers spin new dreams of deeper and deeper cellars. But where they would like to arrive there are no roots at all, there is only darkness, boundless and heartless darkness. But Kafka was a religious writer; in his cellars he was desperately seeking the source of light hidden from human sight.

April

The Brand: The Last Kolyma Tale

*People should not see what I saw, they should not even know
about it.*

*I was frightened by man's frightening strength, his wish and
ability to forget.*

I wanted to be alone, I was not afraid of memories.

—*Varlam Shalamov,* Kolyma Tales

A great writer was dying. He had been dying for three days, ever since he had been taken from the asylum for the old and infirm to the psychiatric hospital on the outskirts of Moscow. He resisted with the little strength he had left, convinced that he was going back to Kolyma, battered and bruised, with his hands tied behind his back. He had been dying for three days without realizing that he was dying. Life was leaving him slowly, it was just leaving; it did not turn back even for a moment, not even for that one moment, however brief, in which a dying man realizes that he is dying. He sat on the bed in striped pajamas, in a small room with bars on the window, facing a padded door with a round spy-hole. By day he was caught between two fires of light, one from the bulb over the door and the other from the frosted windowpane; at night he was entangled by the rays of the bulb. Sometimes steps resounded in the corridor, shouts and curses rang out, keys grated in locks: he did not hear them. The view from the window extended over an empty snow-covered courtyard, separated from the street by a wall; that view was not for him. Occasionally an elderly woman in a white coat came into the room. Effortfully he raised his eyelids and fixed his blurry gaze on the rapid movement of her lips, but not the slightest tremor moved his own. He had long been deaf, he was almost blind, and lately he had begun to lose his speech as well. His stammering had meaning only for the single friend who sometimes visited him at the asylum for the old and the infirm.

He was sitting on the bed, emaciated: you could see that he had once been tall and robust; now he was like a fossil or an enormous icicle with human features. He gripped a small bowl with both hands and pressed it against his striped pajamas, a small bowl of uneaten gruel with a spoon stuck in it. The massive block of his head, overgrown with hair like moss on a rock, hung over the bowl in such a rigid pose, with such tense obstinacy, that his half-closed eyes might have been seeking something precious that had suddenly been lost. Could he have been sitting still in readiness to repel another attack? It was surprising that he did not feel drowsiness or the weakness of the old; and that blows elicited not a moan from him. Was he numbed forever? Had he found a way to keep death at bay with his numbness? Or was he petrified because he was dying without realizing that he was dying?

Immediately after the transfer to the hospital he had been struck by a paralysis of the memory. It was a total paralysis, except for a single image. That image had been the pith of his tale about "landing on the shore of the inferno." Gloomy outlines of rock surrounding the bay of Nagaevo. Somewhere far beyond the ocean, in a different, real world, the autumn blaze of color had gone out forever. Here, at the gates of Kolyma, a dense black darkness dripped from the sky. No trace of human life anywhere around, it was cold and dark, and the prisoners the ship unloaded on the shore of the inferno were swallowed up by endless night. And that endless night, hostile and cruel, filled his heart again now years later, filled it completely and left room for nothing else. It was as if thick black blood flowed slowly through his veins, evoking a dull pain in its passage.

Certainly the writer's future biographer will note that he was dying every day, every hour, every minute of his twenty years in Kolyma. For twenty years he had crawled around the brink of the abyss, knowing what the least false move could mean. But that was not all he knew. "I knew that no one in the world could have forced me to take my own life. It was then that I began to understand the essence of the great instinct of life." It was then, when he was beset by the incessant questions: had he remained a man or not? What then was the essence of the great instinct of life? Not to forget. Not, however, for the purpose of someday showing one's memories to others; no, because there are things that people who have been spared a season in hell should not know. The essence of the great instinct of life was the soul's need to keep alive all it had suffered, to preserve it until the last breath or else risk the loss of one's very identity. The essence of the great instinct of life was life itself, were it the most terrible life, were it even as heavy as the cross borne on Calvary.

When, after twenty years, he returned to Moscow, he found that his wife had left him and his daughter repudiated him. In Kolyma he often seemed to have touched the ultimate depths of loneliness, but it was only on the threshold of freedom that he truly knew what it was to be alone. There is a limit beyond which a man who is totally alone dreads himself and tries to flee from himself. In his case that could only mean fleeing from his Kolyma past. He had practiced fleeing and became so proficient that there were times he was not sure where and how he had passed half his life. Then he was enveloped by the void, the barren weightlessness of giddiness and inner emptiness. Until one night, staring at the ceiling, he felt a violent oppression in his breast. He tried to break free, but the sense of oppression grew stronger, rose to his throat and became suffocating. A gust of dry sobbing finally broke it, combined with a gently falling sensation and threaded with the word "no, no, no." This great writer later described it in one of his tales: "Suddenly I realized that I was now about to forget everything, to cancel out twenty years of my life, and what years! Then I understood, and I won the struggle with myself. I knew that I would never allow my memory to get rid of all that I had seen. I calmed down and fell asleep."

He wrote his tales with no concern for what might become of them in the future. He wrote so that they would "remain in nature," endure, no matter for whom, no matter where, no matter how. The earth does not concern itself at all about who reaches out for it fruits or where or how; the sea does not look back to see what its tide throws up from the depths onto the rocky shore. Every tale had the form of a poem and unfolded in strophes built around the nucleus of an episode or event. In pain and silence, he slowly sought words that corresponded exactly to what he described. "I could not, I could not squeeze even one extra word out of my camp-dried brain." There was not one extra word in all his tales, there was not a single word he did not long and suspiciously weigh in his callused labor camp hand. He was not concerned with what might happen to his tales, and, yet, they reached the world by various paths. He wrote more than one hundred; he could have written another hundred. He became the greatest explorer, cartographer, and chronicler of an unknown archipelago, a hell that people had created for people. If only his strength did not fail him, if only they left him in peace . . . But he was growing blind, deaf, and infirm; and he was required to declare that life had changed and his tales were no longer true. He wrote the declaration, evoking charges of "betrayal" from those near to him. He was still alone. He wanted to be alone, he was no longer afraid of memories, but he agreed to let them fall silent and accompany him, in silence, in his advancing impotence. As a reward for his "betrayal," he was given a place in the asylum for the old and infirm: a warm, cozy room. "In his own way" he was happy there, just as, "in his own way," the blind priest was in his tale "The Cross," where he tried to sleep day and night because it was only in his dreams that he was able to see. On the writer's seventy-fifth birthday his urge to write reawakened. During the visit of his lone friend, he stammered out several short poems, which were published abroad. He was punished for this by semi-imprisonment in a cell of the psychiatric hospital.

He had been dying there for three days without realizing that he was dying. And always the same image, or rather the same vision. A black portal, someone unseen battering a ram against it; a black human procession approaches the portal, stops suddenly, and tries to turn back; the black rocks flanking the portal quake, the black lid of the sky descends on the procession; the portal slowly opens, and behind it, at a distance, swirl black clouds flushed by fire, a black sea rubs against the shore like an enormous animal with bristly hair, the human procession resumes its march forward and disappears as it gradually dissolves in the flaming black chasm.

He gripped his hands tighter still around the little bowl and pressed his feet spasmodically against the floor to stay in a sitting position. He kept his position until the dawn of the fourth day. When the frosted windowpane brightened with daylight, he sank back against the pillow and raised his legs, still clutching the bowl to his stomach. He was wrenched from his shallow doze by something warm touching his face, head, and neck. He no longer had the strength to raise his eyelids: and through the blur he could not even see the elderly woman in the white coat who stroked him and nursed him and monotonously repeated some exclamation. He neither saw her nor heard her but presaged only the coming thaw, and he remembered Anna Pavlovna from Kolyma, a thin little woman who was once passing their squad in the open-air gold mine when she pointed toward the setting sun and shouted: "It won't be long, boys, it won't be long!" "I remembered it all my life," he admitted in the tale. He remembered it all his life as the most beautiful emblem and image of hope. This is what hope meant at that time and that place: to return to the barracks and collapse on a bunk. "You cannot live without hope," the chronicler of the *House of the Dead* had written a century earlier. But can you die? Can you die without hope? He finally understood that he was dying; finally his memories came back to life and briefly swarmed through him; finally indomitable memory recovered its power. He smiled: that faint, barely perceptible smile was tinged with a blend of suffering and triumph. He died the way one falls asleep exhausted after a long voyage, lightly sinking into a pure black flood. The writer's future biographer will certainly make every effort to determine in whose arms he died.

Here he is smothered with flowers lying in a coffin; the priest on the dais is saying the office over him. The room that has been turned into a chapel is small and dark: thirty people with slender glowing candles in their hands form a tight circle around the coffin. It had snowed a great deal on that January day, and at the same time the weather turned warmer. Because of the glaring light outside the windows, the starry candle flames showed dimmer in the penumbra of the chapel, and the faces of the people standing in a circle were also dimmer. One would have liked to read those faces, but all eyes were fixed on the dead man's face.

His face is his own funeral mask. The deep eye sockets, a sharp long nose, furrows seemingly carved in his cheeks, and a bitter, slightly scornful grimace left by his last smile: only from a long-dead face could death take that kind of mask. The priest closed his breviary, blessed the dead man, and left the dais. All was silence. A young man stepped out of the circle of mourners, approached the coffin, raised his candle, which lit a fleet gleam in his eyes, and spoke in a strong ringing voice: "Kolyma has written its name on every face, it has left its mark, it has hewn additional wrinkles, it has impressed a perpetual brand, an indelible brand, an ineffaceable brand!" It was a sentence from that great writer's tale "Silence." And again all was silence in the chapel.

The writer's coffin was carried open as far as the grave; the last flakes of snow fell on his death mask: they melted at once and washed it with streaming little drops. One of the women dried his face with a large kerchief before they closed the coffin.

The writer's future biographer will certainly applaud the young man's choice of that farewell. It is altogether unique in the work of an author who is known to have shunned extra words and mistrusted the exclamatory. The word "brand," used three times, modified by such emphatic adjectives, and reinforced by an exclamation point, resounds in his tale "Silence" like a biblical curse and a subterranean rumble.

May 5 [The death of Nadezhda Mandelstam (II)]

A few days ago I finished my brief "Kolyma tale" about the death of Shalamov: an attentive reader will certainly notice that it is partly an imitation of Shalamov's tale about Mandelstam's death in the transit camp in Vladivostok. Today I received "information about the death of Nadezhda Mandelstam and subsequent events," written by an "anonymous chronicler" in Moscow (an eyewitness and probably a participant in these "events"). I have written so many times about the Russian Antigone in this journal, about her *Hope Against Hope*, her *Hope Abandoned*, and her *Testament*, that it behooves me to add a final toll to the knell I rung at the beginning of last year.

The "events" narrated by the anonymous Moscow chronicler come down to the "posthumous arrest" of Nadezhda Mandelstam. She died in her sleep on December 29, 1980. There were difficulties, clearly inspired by the authorities, in finding a cemetery plot for her, and orders were given to take the corpse to the morgue. There seemed to be no way to circumvent the injunction, since Nadezhda had no relatives and the authorities demanded that the apartment be vacated at once and sealed. But a few friends found a way: they managed to sneak the objects she loved most out of the apartment while awaiting the van that was coming to "arrest" the corpse. The guard on the stairs shouted to his comrades in the apartment: "Watch out that they don't take the manuscripts away!" Some of the people following the coffin were searched on the way out. The building was surrounded by militamen and *druzhinniks*. No one was allowed in the van that took the corpse to the Institute of Human Morphology. Some of her friends followed the van to the morgue; they were not allowed to stay, but they did get a certificate that the corpse had been transported and received. There was no word of what happened to them afterward. According to the "information" from the anonymous Moscow chronicler, a telephone call from the KGB to the director of the Vagonkovsky cemetery blocked the possibility of burying the dead woman there.

Two funeral services were celebrated: one for the soul of Nadezhda, and one (February 8) for the souls of Osip and Nadezhda. My death knoll rings its last over the purloined dust of the two of them, the poet and his Antigone.

Dragonea, July 27 [Dostoevsky's Double]

In his book about the early Dostoevsky, *The Seeds of Revolt*, Joseph Frank dedicates a separate chapter to *The Double*, "The Adventures of Mr. Golyadkin" (in the first version), "A Petersburg Poem" (in the revised second version). Hitherto this not altogether successful story has generally been dismissed as a fantastic Russian variation on Hoffmann's *Doppelganger* or as proof of the accuracy of Belinsky's remark that Dostoevsky himself, like Rousseau, had paranoid tendencies and that, in the "doubled" figure of Golyadkin, he embodied his own firm conviction "that all of mankind envied and persecuted him." Frank subtly and acutely makes clear the true meaning of *The Double* and explains why Dostoevsky so vehemently defended it against his critics and why he attributed such importance to it. When the story opens, the clerk Mr. Golyadkin "looked as if he wanted to hide from himself, flee from himself!" So at once there is the musty acrid scent of "underground man." And then the double appears. "Mr. Golyadkin knew the man perfectly well, he even knew the man's first name, and he knew the man's last name, and yet not for anything, not for any treasure in the world would he have uttered his name or consented to admit that his name was so and so. . . . Mr. Golyadkin was well acquainted with his nocturnal friend. His nocturnal friend was none other than himself, it was Mr. Golyadkin, another Mr. Golyadkin, but exactly like him; in a word, he was in every respect what is called his double." And then: "The man who was now seated across from Mr. Golyadkin was Mr. Golyadkin's terror, he was Mr. Golyadkin's shame, he was yesterday's nightmare to Mr. Golyadkin, in a word, he was Mr. Golyadkin himself, but not the Mr. Golyadkin who was now seated on the chair with his mouth agape and pen stiff in his hand; not the one who worked as assistant to the chief clerk of his office, not the one who liked to sink and melt in the crowd; not the one, in sum, whose very step clearly said: 'Don't bother me, and I won't bother you,' or 'Don't bother me, since I am not bothering you.' No, that was another Mr. Golyadkin, completely different, but, at the same time, completely like the first one . . . so that if the two were set side by side, no one, absolutely no one, would have been able to decide which was the real Golyadkin and which was the false one, which was the original and which was the copy." It is interesting that the later Dostoevsky planned not so much to revise the novella as to recast it completely. Mr. Golyadkin was to become a radical, a member of the Petrashevsky "circle," he was to "dream of being a Napoleon, a Pericles, the leader of the Russian revolt," he was to be a walking font of knowledge and a pioneer of atheism; while, for his double, Dostoevsky foresaw that he would have the task of denouncing the radical "circle" to the police.

"People who wear a mask have multiplied, and it is hard to know a man behind his mask." This is a key sentence in *The Double*. In Dostoevsky's work, Golyadkin was something more than a figure after the manner of Hoffmann or a reflection of his persecution mania. He has the makings of the Russian "hero of our times," the representative of a new race of people. It is not poverty that eats at him but ambition: "He goes mad out of ambition, while at the same time fully despising ambition and even suffering from the fact that he happens to suffer from such nonsense as ambition." Documents at hand, Frank shows Golyadkin as the product of the "true state of the Russian cultural psyche of the time" (the novella dates to the years 1845–1846); a personality that is stifled and maimed by bureaucratic tyranny; and perhaps also (as Dobrolyubov thought) one of the "downtrodden people" struggling desperately to assert their dignity and individuality despite the pressures of the system and the environment. Here Frank refers to the feuilletons Dostoevsky wrote at the time for the *Petersburg Gazette*. In one of them, the author of *The Double*, alluding to Herzen's much-admired philosophical letters, speaks of a "necessary egoism" as a "vital principle" in the process of the formation of a person. According to Dostoevsky (and Herzen), Russian life blocked the human "ego," did not allow it a normal outlet, so a Russian's character was deformed by the gradual atrophy of his indispensable human sense of dignity and responsibility. The "duplicate" Golyadkin was certainly the living image of this, however satirically and grotesquely "exaggerated." Were these the birth pangs and contractions of *Homo russicus?*

August 14 [Kot Jelenski]

Gombrowicz wrote a piece about Kot Jelenski for the French edition of his *Diary* and intended to include it in subsequent Polish editions. This has not yet happened, because of Kot's negligence or forgetfulness, but certainly one day it will, for the *Diary* seems likely to outlast all Gombrowicz's other books. But this is a good occasion to remedy the lacuna. Gombrowicz's text should be a good supplement for readers of Jelenski's *Zbiegowie okolicznosci* [1982, Coincidences], whose more-than-four-hundred pages include almost everything he wrote in Polish between 1946 and 1981 (with the exception of the article about *Kultura*, which was translated from French). In any case it is my supplement as I begin to draw a profile of Jelenski, with his hefty tome on my table.

Jelenski . . . who is he? He appeared on my horizon way off in Paris, and he fights for me. . . . It has been a long time, if ever, since I encountered so decisive and so disinterested a statement of what I am, of what I write. This is not a matter of being particularly receptive and perceptive, such consonance can occur only on the basis of natural affinity. . . . I do not consider it strange that he so easily absorbs and assimilates my ease. . . . He is wholly easy himself, he does not swell like a river at an obstacle, he flows rapidly in secret understanding with his bed, he does not shatter, he pervades, he filters through, he shapes himself to the obstacles . . . he almost dances with difficulties. Now, I too am a bit of a dancer and this perversion (to approach "easily" what is "difficult") is very much my own, I believe it is one of the bases of my literary talent. But what surprises me is that Jelenski has also managed to get in touch with my difficulty, my sharpness; our connections certainly do not come down just to dancing, and he understands me as very few do, right where I am most painful. My contact with him is exclusively by letter, I have never laid eyes on him, and even his letters are for the most part hasty and concrete—nevertheless I know with certainty that there is no mawkish spiritual coddling in our relationship, that it is a stern, sharp, tense relationship and in its very marrow it is deadly serious. At times I associate Jelenski (who seems to be a polished man of the world) with the proletarian simplicity of a soldier . . . that is to say, I have the impression that the ease in him is ease in the face of battle, death . . . and that the two of us are, like soldiers in the trenches, carefree and tragic at the same time.

Yes, of course, "receptive" and "perceptive": that is how almost all of Jelenski's admirers start out. They usually add "his intelligence" or "his infernal intelligence." I remember years ago in Rome his mother, Rena Jelenska, complained: "Good God, such an intelligent boy and he is wild about that wretched Gombrowicz." Did she, in this paradoxical way, intuit and acknowledge as well that the criterion of "intelligence" was a bit insufficient, that her son went far beyond banal labels? Two other such labels were "cosmopolitan" and "polished man of the world." Jelenski cosmopolitan? It was Andrzej Bobkowski who coined the term "cosmoPolish," probably in connection with Conrad. That is Jelenski's breed, the same breed that produced the people who are expressly present or fleetingly glimpsed in his book: the author of the *Saragossa Manuscript*; P. L. Courier's covert correspondent Jerzy Stempowski, secretly in love with that "Mr. Chlewaski" who hoped "to pass through life like a benevolent and beneficent shadow"; Jozef Michalowski, who spent his whole life writing a book about Prince Adam Czartoryski that was never completed and perhaps never actually begun. An extraordinary breed, a felicitous cross between "men of the world" and Poles, but sometimes a tragic breed with a touch of silent pride. I can see Jan Potocki in my mind, staring at the family sugar bowl that was to be melted down to make "the silver bullet." I call Stempowski to mind, the "leisurely stroller" of the streets of Berne, Paris, and Naples, and the bent figure of Jozef Michalowski, barricaded under siege in his library in Vicolo Doria in Rome.

Gombrowicz associated Jelenski, the "polished man of the world" with the "proletarian simplicity of a soldier." That is splendid coming from Gombrowicz, and so is the gradual transition from an "easy" Jelenski, who "almost dances with difficulties," to the one "who understands me where I am most painful." Gombrowicz immediately grasped who and what Jelenski was in terms of mind, moral sensitivity, metaphysical brilliance, and gift for writing, and the grand words that conclude his piece do not even for an instant seem out of proportion. Jelenski is a deadly serious writer (behind the mask of "ease") and unceasingly vigilant; he has a keen ear for ultimate questions, fighting in his own behalf, for his own spiritual essence and truth, through the work of others (if he is fascinated or, more often, deeply impressed). There is no trace in him of the "critic" fitted out with jaws for industriously grinding the printed page into "analytic fibers." He is enthusiastic and stirred when he happens to discover, or even detect, in another writer something he considers important and (nothing to fear in the word) lofty. He dozes off over what is merely the product of ability, skill, and talent. He gets gooseflesh at the mere idea that someone might say he sounded like a "critic." He seeks literary works worthy of love; anything that does not meet this expectation is, and must remain, more or less a dead letter. Hence the perspicacity of that love, a perspicacity that enriches and illuminates the world and himself in several brilliant essays on Gombrowicz (especially on the *Diaries*) and Milosz (especially on *The Land of Ulro*), and in a seemingly minor piece about Elsa Morante's *Arturo's Island*. There is a comparable literary drive in his essays on painting with their solid underpinnings of knowledge and so-called "connoisseurship." And even outside the field of literature and art, for example in his notes on the "May Revolution," and in his pen portraits, for example his beautiful memoir of Jozef Michalowski.

The young Jelenski's classmates at Saint Andrews College used to tease him about his maniacal "theory of coincidence." As many passages in *Coincidences* now make clear, it was no distant relative of Jan Potocki's "theory of miracles": the undeniable fact of the existence of miracles as the sole proof of God's existence. "The two of us are, like soldiers in the trenches, carefree and tragic at the same time." Nonbelievers believe, often with religious intensity, in a mysterious pattern of human life and destiny.

1 9 8 3

Naples, August 9 [Cats, Dostoevsky, and Naples]

"Summer, vacation, dust and heat, heat and dust. It is hard to stay in the city. Everyone has left." So begins one of those "little scenes" with which Dostoevsky loved to diversify "the chronicle of St. Petersburg" in his *Writer's Diary*. And here is my "little scene" from "the chronicle of Naples."

I will call it "Cats." In our parts cats are the scorching heat's thermometer at night. Thermometers are unnecessary by day: the temperature is 100 degrees, half a degree higher, half a degree lower. The sun beats on the head of those obliged to play the part of "occasional passersby." Automobiles give the impression of fleeing in panic from pursuers. The streets and squares are deserted, although not everyone has left. The only salvation is to stay indoors with the shutters closed. In the half-light television screens explode with images of distant fires. Distant and so near that the flames seem to dart out of the forests and creep up to the gates of the city.

At night the cats come out, from holes in the walls, from cellars and basements, and from little wayside chapels. Their cry is the thermometer. It grows louder night after night in step with the increasing exhalation of the heat of the day, scorching and muggy at the same time. The cry is beseeching at first, then desperate, and finally furious. The cats dart past the buildings, they sit stiffly in the corners of doorways, they run up and down the steps that connect the upper streets with the lower ones, and sometimes in their surge they rush into the street (sometimes never to return, just a bloody trace left by a car passing and swerving). They are stray cats for the most part, hungry after waiting all day in their hideaways. Rarely do Neapolitans take their cats on holiday.

This "little scene" from the "chronicle of Naples" will have a slightly more edifying conclusion in the description of the *wee small hours*. It is then that the cat lovers appear in streets and alleys, heedless of the increasing heat, cat lovers with their bags and bundles of left-overs. Where they make their appearance the cat cries abate for a while.

It would be interesting to catalogue the different types of cat lovers. Who are they, and why do they love cats? I know, from an old "Neapolitan chronicle," for example, that a retired university professor was a famous "king of the cats" at the turn of the century. But as soon as anyone said "You, who love cats so much . . ." he would snap back angrily, "Me, love cats? I hate them, I hate them because I must—absolutely must—look after any cat that needs care and help. Any cat I come across, blind or lice-ridden, crippled or full of fleas." It seems he secretly believed that the souls of the dead entered the bodies of cats: he had lived bereft for years after losing his wife and two children in a cholera epidemic.

November

The Miracle

The miracle of Saint Januarius, patron and protector of Naples, has lost much of its former splendor. It used to be that the liquefaction of the two vials of the martyr's congealed blood on September 19, the anniversary of his martyrdom, was the axis around which the Neapolitan year turned: it was a bad sign if a long drawn-out ritual was needed to accomplish the miracle, a good omen and proof of the saint's benevolence if prayer and invocation obtained a rapid effect.

My account-in-miniature of the miracle needs at least a few words of historical, or rather legendary-historical, background by way of introduction. Januarius was bishop of Benevento at the time of Diocletian's persecution of the Christians. In the year 305 the bishop paid a visit to a group of fellow believers in Pozzuoli. He was arrested with them for refusing to do homage to the pagan gods and sentenced to death in the arena of the amphitheater, where in such cases it was lions and bears released from underground vaults who carried out the sentence. At the last moment, the manner of execution was changed to decapitation. On September 19 Januarius and six companions were beheaded in the volcanic area of the Solfatara. A pious Christian woman hid the bishop's severed head, and she poured a few drops of his blood into two vials. The earthly remains of the martyr to the faith were placed in the Capodimonte catacombs in Naples. He was proclaimed patron of Naples in 472, when an apocalyptic eruption of Vesuvius made his tomb a pilgrimage site, the place believers went to make beseeching prayers. But it was not until 1389 that the coagulated blood in the vials miraculously liquefied for the first time. It was then that Saint Januarius became the protector as well as the patron of the city. Appeals were made to him for protection against earthquakes, volcanic eruptions, epidemics of plague and cholera, marauder raids, and the calamities of poor harvests and famine. A silver bust of the saint (with relics of his skull and bones preserved inside) was carried in procession around the city whenever the accomplishment of the miracle was too long delayed.

It is hard to determine what it is that has dimmed the luster of the miracle these past years. It may have had something to do with the See of Peter's distaste for what it considered a touch of "Christian paganism" or a "cult that smacked of something barbaric." Or it might be that the death of the last of the women known as the martyr's "relatives" (the people in the backstreets of Naples called them San Gennaro's "widows") deprived the solemn September ceremony in the Cathedral of Naples of its main element of drama: that peculiar Greek chorus imploring the miracle in humility or demanding it with imprecations and abuse directed at the city's patron and protector on the occasions when he proved sluggish. Or it may be that after so many centuries, the apparently indestructible ritual of an eternally awaited miracle just flagged and dwindled away. Whatever the reason, the fact remains that for some ten years now the miracle in the half-empty cathedral has seemed like a business transaction rushed through in the presence of dignitaries of the church and representatives of the municipal authorities rather than a *festa* with crowds of people at the altar of faith and hope in the presence of the mysterious transformation of dead into living blood.

But something out of the ordinary happened this past September, and the city was suddenly roused from its increasing indifference. Usually the martyr's blood liquefied at the earliest after a half hour of prayer and invocation. This time, to the amazement of the fairly few witnesses of the miracle, the blood was already brewing when the vials were taken from the Cathedral Treasury. The age-old chronicles of the miracle mention only one similar occurrence: in September 1647, after the revolt of the people of Naples led by Masaniello, the blood in the vials was already liquefied at the moment the treasury was opened.

On the threshold of the sixteenth century, the Kingdom of Naples fell to the power of Spain and became one of its dominions, with the sovereign in Madrid and his viceroy in the Royal Palace in Naples. The Kingdom of Naples was not a colony but a "mine." That is what Philip IV called it a century later in a letter to the Spanish ambassador in Rome: "It would be too great a blow for our monarchy to lose Naples, which has always been a living mine, providing our throne with armies to conduct wars and with money and means to maintain our armies. If we lost this realm we could neither defend nor maintain the others."

The problem was how to exploit the "mine." The Spanish Viceroy relied on the counsel and assistance of the Neapolitan patricians in the matter of extorting the tribute that had to be paid every two years into the coffers of Madrid. It was the duty, and at the same time the privilege, of the aristocratic-noble party in Naples to exercise its trust on the "mine" in such fashion that the regular tribute increased each time it was paid, enriching the distant ruler and the local administrators alike.

Their primary resort was to apply the screw of customs and taxes levied on the whole population. And whatever was not squeezed out by that press was gradually crushed under local taxes and duties. The common people became increasingly angry. The last straw came in December 1646, just before the Christmas holidays, when the Viceroy introduced a tax on the fruit brought to Market Square from the surrounding countryside. On December 26, Viceroy Rodrigo Ponce de Leon, Duke of Arcos, went, as he did every Wednesday, to Mass at the Church of the Carmine in Market Square. A crowd of men and women immediately surrounded his coach and made it impossible to reach the entrance of the church. More people continued to pour out of the backstreets. Their shouts grew louder as they pleaded with him to abolish the new excise. Pale with fright, the Duke of Arcos leaned out of the window of the coach and promised to take their request under advisement. Then they allowed him to enter the church. But after Mass, he did not want to risk going through town and returned to the Royal Palace by sea. That evening some hand daubed blood over the royal escutcheon on the newly erected customs house. And in early January 1647, somebody set it afire. The arsonist turned out to be Masaniello.

A fisherman who sold his catch in the market, he was twenty-seven years old at the time. Strong and robust, with a bold glance, he wore ragged sailcloth pants, a blouse open on his chest, and a net slung over his shoulders. Much was made subsequently of his gift for leadership and innate flair, more infallible than the intelligence and education of the well-bred. What else didn't they say, when he soared meteorlike across the sky of seventeenth-century Europe! How strongly he must have spoken to the imagination! Plays about him were written or planned, and Lessing intended to portray him as a kind of *Hercules furens.* The young Spinoza did a self-portrait in the guise of Masaniello.

The Viceroy did not keep his word, and the tax remained in force. Masaniello spent the following months rousing the people to action. The walls of the city were covered with calls to resistance, malicious verse, and protests against oppression and exploitation. Meanwhile, violent disorders broke out against a similar background in Palermo, and that acted as an additional spur. The Spanish garrison in Naples was weak. Masaniello mobilized three hundred youths and coined a slogan that historians considered the key to the successful outcome of the revolt: *Viva il re di Spagna, mora il mal governo* ("Long live the king of Spain, down with bad government"). In the words of one historian,

"Masaniello persistently repeated it until it was engraved in the heart and mind of his boys, who voiced it like the words of a song as they ran through the streets and alleys of the city." Fidelity to the crown of Spain, revolt against the Viceroy and his aristocratic-noble administration: this was how the bogeyman of defensive action from Madrid slipped out of the hands of the Neapolitan dukes, counts, and barons. In addition to the words of the "song," Masaniello's boys spread word that preparations were being made for a bloody reckoning on the occasion of the traditional cavalcade of the Viceroy and the nobles on June 23, St. John's Eve. The Duke of Arcos decided to cancel the cavalcade.

The revolt broke out on July 7. The vendors in Market Square refused to pay the tax and spilled their fruit onto the pavement. Masaniello addressed the crowd: "I was the one who burned down the tax office, now let's burn every custom house in the city." He told them that the hour of freedom was at hand, called for a struggle to the last drop of blood ("if you follow me"), and commended Naples to the care of God, the most renowned Holy Virgin of the Church of the Carmine, and Saint Januarius. He expanded his motto to "Long live God and the King of Spain, down with bad government." He strode out to combat at the head of his boys armed only with clubs. In the course of a single day, thanks to what one chronicler called the "miracle of solidarity," this handful of ragamuffins drew the whole city in its wake, with the obvious exception of the aristocratic-noble party. They broke open the prisons, arsenals, and armories, they ransacked the storehouses, they smoked out the homes and offices of the most hated and servile patricians, they disarmed the guards, they carried out summary executions, and they even forced their way into the Royal Palace. "Naples burned like Troy." The frightened Viceroy was ready to revoke all the taxes and customs that had been introduced since the time of Charles V. But more was demanded now: not just cheaper bread and relief from the press of taxes and customs but "the privileges of citizens" that Charles V had granted to the people. The new vigorous power of the people was pitted against the shorn power of the palace. Historians marveled at the "order," military and civilian alike, that prevailed "in the chaos of revolution." It took only two days more for the city to be in the hands of the people. The aforementioned chronicle speaks of the "miracle of solidarity" in the city;

the common people considered Masaniello the source of the miracle and acclaimed him as Saint John the Baptist or the Angel of God.

The "citizens' privileges" of Charles V, which were to give the people equal rights with the nobility in voting and in elections to lower offices (and allow them to defend these privileges *etiam armata manu*) were more myth than reality. No one had ever seen the charter; tidings had been handed down from generation to generation, and it still survived in popular legend. But now, in the clangor of arms and the glow of bonfires, it was no longer possible to challenge its existence. The church mediator, Cardinal Ascanio Filomarino, Archbishop of Naples, understood this at once. And, with the collaboration of Masaniello and his advisers, he "reconstructed" the mythical "citizens' privileges" of Charles V in twenty-three points of a solemn covenant. It was submitted to the people for ratification in the Church of the Carmine. Those present ratified it all the more warmly, for while the points were being read out, an abortive attempt was made on Masaniello's life at the instigation of the impenitent members of the aristocratic-noble party. The next day the Viceroy appeared on the balcony of the Royal Palace, accompanied by the Cardinal and Masaniello, and before a crowd that overflowed the square swore to uphold the charter. Masaniello agreed to don the braided uniform of "general of the people" for the occasion but made it clear that afterward he would take it off at once to return to his fisherman rags. He kissed the foot of the Viceroy and the Cardinal, called for weapons to be laid down and for absolute obedience to the king's regent in Naples. As a perpetual memorial to the event it was decided to raise a triple monument in Market Square to Philip IV, the Duke of Arcos, and Cardinal Filomarino around a column symbolizing the proud and courageous Neapolitan people.

The revolutionary events I have described in extreme brevity all took place in the course of a single week. Then came the moment of tragedy. The writings of the chroniclers and the opinion of later historians diverge in their view of it: the former speak of the "tragedy of Masaniello's sudden madness," the latter of the "tragedy of the anxieties and misgivings that afflicted the revolutionary leader after his unexpected victory."

On the night between July 14 and 15 Masaniello raved, blathered nonsense as if he were feverish, flailed around in his bed, and frequently reached for the bottle. He arose the next morning and announced that he "wished to continue to command and give orders." And indeed he set about "commanding and giving orders." He called for "the chopping block for traitors lying in ambush," threatened new burnings, made lavish gifts of the confiscated belongings of "suspects," and appointed "trustworthy" men to office. No one dared to challenge his "increasingly extravagant and capricious tyrannical fervor," but people began silently asking themselves the frightening question: Was he going mad? The people were tired; they longed for peace and a respite from violence. At the instigation of the nobles a plot was hatched among Masaniello's companions, and they contemplated the idea of putting yesterday's *triumphator* to death. The Viceroy was initiated into the plans of the conspirators and advised against murder. True, he considered the "general of the people" a "madman who ought to be in chains," but what filled him with dread was the thought of how "such brutish people" might react to assassination. What seemed more advisable, considering the circumstances, was to place Masaniello under guard in his own home and then confine him in some out-of-the-way castle until the "illness" passed. The Viceroy's advice was accompanied by orders to reinforce the garrison of the Royal Palace at once. When Masaniello returned home that night, the trap of confinement slammed shut. He was tied up and his house put under guard. The people made no attempt to free him during the night, nor did they storm the Royal Palace.

And yet Masaniello managed to get free of his bonds and escape. That was the next morning at dawn. He hid in the Church of the Carmine. It was there that the Feast of the Madonna del Carmine was scheduled for noon that day, July 16, in the presence of Cardinal Filomarino. The news of Masaniello's escape led the conspirators to the church; they probably knew where he was hiding. Soon after the Cardinal arrived, the fugitive came out of his hiding place. At sight of him all fell silent. The crowd drew apart in front of the man in the fisherman rags, rope marks on his wrists, as he stepped to the pulpit. And from the pulpit he addressed the assembly. He reminded them of the misery of the city before the revolt. It was thanks to him—his quavery voice grew louder as he continued—that Naples could hope for a better future. And what sort of recompense was he given, what was the reward for all he had done? He was standing before his people like an outlaw in the pillory. He was sure to perish; he might lose his life this very day. Masaniello was about to die, the man in wretched rags who had led the wretched to victory! Would they keep that victory without him?

The subsequent course of the chronicle is rather unclear. Masaniello seems to have shed his fisherman rags and stood naked in the pulpit: he used "vulgar gestures and words to express his indignation and helpless rage, as if he meant to besmirch the holy sanctuary with filth." The hushed penitent grief of the assembly suddenly gave place to scornful shouts of anger. Woe betide the man who dares to desecrate the temple of God! Woe betide the naked buffoon!

The Cardinal ordered him to be taken to the monastery next to the church and placed in an empty cell. Masaniello locked himself in; he was suddenly frightened, dejected, and shaken by bouts of weeping. The conspirators soon appeared outside the door of his cell. The ringleader, a close comrade of Masaniello, asked him to open the door. At the sound of the familiar voice, Masaniello immediately turned the key in the lock. They rushed in and laid him dead with several shots of their matchlocks. One of the conspirators took a knife, cut off his head, and rushed off with it like one possessed in the direction of the Royal Palace. He waved it at passersby and shouted, "Long live the king!" The headless corpse was thrown into a dump on the seashore. A compassionate priest pleaded in vain for permission to "give decent burial to the man who had delivered the city from the oppression of the nobles."

The Viceroy rewarded the conspirators lavishly. The first person to come to the Royal Palace to congratulate him on the occasion of this *fausto evento,* this "auspicious event," was Cardinal Filomarino. The Viceroy rode his horse through the city late that afternoon and was greeted everywhere with cheers and applause. He stopped several times and loudly announced that the twenty-three points of the convenant he had sworn to uphold were still inviolable. As proof of his good faith he gave orders that additional workers be assigned to the construction of the triple monument in Market Square.

Later that evening, however, when the Viceroy was back in the Royal Palace, it transpired that there was no bread to be had in the shops and bakeries. A stunned crowd was making feeble protests in the vicinity of Porta Capuana when Cavalier Sanfelice, a member of that well-known Neapolitan family, rode up on horseback: "You'll be eating bread baked of earth. Now that your Masaniello is grinding the earth between his teeth, we're going to start hanging you." Bread went on sale the next day, but at the old price for a loaf that was much lighter in weight. The crowd stormed the Royal Palace. The Viceroy fled down a secret passage to the fortified castle. "That was enough," writes the historian, "for the people to turn all their thoughts back to their Masaniello. They rummaged his body out of the dump on the seashore, washed it and dressed it in the uniform of the general of the people; they found his head and attached it to his corpse. After which they assembled an awesome and moving funeral procession, and with banners unfurled, drums rolling out to a mournful beat, with torches blazing and bells ringing, they carried the coffin with the earthly remains of Masaniello to its eternal rest in the Church of the Carmine, mourning him as their benefactor and revering him as a saint and martyr."

That September 19—in historical circumstances that are outside the framework of the present account—the blood of Saint Januarius (as I mentioned before) was already liquefied the moment the treasure was opened. Many explanations were offered for such a rapid miracle, and many auguries were deduced from it, but one reflection of the common people particularly struck the chronicler: it was whispered in rapt piety that across the centuries "a holy thread of blood linked the two severed heads."

I return to the starting point of my narrative-in-miniature. This year? In this year's lightning-quick liquefaction of the clotted blood of Saint Januarius the people of Naples sensed a connection with the constant and alarming recent seismic tremors in Pozzuoli and the Solfatara, the places where the Bishop of Benevento was sentenced and executed. Is this to be understood as a good sign or a bad one? Is any one of us capable of answering that question, living in constant suspense between a miracle and a volcano?

1 9 8 4

Plague broke out in Europe in 1348. After the first months of "black harvest," in the autumn of that year, it was widely believed that the Jews had brought on the plague to decimate the Christians. The conspiracy was reputedly hatched in Toledo, and its main artificer was purported to be Rabbi Peyret of Chambéry. A Genevan Jew named Agimet was arrested in Châtel on October 10 and put to the rack. Here is what he confessed. A wealthy merchant named De Ranz decided to send him to Venice to buy silk and other merchandise. Rabbi Peyret heard about it and summoned Agimet to Chambéry. The rabbi gave him a pouch of a particular poison that he was instructed to pour in any wells he passed on his journey and promised a rich reward in gold for his efforts and the risks involved. Agimet performed his assigned task first in Venice, then in Calabria and Apulia, and finally in Toulouse. No efforts were made during torture to extract any details from him; it was plain to the interrogators that every time Agimet poisoned a well along the way, he had to clear out as quickly as he could. They asked only if he had been helped by others of his faith in the towns he visited. He responded with silence, and this answer satisfied them. What mattered in Agimet's confession was the crime in itself. The circumstances were not essential, and they were certainly embarrassing, considering that the Jewish-seminated plague did not spare Jews in the regions afflicted by the epidemic. The chronicler does not give the sentence passed on Agimet and says nothing of the fate of the rabbi of Chambéry.

In 1568 Elvira del Campo underwent prolonged torture before the tribunal of the Holy Inquisition in Toledo. She was descended from a *Marrano* family on her mother's side, but her father and her husband were "pure" Christians. She was arrested and indicted on the basis of accusations by servants and neighbors: granted, she was a virtuous and pious woman, she went to Mass regularly, she confessed, and she took communion; but she did not eat pork, and every Saturday she put a freshly laundered white cloth on the table. Hence she was following "Jewish practices." She admitted that at once and explained that was what her mother had taught her when she was a child. But she did not know how to answer the question her interrogators constantly repeated: What other "Mosaic laws" did she obey in secret? She probably had no idea what they were, because, screaming with pain as the torture worsened, she all but begged the inquisitors to tell her what she should reply. But what they wanted to hear was a fully detailed spontaneous confession. When she had reached the limit of endurance, they settled for an overall declaration of crypto-Judaism. Her sentence was public recantation of heresy and an act of contrition, three years in prison wearing a yellow *sambenito* trimmed with crosses, and confiscation of all her possessions.

Both these paradigms have ideological counterparts in our own times: one is associated with the "Zionist conspiracy," namely, the insidious activities of an open enemy; the other with "Trotskyite diversion," namely, the stealthy work of a covert enemy.

February

The Duke of Milan

*Nonetheless he must be grave in thought and action, nor take
fright of himself, and proceed in temperate fashion with prudence and humanity, so that too much trust not make him in-
cautious and that too much mistrust not render him
intolerable. A disputation follows from this: whether it is better to be loved than feared, or the converse. The response is that
it is desirable to be the one and the other; but because it is
difficult to combine them together, it is much safer to be feared
than loved, when one of the two must be lacking.*
—*Niccolò Machiavelli,* The Prince, *XVII*

I

Filippo Maria Visconti, duca di Milano, nato nel 1392 morto nel 1447.
He did not like portraits or monuments, which makes it all the more
interesting to look at the portrait medallion in which Pisanello preserved the Duke's image. There is something of the wild boar in his
profile, and that impression is heightened by the thick creased neck.
Pisanello caught the play of eye and mouth very well: the penetrating
eye looks straight ahead but slightly downward as if always on guard
to avoid a frank glance; the mouth is twisted in a smile that is an
odd mixture of cruelty and mocking good-nature, without a trace of
sensuality in the clenched lips. The chin is small, with a droopy wat-
tle, and so is the ear, a mere orifice in the smooth block of the massive
head. The nose is straight and regular, set off by bushy eyebrows over
it. The forehead is not visible, because it is hidden by the band of a
cap that has a peak bent forward like an antler.

The medallion depicts only a bust, but we know the whole figure from written descriptions. In his youth there was a certain nobility in his appearance, but with the passing years his large body put on too much weight and became heavy and sluggish. What was striking in a figure of such imposing dimensions were the disproportionately short fingers, as if they had been cropped short in childhood. Capricious nature had also endowed him with deformed legs, so that he almost always had to use a cane when walking or lean on the arm of one of his courtiers. He was known for an odd habit of kicking his foot against the wall when, in meditative peregrinations up and down his chamber, he wanted to set off in the opposite direction.

II

In addition to Pisanello's medallion, there is also a portrait medallion in prose. It was written in Latin immediately after the death of the Duke of Milan by his secretary, *secretarius ducalis,* Pier Candido Decembrio. In *The Civilization of the Renaissance in Italy*, in the part entitled "The State as a Work of Art," Burckhardt calls Decembrio's life of Filippo Maria Visconti "an admirable description" conducted with "mathematical completeness," which has fortunately been left us to shed a rich beam of light on the true circumstances of Italian rule in the fifteenth century. Canetti in *Mass and Power*, in the chapter on the "Elements of Power," draws a lesson from his reading of Decembrio, of which more later.

According to minor commentators, the author of the prose medallion took Suetonius as his model, the secretary of the Emperor Hadrian. There are substantial similarities between the two. Both men had access not only to official material in the archives but were also privy to everything that constituted the *secretum* of the realm in the form of gossip and facts suppressed. Both of them fell from the favor of their princes, on suspicion of insufficient reverence for their sovereigns' wives. In any case Decembrio was always praised, before the meaning of his work was fully appreciated, for his "manifest impartiality," erring neither in the direction of panegyric nor in the direction of implicit libel.

Besides the other virtues mentioned, the prose medallion of the Duke of Milan possesses an additional virtue for me, one that might well be envied. It is surely what led Burckhardt to remark on its "mathematical completeness": it comprises eighty pages, seventy chapters, often so concise that they seem the fruit of years spent honing the text down to sentences that read like scientific formulas. So few well-chosen, pondered words to say so much! It is no small responsibility, then, to try to give a summary of Decembrio's prose medallion.

III

Proclaimed Duke of Milan in his twentieth year, after conquering the city, Filippo Maria was eager from the start to pass for a mild sovereign and meet the expectations of his subjects. He announced at the time that every citizen could have free access to him. But absorbed by increasingly ambitious plans, he soon retracted this magnanimous gesture. Shut within the walls of the Citadel of Milan, he dedicated himself exclusively to affairs of state and military matters. For years he did not show himself in the city, and only occasionally did he visit his many castles in the environs. He sought distraction in the hunt.

He possessed the gifts of the strategist rather than the battlefield condottiere. He did not take personal part in the wars conducted in the course of his thirty-five-year reign, with the exception of two: against Genoa and against Venice, but he kept far in the rear to await the outcome of the operations he had planned. He loved the army, he trusted in his full control over its commanders, and he lavished honors and rewards on them according to their merits, though he was not infrequently guided by impulses that seemed baffling. Constantly at war, he subdued the whole area from the Alps to the Tyrrhenian Sea, including Genoa, and later Emilia and Romagna; and he made sudden raids to harass and devastate the cities on the Adriatic as well as Tuscany and Umbria.

He owed his complete control over his commanders partly to police methods. He availed himself of the services of spies and informers to discover their inmost thoughts and intentions. He also fed and exploited the animosities and rivalries that broke out among them. In addition to this he was unpredictable: he would shower a man with exaggerated praise before plunging him into disgrace or subject him to brutal censure before admitting him to his confidence. A despotic ruler, but "happily," Burckhardt remarks, "his cruel egotism did not degenerate into a purposeless thirst for blood."

IV

Filippo Maria was no less surprising in the role of head of state. He would not, however, have been taken as an exemplar in the description of the "state as a work of art" had he been actuated solely by a sovereign's fleeting caprices. To no one did the last of the Viscontis ever reveal his thoughts. But he impressed his entourage with the conviction that his thoughts always evolved in solitude like the calculations of a chess player. He shunned clarity and guarded his secrecy. No one ever knew what to expect of him; he disappointed those who were sure of themselves, and out of the blue he would befriend those who were unsure. He broke all the rules, as if breaking rules were the one rule he respected, which eluded his seeming confidants. He had a peculiar way of expressing himself so that each word seemed to mask a different one. To monarchs and princes, to popes, and to ambassadors he addressed letters the end of which obscured and blurred what he had said in the beginning. Nor did he shrink from indulging in the same mocking histrionics toward the powerful of the world that he used with his own subordinates, as he shifted smoothly and nonchalantly from cruelty to jest.

Decembrio quotes his letter to Pope Eugenius IV. Assuming the guise of a repentant sinner, Filippo Maria wrote that he was on the verge of the grave, which was untrue, and awaited the Holy Father to impose even the most harrowing penance in order that his sinful soul might be redeemed. The Pope duly prescribed penance and took the occasion to ask for several fortified castles by way of expiation. The response sneeringly acknowledged the success of the simulation: although the Duke of Milan set a higher value on his soul than on his body, it was a higher value still than the salvation of soul and body that he set on the welfare of his state.

For Canetti, Filippo Maria is the prime personification of "the impenetrability and inscrutability of power": "He acted as if he had to safeguard his secrets even from himself." One thing is certain: he preferred to arouse fear rather than love.

V

He inspired fear in others, but he too lived in the grip of fear. Under the effect of Decembrio's work, Burckhardt cannot help but exclaim:

what the "passion of fear" can do to a man of unusual talent and high position!

Filippo Maria consolidated the defense of his own person with strict and complicated regulations. He felt safest within the walls of the fortress at Porta Giovia, and only rarely and reluctantly did he betake himself beyond its compass. Anyone entering the citadel was followed by hundreds of eyes. It was forbidden to appear at a window, for fear that anyone standing at a window might exchange signals with someone outside. Every guest or visitor who was admitted was carefully searched and questioned. Palace dignitaries summoned to the antechamber might or might not be received by the Duke in order to thwart any sense of routine. When it chanced that a visitor left the fortress and had to go back for something he left behind, he had to apply for permission to enter all over again. The servants were constantly screened, and few were authorized to cross the threshold of the Duke's private chambers. Anyone on the way to the Duke's abode who happened to pass any vicinity infected by epidemic had to spend forty days in quarantine before knocking at the gate of the citadel.

"The passion of fear" that Burckhardt speaks of was not, however, connected solely with the specter of conspiracies, revolts, and betrayals threatening his power and his realm. The Duke of Milan made strenuous efforts to drive off even the idea of death; it overwhelmed him with horror, it filled him with irresistible dread.

VI

He did not allow people to die within the confines of the fortress; the mortally ill were sent outside the walls. And in the Duke's presence talk of death had to be avoided at any cost; it was driven out by an exorcism of silence.

From childhood he was frightened of being alone in the silence of the night; he could not sleep unless some protective eye watched over him. He was terrified by the sense of time coming to a standstill, and he organized the rounds of the night watch like the movement of a clock, and if these human clock hands seemed to fade into silence, he would listen in agitation, in a transport of fear. He suffered from insomnia. When he could bear it no longer, he would often pace for hours like a restless beast in a cage, not neglecting the peculiar habit of banging his foot against one wall or other of his chamber. Several times in the course of the night he would move from one to another of the beds he had positioned at different points. He ordered nocturnal birds to be placed in the upstairs rooms that would beat their wings at any suspicious sound. He could not, however, abide ravens and crows, "funereal" birds, and he ordered them all exterminated. He was sickened by the sight of withering trees, and in the citadel it was understood that they must be uprooted at once and replaced by healthy ones.

What frightened him most were thunderbolts and lightning. Decembrio describes him during one of the storms: the powerful sovereign cowering in a corner of his chamber behind a hurriedly improvised screen.

VII

And yet . . . despite all this, Burckhardt concludes that "he died with dignity and grace"; even more, "he deliberately hastened his own death."

Two years before he died, he lost the sight of his right eye and immediately after that of his left one. He was so ashamed of his blindness that he pretended he could see, having his servants whisper explanations to him.

In early summer 1447 he finally began to speak openly of death. He gave orders that room be found for his tomb in a church located near the fortress that was large enough for so big a body and in a position where the feet of the faithful would constantly tread on it.

He fell ill shortly before turning fifty-five. He took a turn for the worse at the beginning of August. It was the opinion of the doctors that blood-letting could save his life. But he would not agree to that; he even demanded that they close a wound in his leg that oozed bad blood. "In the depths of his heart," says Decembrio, "he wished for death, which seemed preferable to life, blind as he was and totally exhausted by so many wars. In the early evening of August 13 . . .

bored by the foolish chatter of those around him, he had one of his servants help him turn over on the other side and face the wall, and after a while he breathed his last." The author of the prose medallion thought he died in a way that demonstrated this prince's "greatness and nobility of soul."

VIII

The next morning his body was put on display between the two draw-bridges of the castle, after which it was borne in crowded procession to the Cathedral of Milan. It was placed on a catafalque in front of the main altar. But in the heat of August the fleshy corpse already gave off the stench of decomposition, and immediately after the "tu-multuous funeral service," the body was taken down from the cata-falque and buried. The Milanese, "emboldened by the demise of their prince," immediately convened an assembly of the people and expe-rienced "a happy foretaste of freedom." "Freedom" is the final word of the prose medallion written by the court secretary of the Duke of Milan.

The expression of this freedom was the Holy Ambrosian Republic, which was proclaimed against the glow of the bonfire in which they threw the papers from the Duke's cabinet, that instrument of despo-tism and captivity. The republic lasted three years. Then Francesco Sforza, married to the only daughter of the last of the Viscontis, as-cended the ducal throne. His predecessor and father-in-law, like Machiavelli, deemed that "it is much safer to be feared than loved," but Sforza instead preferred the love of his subjects to their fear. For that he paid dearly in the end.

But the dilemma Machiavelli suggested is not what matters most for my own little medallion of the Duke of Milan. "He acted as if he had to safeguard his secrets even from himself," is what Canetti says about him. Perhaps there was one great secret the prince kept hidden even from himself: the secret of the sterility of the pure essence of power, power that is coveted, defended, and consolidated with no purpose other than possessing it. That may be what Filippo Maria vaguely sensed, ensnared day after day, night after night, in the spi-der's web of his own fear. At the last he may have revealed that worst secret to himself, when he deliberately summoned abhorrent death, when he turned on his side to the blank white wall.

April 20 [The bishop's kite]

Yesterday in Rome, I happened on an exhibition of "instruments of torture from the Middle Ages to the Industrial Era," in two rooms and the gardens adjoining the Quirinal Palace. The erstwhile designers of instruments of torture that inflicted pain directly by lacerating flesh and breaking bones also applied their ingenuity to plunging victims into absolute solitude (in pursuance of "man's eternal aspiration to the absolute" in all his works and deeds). One perfect product of this ingenuity was the "bishop's kite," which particularly attracted the attention of visitors to the exhibition in Rome. There was no explanation of the odd name: it may have commemorated some medieval bishop as its inventor or, vice versa, as its victim. The designated victim was locked in a human-shaped iron cage. When "the bishop's kite" was empty, it looked like a wrought-iron construct of the human figure, on the order of a modern sculpture or a dressmaker's dummy. Dangling from the top of tall scaffolding with someone stuffed inside, it cut the victim off from the world more radically than a dungeon cell. He was probably given bread and water on the end of a pole. If he held out to the end and refused to capitulate and confess his guilt, a long time passed before his desiccated skeleton was removed from the iron cage. The idea of the bishop's kite certainly arose in unconscious imitation of crucifixion.

November

San Dragone

What is a dragon? An animal, one might say, which looks or regards (Greek drakon*); so called, presumably, from its terrible eyes.*

—*Norman Douglas,* Old Calabria

I

I have just returned from the funeral of Father Ilario Sterpone. There were few people, or so it seemed in the immense nave of Santa Chiara. There was a handful of his students to the left of the altar, whispering to each other, impatient that the ceremony was so long. To the right his sister in black with her husband, relatives from Calabria, colleagues from the university and friends (like me). Farther back there were a few old ladies, the kind you see in church any day at any hour; they like funerals and weddings, no matter who died or who is entering the bonds of matrimony.

The coffin was on the floor covered with wreaths with purple ribbons. The gold lettering on the ribbons bid farewell to "beloved brother and brother-in-law," "wise teacher," "dear colleague," and "loyal friend." When the coffin was carried to the hearse, the dead man's sister and her husband stopped on the steps outside the church, an invitation to express condolences. My turn came: "You came to see him more often than anyone. He always had something to say to you."

The funeral procession cut through the crowds and the line of cars in Spaccanapoli at the moment the bell at the top of the campanile next to the church began to toll noon. Lately the bell of Santa Chiara, which can be heard throughout the city at noon, was the main strand that linked the dead man with Naples.

Yes, it is true, I visited him very often; the last time I went to see him was a week before he died. At the time there was nothing to suggest the end was near, though he suddenly said with sadness: "They have long forgotten that I am still alive. At times I forget myself."

There is an entry in my notebook about my first visit, two years ago, shortly after he was brought back from the hospital (where he had been treated for about six months for a cerebral hemorrhage) to his sister's home in upper Naples.

"He was sitting in an armchair," my entry reads, "slightly turned away from the window, where you could see the whole bay: a lazy sunny September day, a host of brightly colored moored sailboats, and steamboats gliding slowly toward the islands. He seemed glad to see me, though I immediately discerned a tinge of fright in his face. For the first half hour he indulged himself in erudite memory games; it was easy to guess that this was the spoken continuation of an incessant, obsessive verification of the efficiency of his brain. I incautiously asked him to repeat the title of a book. He reached his good right hand to a little pad of paper with a pencil attached, he put it on his knees, and scrawled some letters with difficulty; then he glanced at his help-lessly dangling left hand and resignedly laid the palm over the pad. For the rest of the visit he could not master his irritation, conversation flagged, and the pauses of silence grew longer. When I stared at the bay in my embarrassment, he glanced briefly in the same direction and gave me a look full of desolate pain. A moment of weakness dispelled by a whisper at parting: *Sto bene, sto sempre meglio.*

II

Before his illness welded our friendship, or perhaps something more than friendship, a shared attention to something enigmatic and close to both of us, we had been acquainted for years in an ordinary con-ventional way.

He had long been in frequent animated touch with my wife's family, since 1955, when he came to Naples from Calabria to teach philosophy in a lyceum run by monks. He was thirty-five at the time (almost exactly my age) and had been a priest for ten years. In 1970 he started teaching at the university, but he did not stop teaching in the lyceum and continued to live in the monastic boarding school.

I used to see him on occasions when we were both invited to tea:

our encounters were limited to small talk. Once he gave me his recently published translation of Plotinus with a scholarly commentary, and I decided to go to the presentation of the book at the Philosophic Society. I have no particular recollection of his lecture, except, perhaps, the vague sensation that I heard extremely intimate confidences tightly and intentionally enveloped in very hermetic language. It was a vague and obviously fleeting sensation, since we immediately reverted to the usual small talk at subsequent encounters. Only later, during the period of his illness, he one day remarked quite casually in the course of conversation: "Probably no one at my lecture heard what was truly important in it." He looked me in the eye searchingly as if he were waiting for me to say: "I heard." But I remained silent, and he continued: "Plotinus says that God is only a name if you talk about Him without true virtue. But is virtue enough for God to stop being only a name for us?"

One March morning in 1982, they broke open his door and found him lying unconscious on the floor between his worktable and his bed. He spent five and a half months in hospital. His sister and his brother-in-law went to see him; he did not want other visitors. The doctors let him go back home (that is, to his sister's apartment) and recommended "gymnastic rehabilitation," but privately they did not see great hopes for the future. A passive life awaited him, but his mind was sufficiently lucid for reasonable doses of reading and conversation.

My wife was the first to pay him a visit. She was struck by the fact that he reverted to the distant past, to the years right after receiving orders, when he had been sent to a vacant parish in a small hamlet between Catanzaro and Nicastro. Never before—that is, before his illness—had he mentioned those years; whenever he dipped into autobiography, he always began at a later time, in Catanzaro, when he privately devoted himself to philosophical studies while at the same time teaching religion in the local high school. Besides, Catanzaro was his home town: his parents had died there when he was still a boy, there his childless widowed aunt lived, and there he had finished seminary.

"What is the name of the village?"

"It has a rather strange name, San Dragone. It is rather as if someone had dreamed up the name Saint Demon."

After hearing that "strange" name, I became a fairly frequent visitor in the sick man's home.

III

I had once read an article about San Dragone in an illustrated magazine, too journalistically sensational for a clear picture of the course of events but sufficiently striking for the name of the Calabrian village to remain impressed in memory. I did not know that there was a serious book about San Dragone, and the author of the article could not have referred to it because it was published much later (in England; until now it has not been translated into Italian, nor has any mention of it in the Italian press come my way). This was the very book Father Sterpone mentioned during my first visit, when he was unable to write down the title I had incautiously asked about. I went home with the intention of asking again at my next visit, in what might be more favorable circumstances. My intention proved unnecessary. The next morning I found the book in the mailbox with the sick man's calling card pinned to the cover, *The Hidden God*, a lavishly illustrated volume of more than two hundred pages with a solid "critical apparatus" provided in the notes. According to the blurb on the dust jacket, the young author, George Herbert Grudger, was a specialist in research "overlapping sociology and theology" and had spent two months in San Dragone in 1952.

At this point I might refer the reader to Grudger's book and spare myself the effort of a summary. But anyone can see that would be absurd, for several reasons that are not worth mentioning. All I can do is concisely summarize the salient points of *The Hidden God* (published in London in 1957) and give an account of what Father Sterpone told me in the years of our friendship.

The title is explained by a quotation from Pascal on the frontispiece: "If there were no darkness, man would not sense his own corruption; if there were no light, man would not hope in a remedy. So it is not only just but useful for us that God be partly hidden and partly manifest, because it is equally dangerous for man to know God without knowing his own misery and to know his own misery without knowing God."

Grudger's introductory chapter gives what little information he dug out of the archives about the history of San Dragone and a rather detailed description of the village with cross-references to the corresponding photographs. The ruins of Torre Falconara, all that remains of the tower of the castle of the Falcone counts, date to the late seventeenth century. The village sprang up on a slope near the ruins, in the middle of the eighteenth century, as the continuation of the former castle *borgo,* which had been razed or burned with the castle. It was originally called Falconetta: it was and still is mainly a village of shepherds. The ring of hills surrounding the valley of the Chiariva River (more like a stream) abounds in easy-to-reach pastures for the flocks of sheep and goats. The name was changed to San Dragone at the turn of the last century for reasons that require more detailed explanation. In the ruins of Torre Falconara, in the wall of a vast dark cavern (which must have been the castle dungeons) a deep chasm split open, and now and then ribbons of smoke would rise from its depths. Thus arose the legend of the Dragon; it is Grudger's opinion that the new name of San Dragone was probably an instinctive attempt to placate the demon by entrusting the village to its power and protection. At the time the village did not yet have a church, and rarely did priests come from Nicastro for religious services. The church, dedicated to Saint Michael, was built at the beginning of this century and was too grand for the small number of inhabitants. "Then," Grudger writes, "the manifestations of the semi-pagan cult receded or abated, but the odd Saint Dragon survived in the name of the village." Several stone quarries, which were opened in the middle of the pastures after World War I, had a stimulating effect on the life of San Dragone. After World War II, the village numbered more than five thousand souls. Photographs show little houses banked up like swallows' nests and narrow lanes like sloping stone corridors with steps.

The central figure in Grudger's account is Gioacchino Scauro, who was also called "Scuro" ("Dark") in the village by reason of his gloomy disposition and his stern frowning face. When he was a small boy tending his father's sheep, he was often to be seen near the ruins of Torre Falconara, gazing for hours, without stirring, into the cavern where the chasm had opened, thrilled whenever a ribbon of smoke crept out and briefly wound its way among the rocks and mounds of earth. He married a neighbor's daughter, Maria Minuzio, and set up a carpentry shop. The wedding took place in the newly built church, and it was celebrated by Don Pietro Vitale, the first parish priest of San Dragone. Scuro became the most zealous parishioner, he spent much time in prayer and visits to the rectory, and he did little carpentry and masonry jobs free for the church. He was drafted when

World War I broke out and left the village as a father of three children: two daughters and a son.

He returned from the war an invalid, without his right leg and with a pierced lung. He had difficulty moving on crutches, and work in the carpentry shop quickly tired him. He stayed in his cottage constantly reading books: he had learned to read and write fluently during his convalescence in the military hospital.

IV

The longest chapter, almost a third of the book, is entitled "The Conversion" and contains such a mass of evidence, documents, and detailed description plus authorial digressions and interpretations that it must necessarily be pruned to the essential bare facts. I realize full well that this involves the risk of impoverishing and flattening the whole story as well as substantially diminishing its credibility to the reader. But I see no other solution.

One night in 1930 Scuro had a revelation. A woman dressed in green appeared to him in his dream, pointed to an oil lamp with three spouts, and said, "Light that lamp." Then she said, "Your name is Levi, and you must spread the light with this lamp." The next morning a man Scuro had never seen before in San Dragone knocked at his door and gave him a copy of the Bible. He was an evangelical minister distributing religious literature from village to village in Calabria. Scuro began to read, and by the time he got to the end, he realized that he had hitherto been living in a false faith. "He understood," according to the testimony of one of Scuro's daughters, quoted by Grudger, "that the religion of the Old Testament was at the source of all religion and hence was true, while the religions of the New Testament, Catholic and Protestant alike, were later and hence false." At the time he had not the least idea that there were still Jews existing in the world and was absolutely convinced that God had entrusted him with the mission of giving the true faith back to humanity. He then set out to spread the faith that he had discovered: he inveighed against the "pagans" who adored images and the statues of Our Lady, he admonished them to rest on Saturday and not on Sunday. Grudger quotes a peasant converted by Scuro: "One God only commands us. He says, I'm your Lord God, I saved your life and led you out of

Egypt's land. I'm your jealous God unto the fifth generation. The Last Judgment is going to be held in the Valley of Jehoshaphat. Our God will not forgive people who keep on sinning like the Catholic God does. In the Valley of Jehoshaphat, the Last Judgment will reward the just with eternal life, it will punish the wicked with eternal death." Grudger comments that "what most struck the man's imagination was the inflexible justice of the Hebrew God. The merciful God of the Christians no longer spoke to the peasants of San Dragone: like the ancient Hebrews, they preferred a just and inexorable God."

Scuro, who henceforth insisted that he be called Levi the Teacher and considered himself a descendant of the Levites and priest of his community, converted about fifty people. Not one of them even suspected that somewhere in the world followers of the Old Testament still lived. The first news in this regard was brought to San Dragone by a traveling salesman, and in the teacher's little notebook he wrote the address of a Jewish friend in Naples. Scuro sent him a letter at once and in response received the address of the chief rabbi in Rome. The next letter, sent to Rome, remained unanswered. But the converts of San Dragone did not give up and wrote a second time: again they announced that they had discovered the true religion and asked for help, because they wanted "to become real Jews." This time an answer came. The rabbi in Rome said that at first he had thought it all a joke, but now he thought differently and would soon send a representative of his to San Dragone. And indeed, a few days later the rabbi's envoy appeared in San Dragone, spent the whole day with Scuro, and visited the other converts as well. He sat in silence and listened seriously to what they had to say, but on parting he said: "You are more Jewish than all the other Jews." After this visit religious pamphlets began arriving in San Dragone, one of which was entitled *The Straight Path.* But the printed word was not enough for the converts; they wanted to be admitted officially to the Jewish community. Meanwhile, there was much hesitancy in Rome. The delegate of the Jewish religious community in Rome paid two more visits to San Dragone before the war; and after the promulgation of the race laws, he hid out for some time in the Calabrian village. "In 1938," one quotation reads, "we learned that a law had been made that obliged all the Jews to declare their race. We wrote to Rome that we too wanted to declare our race, because we were Jews like the others and we wanted to suffer together with the whole Jewish nation. But the answer from Rome was no."

So the Jews of San Dragone patiently awaited recognition from Rome and practiced the laws of Moses in accordance with their own interpretation of the books of the Old Testament. It was only late in 1943, after the Allied occupation of southern Italy, that a great change came about in their life. One day they saw eight army trucks with the star of David on the main road straddling the river in the valley and, rubbing their eyes in amazement, they made out a word on the drivers' badges they knew only from books: Palestine. The band of converts went out to greet the new arrivals. The soldiers of the Palestinian brigade had difficulty understanding what it was all about, but out of all those chaotic accounts in a foreign language, they did, in any case grasp the word *conversione* and informed the army rabbi in Cosenza. He went to San Dragone, where he was welcomed with songs of the God of Hosts and the Fortress of Worlds. He was moved and promised to intercede with the rabbi in Rome as soon as the capital was liberated. The perseverance of the converts was finally rewarded in the summer of 1946: the new chief rabbi came from Rome. The ceremony admitting the converts into the bosom of the Synagogue took place on the banks of the Chiariva just before sundown.

But the new Jews in San Dragone felt like their ancestors in Egypt: they were forced to lived in exile among the "pagans." In 1948 Scuro learned that a Jewish nation had been created in Israel. He then conceived the idea of leading his community to the Promised Land and succeeded early the following year. They all went by ship from Naples. When they arrived in Israel, the whole community was assigned to the same farming settlement. (It was there in 1949 that Grudger took their statements, the raw material for the book he planned in London.)

They all sailed away except for Scuro himself. He was widowed before their departure, and his wife's death deepened his infirmity. The idea of parting from the village of his birth suddenly seemed intolerable. A grandson was left with him, the son of his younger daughter, an eight-year-old named Giosuè, a sickly, anemic boy who was gradually losing his sight.

Grudger quotes a letter from Scuro to the rabbi in Rome, dated three months after the departure of the Jews of San Dragone for Israel. There is a foretaste of conflict, if not of rupture: "He who closes the heavens and says that the Vision does not exist, rejecting the God of the Vision also rejects Moses and the Pentateuch. For I say unto you, in the name of my Creator, who is also your Creator, that if we wish to conquer evil, you must proclaim Sight. You must also found a school of prophets. In this way, neither you nor we will blunder along groping in the dark. Certainly you do not believe what I told you, and yet without Sight the shepherd is blind. Since our God is not a dead God but the God of Hosts . . . If you scorn my words, it is not I you scorn but the God of Visions who calls forth the wind and turns it at his pleasure. And none dare ask Him 'what are you doing?' "

From 1946 on, there is no need to refer to Grudger's book. The aged Father Vitale died that year, and young Father Sterpone came to take his place in San Dragone, where he stayed four years. Grudger visited him in Catanzaro in 1952: "He received me in his aunt's apartment: he was reserved, disinclined to talk, and tense, and he responded to my questions with monosyllables, he was almost rude. The people to whom I owed that brief encounter had warned me that after the tragedy in 1950 he left San Dragone, with the agreement of his superiors. He had been on the verge of a nervous breakdown. It had clearly not left him unmarked."

V

There was a particular quality about the things Father Sterpone told me during my visits that was due to his illness. His discourse oozed like clots of blood. There were episodes, recollections, reflections, and feelings that clotted in plaques: first one, and then, after a while, another, and then still another, but the connecting links seemed broken or at least sadly slackened. Each account was a fairly independent whole, loosely and vaguely connected with the others, and it unfolded without much concern for when or where the events took place, often blurring and even mistaking people's faces. It gave the impression (sometimes wearying for me as I listened) of a story reconstructed outside of time and space, detached from its concrete participants. Who knows, perhaps all the clots suddenly linked up again that night, during the sleepless hours of solitary meditation, struck the man's heart, and finally broke it.

So the quality of the things Father Sterpone told me was due to his illness. But not solely. The same resistance the author of the *The Hidden God* had been so drastically subjected to must have been at play to some degree even in regard to me, despite our ever closer friendship. The former parish priest of San Dragone was, I think, defending himself with all his strength from some specific confession, while at the same time yielding step by step to an irresistible need to make it.

Whatever the case, all I can do is trust that my pen may give some order to the dense shapeless mass and single out some distinct strands.

VI

It was said that the old Don Vitale had died of grief after the official formation of the Jewish community of San Dragone. For his successor the apostasy of fifty inhabitants of the village was certainly a surprise but no cause for breast-beating or even scandal. On the contrary, he privately considered it a sign of the enhancement of God's presence in a land where religion had long since either taken the form of a tradition all but drained of any meaning, or become something like a mixture of superstition and magic. He made an effort to approach the members of the community and knocked at their doors the same way he knocked at the doors of his parishioners. He was given a cold reception. But he would not be discouraged, and they began to greet him on arrival and departure with the same words: "We pray to the true God." It was obvious that they were repeating Scuro's words, from whom the young priest had first heard them, on the threshold of the carpentry shop, transfixed by his host's angry glance. From the window of the little house next door, Scuro's wife watched him in silence with what seemed like an embarrassed smile. She clasped her grandson Giosuè to her breast as he squinted his eyes and turned his pale little face toward the sun.

Scuro held his community firmly in hand. They lived in different parts of the village, but every Friday evening and every Saturday morning they assembled in his workshop transformed into a house of prayer. In a corner was a cabinet with a Torah sent from Rome, and a wide strip of grayish linen embroidered with Hebrew letters was nailed on the wall (similar fabrics hung in the cottages above the beds of the converts, in the place formerly occupied by crucifixes and images of the Madonna). Scuro was the priest, and he had established the liturgy: in unison they recited a prayer he had composed in Italian, they listened to his lessons, and then he would read selected passages of the Old Testament. Scuro had also seen to it that a piece of barren land in the environs of Torre Falconara was staked out and a low stone wall built around it to provide for the community's future dead. The first person to be laid to rest in the new cemetery was Scuro's wife, Maria, shortly before the Jews of San Dragone left for Israel.

At first the village treated its apostates with indifference. Few voices were raised in disapproval. It was more likely that someone might shake his head in wonder: "Who can grasp the truth, who can fathom it? We do what the priests told us." The gap that gradually widened later was chiefly the work of the converts. They rejected Father Sterpone with the words: "We pray to the true God." To his parishioners they said: "You pray to a false God." A community of "strangers" had sprung up in San Dragone that aroused fear rather than hostility.

"Fear"—*timore* and sometimes even *timore religioso*—played an important role in Father Sterpone's stories about his first two years in San Dragone. He sensed that fear in the sudden outburst of devotion, almost fervor, among his parishioners: the church was full on Sunday, people prayed out loud, as if they wanted to shout down something dark and disturbing within themselves, they crowded to confession and communion, on mild evenings they would linger on the steps of the church, and they clung too dependently on their curate. He sensed that fear even more acutely a year later in an equally sudden drop in zeal: no, the church was not deserted on Sunday, people did not stop confessing and taking communion, they still lingered on the steps of the church on mild evenings, but they did everything sluggishly, out of fainthearted compulsion. During the Mass, a hasty voiceless movement of the lips replaced loud supplication to God. Father Sterpone then experienced what he called "absolute solitude in the midst of people." I remember his exclamation: "Ah, God needs people so as not to be merely a name!"

Over and over again he wondered how they got that way, what had really happened in San Dragone. . . . He liked the thought of Pascal that Grudger had used as the motto of his book; and there were times that he totally forgot my presence in his incessant, insistent allusions to the "manifest God" and the "hidden God." He was all but convinced that God had revealed Himself in "dual fashion" thanks to the conversion and apostasy of the fifty villagers, only to hide himself deeper than ever at the sight of the growing rupture in the village. "Now," he said, "everyone in San Dragone knew only his own human misery, and slowly the darkness overcame everyone. The apostates were poisoned with the pride of possessing the sole truth: the faithful were consumed by the unconscious fear of living in a false faith."

He stayed up late at night poring over his books, slept little and badly, was debilitated by fleeting bouts of fever, and watched aghast as a spiritless void crept into his prayers. His absolute solitude in the midst of people was accompanied by a lost feeling in the presence of God. He awaited a miraculous recovery, and day after day he lost hope that it would come.

One afternoon in the empty church he dozed off in the pew in front of the altar. It was a sunny January afternoon in 1949, and the windowpanes were splashed with a chill gilt. That morning the Jews of San Dragone had buried Scuro's wife in the new cemetery, and within a month they were to leave their village forever. Father Sterpone was awakened from his doze by a child's shrill crying. He jumped to his feet and rushed in the direction the sobbing came from, a corner sunk in darkness near the door. He saw little Giosuè huddled against the wall helplessly waving his little hands, floundering like a fish caught in a net. He embraced the boy, hugged him to his breast, and took him outside the church. Halfway down the steps Scuro stood leaning on a single crutch, gasping for breath. When Father Sterpone pushed the child toward him, Scuro braced his left hand on his grandson's shoulder and with his right hand menacingly brandished the crutch. That gesture long haunted the priest of San Dragone.

VII

They were loaded down with the remains of their unsold possessions as they walked down the steep lanes to the two buses on the road in the valley. Men, women, and children. The procession was clearly visible from the windows of the priest's house. Scuro led the way holding little Giosuè's hand in his left hand. The "pagans" stood outside their houses. They saw the leavers off the way it has been customary for centuries, in the villages of southern Italy, to observe the course of life from behind the walls of one's own house: with a wan, blank gaze, and without a word.

Father Sterpone sank onto a chair by the window; he was overcome by enormous fatigue and was totally unable to bring forth a prayer for the departing villagers. It was early morning on the last day of February, and a storm was gathering over San Dragone. Muffled shouts and calls came from the road in the valley but were cut short by the growl of engines, and then there was silence.

Scuro came back home with little Giosuè the following evening. Thenceforth he was rarely to be seen in the village, once a week. It was not clear what he lived on after closing his shop; he may have lived on what his community had left him before leaving. He refused to send Giosuè to school; he wanted to teach the boy himself and raise him in the true faith. Whenever the child went to the store, he was asked how his grandfather spent the day. "He reads, writes, and prays to our God." He was seen every Saturday, when he took his grandson to the solitary grave of his wife. It was an effort to walk, and he had to stop every couple of steps; he would choke and clutch his throat in bouts of coughing. A feeble old cripple in a black Calabrian peasant hat and a frail youngster with an unsure step, straining his sick eyes to scrutinize the ground beneath his feet.

Grudger quotes the letter full of bitterness (to say the least) from Scuro to the rabbi in Rome, dated three months after the departure of the Jews of San Dragone for Israel. It was at the time he wrote the letter exhorting the rabbi to proclaim the glory of the "God of Visions" and to found a "school of prophets" that he began to be seen more often with the inseparable Giosuè. They would walk from the cemetery to Torre Falconara, and there they rested on the large rock where Scuro in his childhood had watched ribbons of smoke rise from the dark cavern. Smoke still rose from to time, and in this regard nothing had changed with the passing years; or rather, the only thing that had changed was the fact that the village had all but forgotten the origin of the name of San Dragone. And that (according to Father Sterpone) was why the image of the "shepherd without a flock" staring into the mouth of the cavern, the priest of the "strangers" on the threshold of a dead past, awakened associations for the villagers that were baffling and obscure and rekindled barely smoldering embers in the ashes of memory. Suddenly the figure of Scuro was seen as something ominous; people turned the other way—and occasionally made a furtive sign of the cross—at sight of him.

I suspect that the remark about "rekindling barely smoldering embers in the ashes of memory" was not merely a metaphor for Father Sterpone.

Scuro's shop, formerly used as a synagogue, caught fire one November night. The circumstances of the fire were never cleared up. Was it arson, or was it an accident caused by Scuro smothering with ashes the unburned wood on the hearth before he went home? At this point Father Sterpone lost the thread of his narration; he seemed upset and embarrassed, as if the thing had happened yesterday rather than many years before. None of the neighbors helped put out the fire, that was a fact. Scuro tried to force his way into the burning shed, but a gust of flame blinded him and hurled the burned man against the wall across the street. He was carried home, and the women of the neighborhood cleansed his burns and wounds and dressed them with oil-soaked rags. He moaned and raved and finally fell into a convulsive sleep. Little Giosuè would not be separated from him; the child was in a state of shock. This was the situation Father Sterpone found when at dawn he was finally awakened. He managed to take the boy with him. The injured man was taken to the hospital in Nicastro.

A week later a nun from the hospital in Nicastro came to San Dragone. The injured man was out of danger, but treatment would take several months. Scuro wanted his grandson and refused to take food or medicine until he saw him. What was to be done? The sister had come for little Giosuè.

"During my four years in San Dragone," Father Sterpone would say, "I had never been so happy, so close to God, as I was looking after the boy that week, solacing his memory of the shock he had experienced. At the time I often thought about his unexpected flight into the church and his sobbing in the corner by the door. Was there some sign in it? Did God manifest Himself most fully in the tear-stained face of a child, in those half-blind eyes?" And after a moment, with a tremor in his voice: "My God, how I loved little Giosuè!"

VIII

Scuro's stay in hospital lasted until March 1950. Spring came early that year, the pastures soon turned green, the herds of sheep and goats were taken out, and the warm air revived work in the stone quarries.

Scuro dragged himself to the priest's house with little Giosuè to thank Father Sterpone for looking after his grandson just after the fire. He looked terrible, a skeleton covered with burn-blotched skin. But what was still more terrible than his appearance was the sensation of speaking with someone who was not there. The man gurgled his thanks, would not cross the threshold of the priest's house but leaned against the doorframe, and just stood there, his eyes riveted to the cross hanging on the wall. He caressed the child's head mechanically and stammered something incomprehensible, mangling his words, not hearing what was said to him, and not replying to questions. He left without saying good-bye. On the steps of the church, the child turned around and shouted for both of them: *"Addio, padre."*

A strange calm came over San Dragone with the arrival of spring, a dead calm between the storm that had passed and the storm that was to come. Scuro shut himself up in his house, and little Giosuè appeared rarely in the store. One morning early in April Father Sterpone knocked at the door of their house. There was no response. He knocked harder and harder, suddenly certain, with a certainty like a pang in the heart, that he would never see them again.

The rest belongs to legend. The palpable facts were that Scuro's house was found empty and that a few days later the police were summoned and found a black hat and a child's shoe on the path leading from the rock by Torre Falconara to the mouth of the cavern. The legend that grew up in the villagers' imagination, or the truth hidden from human eyes, was that Scuro followed the trail of the wisp of smoke and, dragging the struggling little Giosuè as a sacrifice, entered the subterranean abyss, the realm of Saint Dragon.

IX

I began to write down the events connected with San Dragone the day Father Sterpone was buried, October 29. I finished writing this evening, a rainy November day, after paying a visit to his sister this afternoon on the pretext of returning Grudger's book. I do not know why, but I was very anxious to have one more look at the dead man's room. My hostess left me alone. The room was untouched, even the notepad with the pencil attached was still on the little table next to the bed, beneath the lighted lamp, as well as the bulky volume of the acts of a symposium held in Bologna in the 1970s: *Studi sulla religiosità vecchia e nuova,* including an address by Father Sterpone. "We hear and read that people's idea of God is constantly changing and that their need to believe in Him swings up and down like a pendulum. In my opinion, it is the face of Satan that is ever changing and altering its expression: and man the pilgrim—be he in eternal flight from that face or in eternal fascination with it—blunders and stumbles, falls down and rises again."

I looked out at the black bay through the rain-lashed window. As soon as I turned off the lamp, the blackness of the bay in the window of the darkened room brightened at once and sparkled with bustling glints of light.

1 9 8 5

"Writing is a form of prayer." Auden refers to this thought of Kafka to explain his decision to destroy everything he had written. "Anyone who truly addresses his prayers to God does not want others to hear them."

A brilliant but strained interpretation, yet the wisdom of Kafka's observation remains. Every authentic piece of writing ultimately takes the form of prayer, I am convinced of that. A prayer in the broadest sense, let us say, is the equivalent of submitting questions to the Creator. However, an authentic writer—believer or not, on his knees with his head humbly bowed or on his feet with a glint of challenge in his eyes—should not be conscious of the fact that prayer is flowing through his voice like an underground stream, sometimes clearly audible and sometimes muffled or totally soundless. When he is aware of it, prayer becomes a form of literature, generally bad literature. A few days ago, to compensate for a trip to Assisi that was postponed for various reasons, I read Julien Green's book about Saint Francis. It is, indeed, prayer in the form of literature. The prayer is certainly sincere, in some points it is even fervent, but it turns the great and dramatic *Poverello* into rustling paper.

May 15 [Caravaggio]

At the exhibition *Caravaggio e il suo tempo* at Capodimonte palace, Caravaggio in the framework of his predecessors and his imitators. Some great pictures are missing in the rooms dedicated solely to his painting, but there is enough to sense who and how important he was.

If someone ever decides to write the *Life of Caravaggio* (despite gaps and several "obscure areas" in his biography), he will have to invent a particular narrative style: hectic, abrupt, throbbing like a heart contracting and dilating. Especially in his last ten years, 1600–1610, Caravaggio lived as if he were in a constant fever of delirium. He was violent, quick-tempered, ever abristle, quarrelsome in bloody fights, pursued for killing a man, and torn between an urge to flee and a yearning to return whence he fled. *Muore di febbre,* they write in biographical accounts. The fever killed him in Porto Ercole, where he was awaiting a pardon and permission to return to Rome. He was not yet fifty years old.

What other painter would have painted his own likeness in a severed head? What is probably his only self-portrait is the severed head of Goliath in David's hand: dead and yet alive, grimacing in rage, a strangled shout on his half-open lips and a frantic glint in the wide-open eyes. In addition to David and Goliath, he painted Judith decapitating Holofernes and Salome with the severed head of John the Baptist. He put his signature in the blood dripping from the head of John the Baptist. Decapitation scenes attracted him. And scenes of the flagellation of Christ. In the Naples *Flagellation*, one of three he painted, he endowed the figures of the flagellators with an uncanny expressiveness that erupts with desperate fury. A far cry from Piero della Francesca's glacial, metaphysical *Flagellation* in Urbino!

His handling of chiaroscuro is considered a way of revealing the invisible. At the same time it is a form of veiling the visible with mystery. Caravaggio's chiaroscuro throbs with the need to make religious sensitivity and imagination part of the commonplace and to dramatize them tangibly in life. The realism of the flagellated Christ's pain is expressed by the fierceness of his flayers. Caravaggio was commissioned to paint the *Death of the Virgin* by the Church of Santa Maria della Scala in Rome: the canvas was considered scandalous, perhaps blasphemous, and was rejected. It depicts the dead Virgin as a woman crushed, worn out by life, with a slender ring of a halo around her head, an almost unnatural sign of sanctity in such an earthly image of death.

What comes to mind is the *Madonna del Parto* in the cemetery chapel at Monterchi. Piero della Francesca's Tuscan peasant girl, her gown unbuttoned over her pregnant belly, imparts a note of gentle and serene earthliness, while in Caravaggio faith clashes violently with human life and death.

1 9 8 6

Rome, January 10 [A sunny day in Rome]

A marvelously sunny day in Rome, and before my round of appointments and visits, I spent the whole morning between Castel Sant'Angelo, Piazza Navona, and Campo dei Fiori, from the yellow Tiber to the colored stalls around the monument to Giordano Bruno. I come to Rome infrequently, so when I do I am able to measure the precise fluctuation in its "temperature."

There are slight fluctuations in the climate. Nicola Chiaromonte captured the "norm" in the conclusion of his story "The Jesuit": "The Roman streets and squares: the Roman space, so generous, so free of compulsion, rejecting nothing, asking nothing of the individual, except that he put on a costume and play a role, forgetting himself in it. The cast is innumerable, the stage set once and for all. There is room for the Fanatic on it, and for the Cynic. Only the person who wants to be himself is excluded: the Heretic."

Costumes and roles, what are they like today after a round of appointments and visits? There has been a robust increase in the degree of anti-Americanism, ennobled with patriotism in the name of offense to "national sovereignty." A little tear is shed over the decadence of Western Europe and then a flood of tears over helplessness in the face of international terrorism, followed by a sigh that Soviet participation is essential in the work of "stabilizing" the Mediterranean basin. The notions of "stabilization" and "destabilization" rose several points on the market of costumed players, who have the Roman gift of forgetting themselves altogether in the various roles they play on the same stage ever and again.

Europe was divided, nothing can be done about it; "that" Europe was separated from "this" Europe, yet there is no way to preclude Moscow from mutual concern for the future of the western half of the Old Continent, and "stabilization" or "destabilization" is becoming just as important *there* as it is *here.* I was invited to dinner at V.'s, and O., an Italian monsignore from the Curia who is particularly enamored of the expression *"vogliamo sperare,"* laid particular stress on this. "A year and a half from now the Pope will make his third visit to Poland. It will, *vogliamo sperare,* be a stabilizing pilgrimage. And the doors to the other socialist countries will, *vogliamo sperare,* open wide to the Holy Father." One of the dinner guests, a liberal journalist with an anti-clerical streak, enthusiastically exclaimed, *"Sacrosante parole!"* Our host gave me a slightly embarrassed glance and promptly poured me some more wine. Roman costumes and roles come close to the essence of Pirandello's theater; that is, the identity of the figures on the stage is gradually undermined. Does this identity exist at all? Nicola was right: the man who would be himself in Rome must be reconciled in advance to being a heretic excluded from the play.

I am writing this at night in Trastevere, in the upstairs room of R.'s apartment. You can hardly see a thing from the terrace. Might there have been an announcement that the house lights are going out in the theater of the Eternal City?

Maisons-Laffittes, March 26 [Lanzmann's Shoah]

Today I saw the first part of Lanzmann's film *Shoah.* The real theme, several decades after the Holocaust, should be the world's indifference. It should be, but it is not. Instead it is willfully limited to the indifference of the Poles. This made it easier for Lanzmann "the artist," whose chief concern had to be the "rigorous construction" of the film.

This "rigorous construction," limiting the picture of the Holocaust to the country in which it was technically perfected, equates the world's indifference with Poland's (mainly economic and ecclesiastic) anti-Semitism. Lanzmann pushes reductionism so far that anyone seeing the first part of the film would never guess what really happened to "Aryan" Poles during the Holocaust: they too were condemned to gradual extermination by the *Untermensch*, they strove to resist, and they perished in the unequal struggle; or else they lived rather quietly tilling the earth in the neighborhood of the smoking crematoriums and looked the other way, privately satisfied that the descendants of those who had nailed Christ to the cross were being crucified every day in the gas chambers. Lanzmann seems to think his view of the tragedy—what's more, against a background of aesthetic panoramas of Indifferent Nature—is richer "artistically." But an enormous amount of truth is cropped outside the frame of his "rigorously constructed" film. This "artist," to whom "art" is dearer than "anything else," turns out to be mean-spirited, blind in one eye, and mendacious.

The "anything else" includes two books, Laqueur's *The Terrible Secret* and Wyman's *The Abandonment of the Jews*, and the Ophuls film *Le chagrin et la pitié*. (This is what I wrote about it in the journal in 1978: "For viewers from our part of Europe, *Le chagrin et la pitié* suggests one reflection: if Hitler's 'final solution' had been carried out in France with the same methods and the same terror used in Eastern Europe, the French contribution to the operation would have gladdened Himmler's heart. As for England, had it been occupied by the Germans, only the imagination of the author of *1984* would have been equal to the theme.") And there is Orwell's observation in 1945, that the war—with the Holocaust in full swing—*intensified* British anti-Semitism. Karski's testimony in the second part of Lanzmann's film breaks off, as Ewa Kuryluk remarked in the *New Criterion*, where it should rightly begin. Karski himself mildly complained in *Kultura* that the most important part of his account was sacrificed to the "rigorous construction" of the film.

The whole of *Shoah* reflects an almost universal stance of Pilate in the face of the Holocaust. Perhaps no one will ever fathom its deepest essence, measure its enormity, or gauge its terrible weight. But it certainly cannot be done by someone to whom the idea is alien that the extent of the contamination and poisoning of human hearts was nearly universal in the midst of an unbridled and consciously fomented orgy of mass atrocity, when the single individual had to grope his way through the exhalations of collective madness among the shattered and smashed Tablets of the Law. You have to abhor, perhaps even hate, all forms of the totalitarian plague in order to look at the Holocaust and see more than its Polish "setting." I doubt whether Lanzmann would have the capacity to take that kind of look, which comes naturally to people of Orwell's stamp.

Naples, April 13 [The synagogue on the Tiber]

Gregorovius described a practice that had been customary since the early Middle Ages, the homage the Jews of Rome paid to each newly elected Pope. They came out of the ghetto singing hymns of praise and carrying the Pentateuch, and they stopped at a designated place on the route of the papal retinue. They were sometimes heaped with jeers and insults in the crowd. As soon as the Pope arrived, they fell to their knees and lifted up the Scroll of the Law to him. He would read (or pretend to read) for a while, hand the roll of parchment to someone in his retinue, and pronounce the ritual formula: "We confirm the Law, but we condemn the Jews and their interpretation of it."

Some journalists quoted Gregorovius in the morning papers in connection with John Paul II's visit this afternoon to the synagogue on the Tiber, while others journalists, who had talked to historians, reproached Gregorovius for inaccuracy. The correction has it that the Pope waved his hand in scorn and wordlessly disdained the Scroll of the Law that was offered to him.

Whatever the case, today's visit was given this frame from the past to illustrate its "historic" nature. Meanwhile John Paul II offered something marvelously natural in place of what the press thunderously trumpeted as "historic." He spoke and acted as if a simple embrace between "younger and older brothers" had the power of disdainfully rejecting the mad follies of history once and for all.

Naples, August 26 [The eighth death of Maxim Gorky]

R. sent me an excerpt from Edmund Wilson's *Diary* published in *The New York Review of Books*. On the margin he wrote: "In case you want to know the truth about the eighth death of Maxim Gorky."

Wilson describes his visit to Malraux in 1954. At dinner they talked about Stalin, whom Malraux had met twice when he visited Gorky in Moscow. Malraux's opinion was that Stalin was very "abstract," while Wilson's opinion was that he was too primitive. Wilson asked if Stalin had ordered the poisoning of Gorky. Malraux answered decidedly not. Yagoda got rid of him, because he wanted to marry Gorky's niece, so he first murdered her husband and then Gorky.

Malraux's "expert" opinion in Soviet matters (for Wilson seems to have considered him an expert) is just as idiotic as his "abstract" picture of Stalin. R. is wrong about "the eighth death of Gorky": in my historical crime story "The Seven Deaths of Maxim Gorky," the version in which Yagoda is the murderer appears in the subsections of Death Number Two and Death Number Six. Moreover, Malraux confuses even this version, which came out at Yagoda's trial. The then head of the NKVD was accused of ordering the death of Maxim Peshkov, Gorky's son (married to the beautiful Nadzedzha), and Gorky. Yagoda allegedly had an affair with Nadzedzha, but there was no reason to rush into marriage with the writer's daughter-in-law, since he could bed her at his convenience without disturbing her husband (a notorious cuckold). In any case he would not have dared to raise a hand against him, much less against the father, without Stalin's tacit agreement or clear instructions. Malraux took the garbled version of Yagoda's trial for gospel (in 1954!), despite the fact that in conversation with Wilson several years earlier he had dismissed the Moscow trials with the brief remark *ce sont des mensonges*.

1 9 8 7

If Shakespeare in his later years had happened on Paul the Deacon's *History of the Langobards*, written in the eighth century, toward the end of the more than two-hundred-year Lombard occupation of Italy, he would have lingered over a chapter in which two strands come together. . . .

It was the second half of the sixth century. Pavia had withstood the siege of King Alboin for more than three years. In the end it surrendered. When the victorious Alboin entered the city, his charger fell in the middle of the gateway, and kicks and spurs could not get it back on its feet. One of the Langobard warriors then turned to the king: "Remember, sir king, what vow you have plighted. Break so grievous a vow and you will enter the city, for truly there is a Christian people in this city." In the course of the siege Alboin had vowed that he would put all the people to the sword for their obstinate refusal to surrender to the invaders. He now heeded the warrior's advice, broke his vow, and promised indulgence to the conquered people. His horse rose from the ground at once and carried the invader king into the city.

Alboin received the homage of the inhabitants of Pavia from the balcony of the palace built by Theodoric. He reigned in Italy for three years and six months. He perished at the instigation of his wife Rosemund. He was banqueting in Verona, tipsy and merry beyond measure, when he suddenly ordered that Rosemund be served wine in a cup made of the skull of her father, King Cunimund. (The deacon does not mention why and in what circumstances Alboin dispatched his father-in-law.) The queen's head reeled with pain, she seethed with rage (but gave no visible sign of it), and she privately decided to kill her husband and so avenge her father.

Later she revealed her intentions to Helmechis, Alboin's foster brother. Peredeo the designated assassin, known for his enormous strength, refused to lift his hand against the king. Rosemund resorted to a clever stratagem. Knowing that Peredeo crept into her maidservant's room every night, Rosemund took the woman's place in bed. In the darkness and silence the lover was unaware of the identity of the woman with whom he took his pleasure, until after their amorous embraces he heard the terrible words: "I am Rosemund. You have perpetrated such a deed . . . that either you must kill Alboin or he will slay you with his sword." He chose to save his own skin. He slew the king with the queen's help. Amid the grief and lamentation of all the Langobards, Alboin was buried beneath the steps of a staircase in the palace.

Helmechis married Rosemund and, abetted by her, attempted to take the royal crown for himself. In the struggle for the throne he barely escaped with his life, with Rosemund and with the treasure of the Langobards. They fled to Ravenna, where they were given refuge by the imperial prefect Longinus. Rosemund wished to become mistress of Ravenna at least, and she let herself be persuaded by Longinus, who promised to marry her in exchange for slaying Helmechis. She offered Helmechis a cup with poisoned wine. After the first draft he guessed the assassination plot and at sword's point forced Rosemund to drink the rest. "Thus," Paul concludes, "these most wicked murderers perished at one moment by the judgment of God Almighty."

What threads, then, would Shakespeare have found in this episode of the *History of the Langobards*? First, in Verona, the shade of a Langobard Hamlet in a petticoat. Then, in Verona and in Ravenna, the shade of a Langobard Lady Macbeth.

January 9 [Hamlet]

One day there may appear a bulky catalogue of the greatest stage Hamlets. Richard Burbage will open it, the first actor to play Hamlet, straight from Shakespeare's dramatic forge. Burbage was thirty-five years old, but he looked like an old man. He was obese, wore a beard, and suffered from shortness of breath. Since this Danish prince had his creator's blessing and approval, we ought to have some reservations about the tradition Goethe initiated of a Hamlet "fluttering like a candle flame," Hamlet as the personification of "hesitation and indecision." Besides we have made that tradition our own in an age of manifold, and still multiplying, versions of Hamlet "our contemporary." The Hamlet that spoke to me most strongly was the one whose "key" to stage interpretation was suggested by Salvador Madariaga in a little volume about Shakespearean tragedy published after the war. I saw it in London about 1950. I should say I managed to see it, because it was hissed by the public and taken off the boards after two performances. Alec Guinness played Hamlet with a pointed Spanish beard and a round tummy, a cunning thoroughly Renaissance prince, an inveterate gambler accustomed to intrigue, a man who could wield a word with more than one meaning as if it were a poisoned foil, with a host of masks to choose from (among others, a mask of "morbid indecision"), while holding back his own feelings like a brace of dogs ready to leap. This Hamlet was intolerable in Gielgud-Olivier London.

How many faces does Shakespeare have? As many as human passions ever have anywhere when they are "out of joint."

January 28 [A new Job]

Yesterday I learned by chance from an acquaintance that it was the hundredth birthday of P. the architect; ten years ago he lost everything he had in a matter of weeks, including his family (never mind the circumstances), and soon after left Naples for the Abruzzi village of his birth. Since he was known for his piety, he was then dubbed the "new Job." I never met the man, but once after the tragedy he was pointed out at a distance, sitting alone on a bench in the city park.

So why did I dream, and such an outlandish dream, about someone who was a complete stranger to me?

There is a particular variety of dream, fairly rare, whose unreal atmosphere has something of what Kubin calls "that other shore" about it. Anyone who knows Kubin knows that it is a matter of symbiosis between the reality of this life and (what I call) that after death. The secret depends on the degree of one time or the other, one still running and the other already stopped. They permeate each other so exactly that it is impossible to experience either of them separately. "The other shore" is our shore, our shore is the "other shore." Not only is the bridge between them unbroken, but it is actually the only bridge that looks likely to endure. It is the bridge built of the material of dreams.

In my dream I climbed an icy, slippery, narrow road to an Abruzzi village, sliding back and obstinately going up again, and often had to grasp the bare branches of trees on the slopes. There was not the slightest sound of life from the village, though I could clearly see the buildings and the church in the center. There were several motionless figures, it was a totally lifeless scene. I guessed that the centenarian lived at the very top of the village; the windowless house on the escarpment, at a distance from the other houses, was surrounded by a wall and looked like a small fortress. I did not take my eyes off it, off it or the cross on the church. I passed by the forlorn church and went into the lane leading to the small fortress. I was accompanied by staring faces behind the windowpanes in the houses on both sides of the lane; all the faces were very old.

The door of the little fortress was opened by a short, stooped, wizened old woman. She let me in without a word, and without a word she led me to the centenarian's room. He lay fully dressed on the bed with a fur over him, looking remarkably hale, only his eyes were faded and dim. Across from the bed an old-fashioned clock with a golden pendulum ticked loudly. *"Come sta?"* I asked instinctively. He smiled: *"Sto morendo."* And after a while, "I am philosophical enough to understand that it would be awful if a person could never die and remained confined in the prison of life." Those, he explained at once, were the words of his "favorite philosopher." I noticed an open book on the floor by the head of the bed, as if it had slipped out of his hands before I entered the room. "That is the Book of Job," he said. "I read it all the time! I have probably read everything that has ever been written about it. I never part from it, because it instills a sense of pride. Too much talk in it, decidedly too much: Job talks too much, his friends talk too much, even God talks too much. I have found a more dignified way to be faithful to God in hardship and misfortune. Silence. The reason I have lived so long—a hundred years—is that God is surprised by my silence, he keeps on waiting for my lamentations. He has heard not a one. So eventually he will have to respect the dignity of my silence and reward it by releasing me from the prison of life." At that moment a peal of someone's laughter rang out. The louder the laughter became—and it made the walls of the house tremble—the slower the clock pendulum swung, until it stopped and the ticking came to an end. The last thing I remember from my dream is the "new Job's" face twisted in horror.

February 3 [Joseph Frank and Dostoevsky]

Joseph Frank's *Dostoevsky*, in several volumes, is on the way to becoming what is usually described as a "definitive work." In the recently published third volume, *The Stir of Liberation, 1860–1865*, Frank devotes a separate chapter to the generally neglected *Winter Notes on Summer Impressions*, which he rightly considers the prelude to the turning point in Dostoevsky's career, *Notes from Underground*. In the 1863 *Winter Notes* Dostoevsky describes his journey through Western Europe the previous summer. He visited Herzen several times in London. And as he wrote, Herzen's *Letters from France and Italy* were ever-present in his mind (and on his writing desk), though considerations of censorship prevented him from mentioning them. What did the Christian *pochvennik* have in common with the enlightened atheist and liberal enemy of czardom? An aversion to "soulless" Western rationalism and materialism, the poisoned springs of Russia's growing nihilism. It was in the West that the "fathers" descried the illness that was soon to invade their country and gradually overwhelm the organism of the "children." No matter what each in his own way believed to be the cure, they were at one in their dismay at the spread of soullessness, indifference, and moral relativism under the influence of triumphant, all-powerful reason.

I have just read that Milan Kundera has filed a brief against Dostoevsky in defense of the Western treasures he scorned: rationalism, skepticism, and common sense. He turns upside down the whole construct of what I summarily described in connection with the third volume of Frank's book. For example (one is free to presume, skipping ahead), it was not followers of the rational "fads" and "ruffianly" books smuggled into Russia from the West who made "scientific socialism" their own and later put it into practice, but readers of Dostoevsky. But how on earth did those readers of Dostoevsky do it, when his world is the antithesis of "scientificism" and omnipotent reason? For that is how Kundera remembers reading Dostoevsky after the 1968 invasion of Czechoslovakia: "the very *climate* of his novels annoyed me in Dostoevsky, a world where everything turns on feeling, in other words, a world where feeling rises to the level of reason, value and truth." That "climate" also annoyed Lenin, nay, it infuriated him. Clearly this "climate" was responsible for the ban on reprinting *The Devils* under Stalin, until after the German invasion in 1941, when the way was cleared by an introduction that spoke about "the distinct prefiguration of Hitler in the novel." Kundera's accusatory tone is almost a parody of common sense (which he values highly). You can like Dostoevsky or not; Nabokov did not like him. You can, as Kundera did in 1968, turn in relief from *The Idiot* to Diderot's *Jacques the Fatalist*. But it does seem upside down to look at Dostoevsky through the prism of Soviet tanks on the streets of Prague.

"Was that," Kundera asks, "the anti-Russian reflection of a Czech who was shocked by the invasion of his country? No," he answers, "because I never stopped loving Chekhov." And yet, I suspect, it was. It seems that after 1968, Czech Russophobia was reborn and soon caught up with Poland's unaltered Russophobia. And it may now have taken the lead, considering that what was once the most Russophile nation in that part of Europe experienced the shock of frustrated love, something that certainly cannot be said of the Poles. The false "Dostoevskyan" stereotype is grafted onto the false—like all national stereotypes—picture of the "Russian in general," which obscures the Soviet face of the invader and enemy. That is why I somewhat mistrust Kundera's suddenly unfurled banner of nostalgia for Mitteleuropa; it smacks of a way to ignore the Russians in the name of "our bonds with the West." For countries conquered and enslaved by the USSR, this would be a grave, if not disastrous, sin of shortsightedness.

April 3 [Bertrand Russell and Bolshevism]

Bertrand Russell's forgotten *The Practice and Theory of Bolshevism* was mentioned en passant today in a splendid lecture by O. Bechenski, whose eighty-fifth birthday was being celebrated by the Pallottine Fathers. He spoke highly of the book, and that gave me real pleasure. Russell's book was reprinted in England in 1950, thirty years after its first publication, and in an article entitled "The False God," I wrote about it together with Carew Hunt's *The Theory and Practice of Communism* and the collected memoirs of six ex-communist writers, *The God That Failed*.

Russell's foresight amazed me at the time. He had spent barely a month in Russia in 1920. You have to remember that the atmosphere of the Labour Party junket he went with was one of sympathy and even admiration for the Russian revolution (1917 is called "one of the great heroic events of the world's history" in *The Practice and Theory of Bolshevism*), and the junket was part of the polemics against attacks on Bolshevism in the British conservative press. And yet Russell saw immediately in Russia what three years after the overthrow of the czars might have been clear only to an exceptionally acute and understanding observer of the "unbiased left" in the West and what thirty years later made it still worthwhile to read his pre-Gide "journey to the USSR."

Russell thought that Bolshevism might be defended as a cruel discipline thanks to which a backward country may quickly be industrialized: but as an experiment in communism it was a disaster. What he saw in the "cruel discipline" was the exhumation of the methods of Peter the Great. And the experiment in communism? It immediately turned into a religion. What Russell meant by religion was the complex of beliefs of a dogmatic character that direct the life of people, transcending the obvious proofs or going against them, and making use of sentimental or authoritarian and not intellectual methods. Bolshevism was a religion in the sense that its dogmas transcended clear proof or were contrary to it. Those who embraced

Bolshevism became insensitive to scientific proof and committed intellectual suicide. Even if all the doctrines of Bolshevism were true, Russell said, it would still not change the shape of things, since the Bolsheviks considered impartial investigation unlawful.

By the time Russell's small volume was reprinted, his view was widely shared. Carew Hunt wrote about communism as a religion in his book. The iconoclastic ex-communist writers execrated the "bankrupt god." O. Wetter of the Paris Oriental Institute called Lenin's dialectical materialism a "periphrasis of God" and likened the dogmatic and authoritarian tone of Soviet philosophy to the role of authority and dogma in the Catholic Church.

What has remained of that "religion" in the decades since the death of Stalin, the new god in the old crown of Peter the Great? A "priestly" caste of exploiters in the Nomenklatura around the altar of naked power. And millions of "believers," whom Gorbachev recently referred to as a "mob." Russell's farsightedness is still praiseworthy, but its range has proved to be not wide enough.

Naples, May 4 [The death of Kot Jelenski]

Kot [Konstanty Jelenski] died.

Pain, genuine pain that is already clotting forever, it will awaken later, time settles pain but does not allay it. First it is numbness, as after a physical injury. And stupor and disbelief alloyed with panic. What will Paris be like without Kot? Our Polish world without him? Has he really gone? No, it is impossible! The image of a black hole, a dry spasm in the throat, a thick pall outside the window, the dead silence of *le piccole ore,* the small hours between midnight and dawn, a silence disturbed only by the scuffling of stray cats in the bushes along the wall of the house next door.

Kot emerges from the black hole of stupor and disbelief in the form I must impress in memory before he is covered by earth in the cemetery of Saint-Dye on the Loire, on that Loire where we walked at twilight many years ago, reminded of our native rivers by shouts echoing from the opposite bank and upright columns of smoke. I stood by his future grave, he pointed it out with a short serene smile: "This is where I'll be laid to rest." He could not bear sentimental-dramatic tones, he had a lordly loathing for them, and he had lived according to a rigorously observed but unuttered code of individual valor. Under that cuirass beat a warm, feeling heart.

He was incredibly intelligent, brilliant, quick to recognize and grasp the real essence of things; inconceivably widely read and informed in all branches of art and thought (though humorously disdainful of "professional erudition"); bursting with energy, and so quick in speaking and writing, as if he could not keep pace with his racing mind; thirsty for "novelty" but ruthless if it was tainted with anything showy or sham, head-over-heels in love with his favorite artists, hating lies and hypocrisy, sensitive to any sign of violence or abuse. Does this sound like a sketch for a portrait of the artist? I am not sure that Kot really wanted to be one. In 1961, when *Kultura* announced a forthcoming volume in honor of Jerzy Stempowski, Stempowski wrote to me: "I am very moved by all this, but I am embarrassed at the same time, because I have always preferred to stay out of the limelight like Mr. Chlewaski, as Jelenski so rightly observed." It may be that Kot observed it so rightly because Mr. Chlewaski, Courier's secret correspondent, was so very much like him, a man who hoped "to go through life like a benevolent and beneficent shadow," faithful to the Voltaire's motto *aimer et penser c'est la véritable vie de l'esprit.*

Like Stempowski, then, Kot never "fell for (a pet expression of his and his mother's) inking paper." He was a fine essayist, one of the finest in modern Polish literature, but he preferred conversation to writing. And he was potentially not only an essayist. There is a thirty-page autobiographical piece about his childhood and early youth, dating from 1979, handwritten in Italian in feverish haste. I read it again today. It is exquisite, and it has the dash of a novel about it with scenes already set out. What did he do with it? There are two copies, the original for an Italian friend and the other for a Polish friend.

Not very long ago I was present when a well-known Paris publisher proposed publishing a volume of his essays in French. He shrugged his shoulders and received the offer with a conventional expression of thanks but was not interested in the slightest. Later the two of us went to a café, and I tried to persuade him to reconsider the offer. He laughed: "Too much is written and published now, we could drown in a sea of printed paper." And yet . . . in the "symposium of polyglots" organized by Stempowski in 1961 in *Kultura*, this is what Kot said: "Why doesn't the polyglot-writer in exile always decide to do his writing in one language? It happens occasionally— and the results are often excellent: Pietrkiewicz in English and Cioran and Ionesco in French. In my case, that of the 'critic' or 'journalist,' it is a rather different matter. My greatest satisfaction comes from writing in Polish for *Kultura*, for the simple reason that my articles evoke some response from a circle of friends, however small. . . . I may have more French or English readers, but for them I am just one of a thousand anonymous hacks." He had a cult of friendship, he was lavish with it, sometimes even extravagant.

I also remember the day I brought him the author's copies of his *Zbiegowie okolicznosci* [Coincidences]. He barely gave them a glance, but when he accompanied me to the bus stop after tea, I watched from the window of the bus and saw him draw out a copy from under his raincoat; he avidly leafed through the pages as he walked, closed the book, opened it again, weighed it in his hands and smoothed it out. If he had looked up for a moment, I am sure I would have seen totally unbridled joy.

> If I had to tell what the world is for me
> I would take a hamster or a hedgehog or a mole
> and place him in a theater seat one evening
> and, bringing my ear close to his humid snout,
> would listen to what he says about the spotlights,
> sounds of the music, and movements of the dance.*

These were probably his favorite lines of Milosz. And this is what he had to say about the verse: "No one has expressed more beautifully the sole philosophical revolution of our times (compared with which neo-Marxism, existentialism, and structuralism are the equivalent of shorter or longer skirts in women's fashions)—arising from the conviction that man is neither the 'lord of all he surveys' nor the center of the universe, so that any 'humanism' is now impossible."

In our age of "impossible humanism," the friendship of beautiful

*Czeslaw Milosz, "Throughout Our Lands," in *Selected Poems*, tr. Milosz and Peter Dale Scott, New York: Ecco Press, 1980.

and noble people like Kot is a boon and a treasure. A treasure whose worth is hard to measure in words and whose loss will be mourned in silence to the end of life.

May 15 [Villa of the Mysteries, Pompeii]

Years ago, the first time I went to Pompeii, there was a large glass display case outside the entrance to the excavations with the petrified corpse of a sleeping man. It looked like a sculpture. The Pompeiian was swamped in his sleep by the flow of lava and earth, and his stone sheath preserved his gesture of terror at the moment of death: his hand over his head and a grimace as he opened his mouth to scream. Yesterday I found the display case in a dark side chamber of the Villa dei Misteri. It was fair to move it out of daylight into the shade, but is almost impossible to see the grimace of the mouth.

The large fresco in the Villa dei Misteri, apparently the only (and splendid) specimen of ancient painting, unfolds in ten scenes against a background of "Pompeiian red" so thick that it suggests clotted blood. The meaning has never been unambiguously deciphered, beyond the conviction shared by all scholars that the scenes show the rites of a newly wed woman being initiated into the Dionysian mystery cult. All that can be made out are the main motifs of a religious mystery: a sacrifice, physical love, the mystical secret of fertility, masks, an orgiastic dance, and a winged demon holding a scourge. The first and penultimate scenes of the fresco must certainly link the hidden connections. The first shows the preparatory reading of the ritual; the penultimate shows a cupid presenting a mirror to a woman about to marry. It is the cyclical continuity of the fresco that is elusive and religious. And the dark chamber with the display case next door? It is a dark mirror of the end of Pompeii appended to the fresco cycle two thousand years later.

May 19 [Flaubert and his parrot]

Flaubert was dubbed "the father of realism": "It is because I hated realism that I wrote *Madame Bovary*."

Flaubert exclaimed: *"Je suis mystique et je ne crois à rien!"*

From a Flaubert letter (1876): "Do you know, Madame, what I've had on my table in front of me for the last three weeks? A stuffed parrot. It sits there on sentry duty. The sight of it is beginning to irritate me. But I keep it there so that I can fill my head with the idea of parrothood. Because at the moment I am writing about the love between an old girl and a parrot."

In *Flaubert's Parrot* Julian Barnes has contrived a splendid cross between a critical study and a novel. The "straight" novel is the lament of the narrator, a doctor by profession and an enthusiastic scholar of Flaubert's life and work, after his wife's suicide: a modern, unloved, and cuckolded Dr. Charles Bovary mourns his beloved Emma. The critical study is constructed by Barnes (rather by the narrator, Dr. Braithwaite) largely of quotations from Flaubert and fragments of his biography. The solitary "bear" of Croisset could not bear biographical intruders and snoops; he knew (every distinguished writer should know this) that only the work counts. Yet thanks to Barnes's skill in getting the right mix, his critico-biographical mélange is surprisingly revelatory. Here is Flaubert, at last the authentic Flaubert, "When you write the biography of a friend, you must do it as if you were taking *revenge* for him." Barnes takes this sentence from a letter of Flaubert as the motto of *Flaubert's Parrot.* Here the "revenge" is for Flaubert's purge of commonplaces; all his life he hunted them down and exterminated them without pity, and they invaded him like vermin after his death. Having purged himself of commonplaces, Flaubert stared at the stuffed parrot on his desk and tried to fathom the "idea of parrothood" as he worked on a tale about the "love between an old girl and a parrot." And Barnes hoists the parrot of "A Simple Heart" into the title of his book. In some way he considers the tale the most important work of the author of *Madame Bovary* and other novels that are far more famous than "A Simple Heart." So do I. Exactly seven years ago, in a journal entry of May 1980, I tried to explain why.

Why is it the most important for Barnes, and why is it for me? Barnes seems to see it mainly as the source of the "idea of parrothood," which he would extend to several other characters in Flaubert, even to the whole world as viewed by the great writer. I limit myself to the servant Félicité and her parrot Loulou in "A Simple Heart." As long as Loulou is alive, one is free to speak of the "love between an old maid and a parrot," understanding love as an alloy of attachment and loneliness. When the parrot dies and is stuffed, a sense of deification is born in Félicité's simple heart and sinks its roots deeper and deeper with the passing years. She discerns a similarity between Loulou and the Church's image of the Holy Ghost. She falls into the habit of kneeling before the parrot to say her prayers. In ecstasy a light frames it, sparked by a ray of sunshine in the bird's glass eye. Maggots rot Loulou, one of his wings is broken, and the stuffing bulges out of his stomach. But Félicité (in the marvelous scene of her death during the Corpus Christi procession) inhales the scent of the incense of "mystical union," and "as the heavens opened for her, she thought she saw a gigantic parrot hovering above her head."

There was a need to go *beyond,* and in Félicité's simple heart the need was linked with faith. Flaubert did not feel the need and did not wish to; he rejected it even violently. This is why Barnes did not notice or chose to ignore the exclamation: *"Je suis mystique et je ne crois à rien!"* That is one feature of Flaubert's portrait I miss very much in the British writer's book: the mystic perch with the parrot on a chain ceaselessly repeating his squawky *rien, rien, rien.*

Dragonea, August 23 [Mystics, Buber, and Musil]

At the beginning of this century Martin Buber edited an anthology of mystics of all faiths, *Ecstatic Confessions (Ekstatische Konfessionen).* Borges considered it one of his fundamental readings. What is much more interesting is that Musil drew on it by the fistful in the course of writing *The Man Without Qualities.* Independently of the Buber anthology, Musil collected his own *Borderline Experiences* in 1921, one hundred and ten mystic quotations. What interested him particularly was the "verbal aspect" of ecstatic experience.

He was right to be interested, for Buber himself admitted in the introduction to his anthology that ecstatic mystics are unable to leap over the wall of speech. They are confined within the compass of experiences and visions separate from speech that are especially powerful in moments of "going beyond oneself" and "entering into God" (*ekstasis*), and at the same time they are powerless in their attempt to achieve linguistic expression, so they constantly fall back on qualifications such as "ineffable," "inexpressible," "unutterable," and (literally) "ungraspable." Angela of Foligno (second half of the thirteenth century) complained that she felt as if her "tongue had been cut off" in her mouth. Others used such turns of speech as "I see nothing, and I see all; I hear nothing, and I hear all." Heinrich Suso (first half of the fourteenth century), speaking of himself in the third person, avowed that "then he caught sight of and heard something that is not accessible to any language. It was without form and without appearance, and yet it encompassed the exultant delight of all forms and all appearances." Whenever ecstatic mystics attempt to grasp the shadow of an ungraspable shadow, to express even a crumb of the inexpressible in their accounts, two elements emerge: light, a flood of light; and a vision of absolute oneness with God merging one's own "I." The "Spanish" Teresa (sixteenth century) may have tried hardest of all to capture the sense of ecstatic experience in the letters to her confessors. But she finally threw up her hands: "All this cannot be explained except by comparisons, which are certainly coarse and uncouth, but I cannot find any other way to do it."

"*Das Wort schneidet nicht*" ("Words do not cut through") Musil sighs helplessly, adding that "mysticism and narratability do not get along well with each other." He surmounted the difficulty by quoting, often word for word, from Buber's mystic extracts and his own, without naming the authors of the "accounts of ecstasy." The thing "works," indeed unexpectedly well, in the poetic context of the novel. States of mystic ecstasy possess only one alternative: poetry or silence.

Naples, October 19
[Stendhal and Giulia Rinieri Berlinghieri]

Giulia Rinieri Berlinghieri, the woman Stendhal loved (requited) during the last fifteen years of his life, was of course known to Stendhal buffs. But rather superficially, it now seems, since a living descendant of the Sienese family of the Rinieris has opened the family archives. The *Storia di Giulia* is an engaging and sometimes gripping portrait of a woman, all the more interesting in that Stendhal hovers in the background and leaves center stage to the only woman in his life he might have married.

She came from Siena, she was good-looking and exceptionally intelligent, and she was twenty-six years old (in those days a warning bell of spinsterhood) in 1827, the year she met the nearly fifty-year-old M. Beyle in Paris, where she lived with her guardian, a family friend and later stepfather, a minister of the Grand Duke of Tuscany at the court of Charles X.

It was a *coup de foudre* for both of them. She: "You are old and ugly, but I love you." He, an old confirmed bachelor was suddenly ready to accept "a connection that is rather singular and I even venture to say against nature, such as marriage." Nine years after their love story began, he admitted in the pages of *Henry Brulard* that Giulia stood out among the women he had loved *par la force du caractère*.

The start of the romance is amusing, embellished with one of those signs of the times that delight connoisseurs of curious customs. Charles X received a giraffe as a present from the Pasha of Egypt. The inspection of the exotic gift in Villeneuve-Saint-Georges was to be a social event. At the last moment the date of the presentation was postponed, and M. Beyle wrote to the Tuscan minister to inform him: "Lofty personages, as you know, Excellency, are accustomed to changing their plans. And I write now to inform you that a very lofty giraffe will be going to Villeneuve-Saint-Georges on Saturday and not on Friday." Stendhal was looking forward to another rendezvous with Giulia, whom he had just met, and the postponement thwarted his plans.

I have no taste (to put it delicately) for disemboweling the private life of great writers, so I will skip all the stages of the romance that Stendhal buffs have detailed so exactly, and so easily since Stendhal dated the many marginal notations he wrote in the books he was reading: "sieges," "battles," and "victories," together with the first English communiqué of Giulia's defloration: "1830, 22 mars, a time, a first time." What interests me is the woman of "strong character." She soon concluded that Stendhal did not have the makings of a husband in the sense of the term that was traditional in her milieu. She loved him, and she never stopped loving him, but a lover was one thing and a husband another. She considered him a "frivolous original," she was fascinated by him, but he did not quite suit a Sienese landed-bourgeois family with extravagant ambitions. Her guardian and later stepfather, the Grand Duke's Minister in Paris, to whom "a certain M. Beyle" had officially made his request for the young woman's hand, wrote to Giulia's natural father in Siena and described the suitor as "a witty and good-hearted fellow, with quite curious ideas," and "the author of rather poor novels and excellent observations in the area of the fine arts." Giulia understood that it was better not to insist. There were also financial considerations involved: prospects were rather poor for "the author of rather poor novels," and a consulate appointment in Trieste and Civitavecchia would not do much to improve the situation. The woman of "strong character" decided to separate heart from altar. She took the "frivolous fellow with quite curious ideas" for her lover and her Sienese cousin Martini for her husband. She consistently maintained this division of roles until Stendhal's death. All indications are that Stendhal reconciled himself to this solution and may even have found it rather agreeable. Shortly before his death he was still able to make the following annotations on the margins of books: "Battle and victory of third August 1839"; a year later "4 juillet 1840, a time"; a year before his death, prophetically, "Two and tenth August 1841, perhaps the last of his life."

The *Storia di Giulia* ends with a quotation from Stendhal's *De l'Amour*: "*Il est beaucoup plus contre la pudeur de se mettre au lit avec un homme qu'on n'a vu que deux fois, après trois mots latins dits à l'église, que de céder malgré soi à un homme qu'on adore depuis deux ans. Mais je parle un langage absurde.*"* At least for Giulia that was not "absurd language." Stendhalists see her as the model for Mathilde de La Mole. And the Sanseverina? And Vanina Vanini?

She died in 1881 at the age of eighty, alone, her children almost all dead, a stern matron occupied mainly with philanthropic work. Her grave on her husband's estate in Tuscany ought to have the following inscription: "She lived fifteen years loving and beloved of Stendhal and forty years remembering that love."

October 28 [Tocqueville, the Grand Inquisitor, and others]

Tocqueville, describing the year 1848 in his *Mémoires*, wrote that "revolutions arise when a widespread illness of the mind suddenly reaches

---

*"It is far more indelicate to go to bed with a man you have seen two times only, after three Latin words uttered in church, than to surrender despite yourself to a man who has loved you for two years. But I speak an absurd language."

a critical state evoked by some casual, unforeseen accident; and as for those who are supposed to have inspired and led revolutions, they inspired no one, they led no one, and their only merit is the same as that of the impudent fellows who discovered unknown lands."

The remark about "impudent fellows who discovered unknown lands" is the sole and probably last "compliment" to be encountered in articles by "sympathizers" on the occasion of the seventieth anniversary of the October Revolution. Obviously, with the melancholy reflection that the unknown land that was to have been "the realm of freedom" instead turned out to be . . . no, better not say what it turned out to be; and, in any case, disenchanted and embittered "sympathizers" do not wish to go into the details, despite what are, after all, amicable winds blowing in from Eastern Europe. They are like rain-beaten bantam cocks, their crests bowed and their tails between their legs. With nothing left over, and evidently irreversibly, the admixture of revolutionary "pathos" has disappeared from the yearly celebrations. On the other side of the barricades, though, there is an orgy, emboldened by the Gorbachev "reckoning." "From the Winter Palace to the Last Empire." "The October Counter-Revolution against the February Revolution." "The rise and fall of the Ottoman Empire." "From the Russian woods to the Soviet barracks." And a hefty book published in England has put the finishing touches on the rehabilitation of the much-ridiculed Kerensky. Since Lenin studied in Symbirsk in a classical gymnasium whose director was Kerensky's father, the author of one of the articles sighs "a bad student in a good gymnasium." Before long we will witness a wringing of hands over the recalcitrant student at the respectable ecclesiastic seminary in Tiflis.

Considerations of the October Revolution commonly refer to Dostoevsky's "Grand Inquisitor." The "philosophically" inclined Soviet heirs of the Grand Inquisitor repeat after him: "man is vexed by no greater anxiety than to find someone quickly to hand over that gift of freedom with which the ill-fated creature is born. . . . Nothing is more seductive for man than freedom of conscience, but nothing is more excruciating either. . . . We shall convince people that they will become free only when they relinquish their freedom and submit to us."

It would be interesting to bear in mind these three teachings of the Grand Inquisitor (especially the third), which were heeded by

Lenin and Stalin, and take a careful look at the situation seventy years after the October Revolution. The imperative of the moment, according to Gorbachev's advisers and intimates, the indispensable condition for overcoming stagnation and immobility and breaking up the monolithic structure of the system, is to reawaken in its subjects those "vexing" human aspirations, which were taken away from them at the advice of the Grand Inquisitor (nay, which, according to his plan, they themselves had handed over, they themselves had relinquished to the authorities). But is that possible without convulsions? Are verbal and as yet empty promises and enticements sufficient to overcome the routine of servitude and the habit of the yoke? I read several pronouncements by the brightest of Gorbachev's team. Tatiana Zaslavska bemoans the "psychological inertia" of Soviet citizens. Abel Aganbegian claims that they "dread independence and autonomy." Nikolai Shyshlyn grants that, thanks to Khrushchev, the Soviet ship of state was purged and lightened when superfluous ballast was jettisoned, but insists that it must now be thoroughly overhauled and equipped with new machinery and new instruments of navigation. How is this going to be done, when the captain can in no way shake the "inertia" of his frightened passengers and his frightened crew? Must we wait for some new "impudent fellows" to spring up at the critical stage of a "widespread illness of the mind" and stir others to "the discovery of unknown lands"?

1 9 8 8

Naples, January 5 [Brodsky's Nobel speech]

What is endearing in Brodsky's Nobel speech is his belief that only poetry (or literature generally) can "save the world." Brodsky facetiously claims to have dreamed more than once about replacing the state with a library. But he sounds less facetious when he suggests that if we could choose our rulers on the basis of their experience as readers, and not on the basis of their political programs, we would live in a happier world. Brodsky thinks that any potential ruler of our destinies should be asked first of all not how he conceives foreign policy but what he thinks about Stendhal, Dickens, and Dostoevsky. The plan this year's Nobelist advanced for improving our less than "best of all possible worlds" gave me goose flesh. I had the same reaction once before, to the statement by the great Nobelist Thomas Mann that political regimes should be measured by the yardstick of their relationship to the "classics of literature." Silone called this the stupidity of the "mandarins."

Reading is a misleading criterion of man's wisdom, noble-mindedness, and honesty. I imagine that the writers Brodsky mentioned were also read by Lenin and Stalin, who generally liked to read so-called "beautiful literature" when they were young. Trotsky certainly read them and would have had something quite interesting to say, for, while he was a one-track reader, he was acute and penetrating. As for Stalin, he had an outright weakness for poetry and may have tried his hand at writing poems in his youth. (Mussolini too had a weakness for literature and wrote a novel, *The Cardinal's Mistress*, when he was young.) And it must mean something that Stalin, in his famous telephone call to Pasternak, asked quite humbly if Mandelstam should be considered a "master." And that Brodsky should move from his real homeland to a homeland of his choosing. President Kennedy was an avid reader (together with his extremely well-read wife, who even set up something on the order of a literary salon in the White House). Setting aside his personal charm and tragic death, I do not think he deserves to be considered an outstanding president: in any case, he was less outstanding than (say) Truman, who probably read only one book in his life, the Bible.

The yearning for a well-read "ruler of our destiny" should be left to the literati. Such a splendid poet and wise essayist as Brodsky must in the wake of his predecessors "save the world" by turning toward other readers and as much as possible away from "crowned" readers.

January 15 [Hogarth at the Tate]

An intelligent Italian literary critic stopped to consider the affinities between drawings and stories on the occasion of the publication of an album of drawings by Gustave Doré, the theme of which is Dickensian London. Last month at the Tate Gallery in London, William Hogarth put me on the identical spoor. What particularly enchanted me was the renowned cycle of eight pictures of the *Rake's Progress*, which I saw for the first time in the original. I found that Hogarth claimed to have invented his subjects the way writers do. The picture was his stage, and the men and women were his actors, who with the help of certain gestures and expressions presented a "dumb show." In his eight chapters from the life of the rake, there are two striking features: the "dumbness," the silence, heightens the expressive power of the "show" (which is obvious), and each episode is open (which is less obvious). What this means is that perspectives are opened only partially in the service of the sequential "action of the actors," so that the actions and events illustrated, or rather narrated, by the brush leave a wide margin for what is not narrated and illustrated. The whole painted cycle, the whole narrated story, is a whole and at the same time it is not: Hogarth shows and simultaneously veils, he quietly interweaves the mute and the living expression of dead and mysterious silence. A splendid painter, he was not afraid of the contagion of literature, and writers might learn something from him in return.

January 16 ["The Pit and the Pendulum"]

Someone remarked that a good title is a prerequisite of a good story *before you begin to write it.* Aside from a good title, it is immensely important to have a good "key" to the narrative and that it be "offered" as soon as the story begins. Edgar Allan Poe's "The Pit and the Pendulum" is an example of the combination of both. "Arousing from the most profound of slumbers, we break the gossamer web of *some* dream. Yet in a second afterward (so frail may that web have been) we remember not that we have dreamed." These are the words of a prisoner of the Inquisition in Toledo, suspended in a dungeon between a black pit beneath and the guillotine of a pendulum above. From the first pages of the tale, actual torture rubs shoulders with a dreamed-not-dreamed nightmare, which follows it to the end like a subtle and absolutely indispensable accompaniment.

January 17 [Chekhov and Canetti]

Some years ago I was given a lavish edition of Chekhov's *Zapishnyje knishki*, the notebooks in which he jotted down little details of everyday life, laconic germs of literary ideas, character traits he glimpsed in people for possible use in plays or stories, and random reflections and maxims. The volume was published with such piety that each page faithfully reproduces the corresponding page in the notebooks: "Where is Masha?" and nothing more, the rest of the page is blank. Sometimes, very rarely, there are interesting remarks: "Between the God who is and the God who is not, there is a broad expanse measured in anguish by the wise man; the Russian instead knows only one of the two extremes, he is not interested in the expanse between them." Ultimately, however, if anyone had suggested to Chekhov, when he was alive, that his notebooks be published, he would have told the man to have his head examined. He treated them like workshop scraps and crumbs of life, legible and meaningful solely to the owner and after a while destined for burning. At most he might have agreed (with reluctance) to leave the notebooks to an archive accessible one day (after his death) to students of his work. He was the antithesis of the vain writer. He was the personification of modesty, reserve, and what is most essential here—he habitually bestowed a sad and embarrassed smile on any excessive exaltation of the role of the writer and the importance of literature.

Elias Canetti, the 1981 Nobelist, is still alive, thanks be to God. He is alive and has published his notebooks for the years 1973–1985. The volume is entitled the *Secret Heart of the Clock* and thus promises an exploration of its delicate mechanism. In addition to several lengthy notes that just might stimulate a moment's reflection, it includes a host of opinions, taken out of who knows what context, that certainly say something to the author, but nothing or almost nothing do they say to the reader. It is not clear why Canetti thinks these randomly chosen remarks should also speak to us: "While others starve, he writes; he writes, while others die." "I am not vain said the vainest of all, I am sensitive." A splendid writer, I have no doubt about that, he deserved the Nobel laurel, but the meager fare of his notebooks only seems to confirm a wider phenomenon. That is to say, I have long suspected that just as the influence and the meaning of literature have diminished, the good opinion that renowned writers have of themselves has constantly and unexpectedly increased. They seem to be convinced that anything they say will be greeted with shouts of wonder, that in even their most banal remarks we will hear the beating of the "secret heart of the watch."

February 18 [Van Gogh: "The night is richer still in color than the day"]

"The night is richer still in color than the day." Van Gogh's statement seems on the face of it to clash with what the two Dutch biographers

Hammacher write about his life and painting. "He adored dawn and sunset," according to the biographers, "the first and the last light of day were a source of ecstasy to him." He often arose at four in the morning to greet the dawn; and he might loiter hours waiting for twilight to fall. There were times he sat up all night—by a pond, in the fields, or in the cemetery—until the first morning birds sang. So what brought him "ecstasy" was the moment when night subsided into day, then day into night, rather than nighttime richer in color than the day. And yet I think he had a right to his statement. The night heightened in him the spasmodic sense of veiled color crammed and vibrating intensely beneath his eyelids. The church in Auvers was painted a month before his suicide attempt and death: the sky is "nocturnal," the walls are "nocturnal," and if it were not for the reference in a letter to his brother to "the sun-drenched pink gravel" on the path, it would be hard to imagine the presence of a natural source of light.

Van Gogh has to be looked at in large doses and not haphazardly, but I never had the occasion until the recent exhibition in Rome. Now I know that he was the greatest painter of the modern period. His greatness eludes "technical" and "formal" criteria. I admire artists for whom art is a ceaseless struggle to reach the other shore. Firmly rooted in reality and in nature, they stubbornly strain toward something that is felt but not known. In Van Gogh's eyes everything contains a fleeting shadow of mystery: a peasant face, a landscape, roots, uprooted trees, sunflowers, a chair. Albert Aurier, the author of the *only* article written about Van Gogh in his lifetime, spoke of the painter's "audaciousness." Aurier was struck by the "excessive" in Van Gogh's painting: excess of strength, excess of nervousness, excess of vehemence of expression. Van Gogh for him was a "drunken giant," "a mind in a state of ferment," "a frenzied terrible genius," "a visionary on the brink of the pathological," soaking up the surrounding world "in abnormal and perhaps painful tension." When he read this description of himself, the painter wrote a letter to the author, in which he championed the role of Gauguin and described his own place in the future of art as "very secondary."

During his year's stay in the asylum in Saint-Rémy for people with nervous ailments, he audaciously looked straight at the sun. Is there also a reflection of "nocturnal colors" in the blazing landscape of the field with harvesters? He was convinced that "pain proves to be stronger than madness." Pain? Yes, pain, the inseparable feeling that the blinding sunlight is intertwined with the splendor of the night. For Van Gogh the portrait of an old villager, painted in full sunlight, had "something eternal, something whose symbol used to be the halo." The evening scene of peasants at table eating potatoes in the light of an oil lamp hanging from the ceiling makes one think of Rembrandt's canvases: the faces here are also eternal, as if they were illuminated from within. But the pinnacle is the self-portrait he painted shortly before death: he looks at us with a stern glance, this painter and onetime itinerant preacher, bitter, concentrated in pain, thirsting for eternal rest after years suspended between bright darkness and dark brightness.

Maisons-Laffitte, March 7 [Plague years]

Kochyna, a thirtyish Leningrad schoolteacher, married to an engineer and mother of a small baby, kept a *Journal of the Blockade* from June 1941 to April 1942. These bare matter-of-fact notes survived, and they are something on the order of a "report from a city under siege," a gripping and truthful report like Defoe's *Journal of the Plague Year*. "The dead are no longer taken to the cemetery, they are just stacked in piles outside front doors. The piles rise every day in front of almost every building. From time to time trucks go down the streets and collect these heaps." The entry might have been taken word for word from the great English writer's book! The ironic-philosophical motto that Kochyna borrowed from Georg Christoph Lichtenberg would have been perfect for the *Journal of the Plague Year*: "Terrible things happen to us dwellers of the earth." One other book came to mind when I read the *Journal of the Blockade*: in John Hersey's novel about the Warsaw ghetto, *The Wall*, the author makes use of a particular literary device—namely, he claims to have "unearthed" from the rubble of the ghetto the "Lewinson archives," a chronicle history of the cut-off quarter under siege. When I reviewed *The Wall* many years ago, I compared it too with the *Journal of the Plague Year* and wrote: "Defoe's journal ends with the sole *personal* comment in the whole book, a simple remark on 'the perseverance of human nature'; it resounds like a powerful chord against the background of his *impersonal* account, and it swells almost to the scale of a finale to a medieval morality play: the last notes of the Lewinson chronicle sound the same."

The number of victims of the Leningrad blockade—people who died of hunger and illness—is estimated at about two million. Julia Lajuk, the Polish translator of the *Journal of the Blockade*, supplemented her translation with a wealth of information. Two items, one after the other, will suffice: "People carved cutlets from their dead to trade for bread in the market; there were cases of conscious cannibalism, but for this purpose they kidnapped small children." "The few Uniate churches that survived after the revolution were jam-packed around the clock; no one made trouble when people practiced their religion." An incredible condensation of the human condition in extremity.

Kochyna does not speak of the "perseverance of human nature"; the moral of the "city under siege" is expressed otherwise in her journal: "It was clear that there is a limit to physical endurance, beyond which a person becomes insensitive to everything except his own suffering. Heroism, self-sacrifice, and good deeds can be expected only from someone who is well fed or has not been starving very long. But we learned what hunger is, it mortified us, crushed us, and made beasts of us. You who come after us and may read these words, try to be forebearing!"

Primo Levi entitled his Auschwitz memoir *If This Be a Man*. Despite any "humanistic" illusions, this *too* is a man. *My World Apart* talks about the difficulty of judging a person by how he behaves in inhuman conditions. It may be hard to judge, but at least one must know; to forget even for an instant is inadmissible. Indeed, "terrible things happen to us dwellers of the earth."

March 11 [Hannah Arendt]

Hannah Arendt's *Eichmann in Jerusalem* has finally been published in Poland; the author of the *Origins of Totalitarianism* has been granted a posthumous pardon by the censors on the Vistula. Her excellent and, in a certain sense, revelatory book shed much new light on the Holocaust by way of the Eichmann trial. The revelation is adumbrated in the subtitle *A Report on the Banality of Evil*. The "demon of our age" (the title of an article I wrote in 1963 about *Eichmann in Jerusalem*), the *hostis generis humani* as he was presumed to be at the trial, actually turns out be a terribly banal bureaucrat of the *Endlösung*, the extermination of the Jews, the personification of alarming human normality in the century of organized ideologies, a déclassé member of the petite bourgeoisie, who mentioned Kant in the Jerusalem courtroom, considered repentance fine for small children, and at the foot of the gallows bid farewell to those present with the words: "We shall all meet again. Such is the fate of all men." What meeting could he be speaking of, since he did not believe in life beyond the grave? Hannah Arendt's opinion was that a banal evildoer had fallen back on the last banal cliché of funeral oratory, forgetting that he was speaking at his own funeral. May he have been announcing his return in other people?

The revelatory character of the book is dimmed by a single error, typical of students of totalitarianism with rather limited direct experience of it. Hannah Arendt believes that the magnitude of the *Endlösung* would not have reached such a monstrous peak if the Jews had been disorganized and lacked leaders: chaos would have been the only possible form of struggle for unarmed people against such carefully ordered extermination. A host of reasons could be given to show that the theory of passive resistance and disobedience is vitiated by deskbound intellectual abstractness and is hard to practice in such circumstances. I mention one very essential and important reason as I formulated it in my essay a quarter century ago. It concerns the politico-historical model of the "city under siege" and offers a response to the question, why Jewish organizations were transformed from an instrument in the hands of the besieged victims to an instrument in the hands of the besieging tormentors. In several countries of Europe—not in all—the locked cities of the Jews were doubly besieged: physically by the Hitlerians and psychically by the conquered nations that surrounded them. The crime was the work of Hitlerism, but the toxins fostered by the crime had been polluting the air of Europe long before Hitler's "final solution." The architects of the Holocaust suffered several setbacks in its organization and implementation. In Denmark the king said that if the Jews had to wear a yellow badge, he would be the first to do so. In Italy and Bulgaria anti-

Semitism never found too hospitable a ground. Mechanical comparisons are risky from several viewpoints, but Rymkiewicz's *Umschlagplatz* still suggests some bitter reflections.

March 18 [Irina Ratushinskaya]

Thanks to a French publisher friend I was able to read the typescript of the English translation of Irina Ratushinskaya's memoirs *Grey Is the Colour of Hope*. It will come out in Great Britain and the United States later this year and in French early next year. A Russian edition also seems to be in preparation.

The young Russian poet of Polish descent, whom I singled out as soon as I read in *Russkoj Myshli* several of her poems smuggled out of prison, was arrested in the autumn of 1982, sentenced to seven years in a labor camp plus five years of internal exile, and given early release in the autumn of 1986. Soon after her release she was allowed to leave for the West with her husband. Woroszylski first translated her poems into Polish for *Kultura* two years ago and recently in a small volume *My Hateful Motherland* published by Aneks.

The "Small Zone" of the women's camp in Mordovia, detention, prison. The group of women prisoners: two Lithuanians, two Ukrainians, three Russians (including Irina). A certain ineluctable sameness in Ratushinskaya's memoirs is vivified by her splendid sense of observation and a poetic memory based on love of detail. There is an ease to the writing and an unflagging air of inner freedom, as if barbed wire and bars were no longer able to serve their intended function. Surely, "gray is the color of hope" in "my hateful motherland," yet hope does surge. I was struck by an unusual antithesis in Ratushinskaya's book: there is a sense of weakness, vacillation, and sometimes dread of the prison guards; on the other hand, there are women prisoners, members of the "Defenders of Law" group, who have overcome their dread, are conscious of their human dignity and unyielding. "Realistic" scorners of "paltry groups of hotheads and crazies" have something to ponder. And so does anyone who believes that the standard "Soviet person" has been formed once and for all.

Twenty years ago another Russian poet, a soul sister of Ratushinskaya, went into Red Square with a handful of friends to protest against the invasion of Czechoslovakia. Natalia Gorbanievska's *In the Afternoon*, testimony of that demonstration, might well have given the impression of black hopeless courage. Today gray is the color of hope not because perestroika has been decreed on high but because people of the stamp of Gorbanievska and Ratushinskaya spring up with heads held bravely high.

Maisons-Laffitte, September 29
[The seven deaths of Maxim Gorky]

During a break in the shooting of her documentary about *Kultura*, Agnieszka Holland asked me if I would agree to a television film of my "crime story" "The Seven Deaths of Maxim Gorky." Obviously I said yes, but most likely other projects caught the director's fancy, because she never again mentioned the idea of a film about Gorky's death. Besides, she made the suggestion before the era of glasnost, so I doubt that she would have found any Western television backing. Now the situation is different. I am convinced that—if the victorious opponents of Gorbachev do not sound retreat—the mystery of Gorky's death can finally be expected to be cleared up in Moscow. The harvest season has opened for historic, literary, theatrical, and film buffs of Kremlin crime. There is a touch of the "thriller," for example, to the story of Eisenstein's film about Ivan the Terrible, so it seems from a curious stenographic account published in *Moskovski Novosti*.

At eleven o'clock on the night of February 25, 1947, Poskrebyshov, Stalin's secretary, took the film's director and Cherkassov, who played the title role, to a room in the Kremlin. Stalin, Molotov, and Zhdanov were sitting at a table, and the scene that ensued might have come from Bulgakov's *Master and Margherita*. It should be mentioned that Stalin liked part one of *Ivan the Terrible*, and it won Eisenstein a Stalin Prize. The scenario of part two drew a dangerous wrinkling of the leader's eyebrows. He did not reply to the letter Eisenstein sent with the scenario, he preferred to "discuss" the matter *viva voce*.

"Comrade Eisenstein," Stalin began, "you show the *oprichnina* in an incorrect way. The *oprichnina* was the czar's army, a regular progressive army. But in your film it looks like the Ku Klux Klan."

Eisenstein dared to interrupt. "Members of the Ku Klux Klan wear white hoods, in my film the *oprichniki* have black hoods." Zhdanov rightly observed, "The difference is slight." Stalin: "Your czar, Comrade Eisenstein, is indecisive, he reminds one of Hamlet. After all Ivan the Terrible was a great and wise leader, he was ten times as smart as Louis XI. He knew how to maintain a national point of view, he did not allow foreigners into Russia, and he screened the country from the penetration of foreign influences. Peter I was also a great czar, but he was too liberal with foreigners, he allowed Russia to be Germanized. And Catherine went even farther, and the courts of Alexander I and Nicholas I, were they Russian courts? No, they were German courts. Besides that, Ivan the Terrible had an enormous merit: he was the first to introduce a monopoly on foreign trade. He was the first, and Lenin was the second."

Fanciers of the artistic development of the theme "the leader and the director" ought to stress several other strands in the Kremlin meeting. Stalin: "Ivan the Terrible was immensely cruel. The film may show that he was cruel. But the public must realize that he had to be cruel. One of Ivan the Terrible's mistakes was that he did not finish killing off the five leading Boyar families. He killed, and then he prayed and went on to beat his breast in remorse. God was a hindrance to him in this work. He should have been even more absolute." Molotov called for "a just historical light": "one cannot mock Russia's baptism, which was a progressive event in that distant time." And here is Stalin: "Of course, we are not very exemplary Christians. Yet that is no reason to deny the progressive role of Christianity in a certain circumscribed phase of history." It is no problem, Zhdanov said, that the director takes too much delight in looking at religious rites. And Molotov added that the film was tinged with too much mysticism. But let us get back to the serious problem of the *oprichnina*. Stalin: "When the *oprichniki* dance, they are like cannibals, they might be Phoenicians or Babylonians." The famous actor Cherkassov spoke up, "There is a scene in our script where Maluta Skuratov strangles the metropolitan Philip. Can we keep it?" Stalin: "Yes, it is historically accurate and true." Molotov added this comment: "In general repression can and should be shown, but you must point out in whose name it was committed and why it was necessary. In other words, the wise conduct of affairs of state should be brought out." Zhdanov took up the defense of Maluta Skuratov: "In your film he is a clown, and that is inadmissible." And he castigated the director: "Comrade Eisenstein, you take too much delight in nuances, and you distract the public from the action of the film with that business of the czar's beard. Ivan the Terrible lifts his head too often to show off his beard." Eisenstein: "I will trim the czar's beard." Stalin: "God help you."

The scenario of part two of the film was never revised. Eisenstein died a year after the conversation at the Kremlin. The film came to the screen after the Twentieth Congress.

Maisons-Laffitte, December 6
[Solzhenitsyn, Chiaromonte, Camus, et al.]

It is Solzhenitsyn's seventieth birthday. I have written several times about his books. Some years ago *Kultura* published my conversation with Nicola Chiaromonte about Solzhenitsyn, and it was later included in that outstanding essayist and critic's posthumous book *Silenzio e parole*. Three extracts of our dialogue strike me today.

NICOLA: "In Solzhenitsyn's books you catch sight of a response—or rather, the clear indication of a response—to the infernal torment that, even if it is not imposed by an autocratic system, oppresses every conscious human being: the torment of living day after day a life without sense, a life in which the individual feels he is losing his soul day by day."

I: "Simple, sensitive and attentive readers of Solzhenitsyn's books in the West are moved and forced to think by what they read, because the Russian writer restores meaning and something like a clear sound to concepts that seemed irremediably outworn: soul, human personality, good and evil, justice, honesty, love, truth, the thirst for immortality. In other words, admiration for Solzhenitsyn expresses a latent and often unconscious rebellion against a world that (in the words of Witkiewicz) 'kills in human beings any intuition of the future, any capacity to integrate the separate moments in a construct of life in the long term, and pulverizes the self into so many moments each separate from the other . . . so that it will all the more easily submit to any mechanical discipline.' "

NICOLA: "For the literati Solzhenitsyn's novels are nobly documentary, and that is all. Now it is common knowledge that contemporary literati have no particular respect for either morality or truth. It is no accident that it was an Italian writer who invented the formula of "literature as falsehood." It is a much more traditional formula in Italy than it might seem, but it can be applied to almost everything that is written today in the West. Did we not hear recently that an eminent French intellectual, Michel Foucault, was called to the honors of the Collège de France, and in the austere walls of that institution gave an inaugural address in which the 'desire for truth' was considered a form of repression of freedom of speech?"

On the occasion of Solzhenitsyn's birthday, one wants to ask if any trace of his books still survives in the West. In the minds and hearts of his readers, yes, I have proof of that. For the literati they remain "nobly documentary," perhaps something slightly more than "noble" (in other words, powerless), since they are now clearing a channel for the streams of Soviet glasnost. But I do not think that Solzhenitsyn and those who are akin to him in spirit, however different from him as well—such writers as Camus, Orwell, and Pasternak, for example—put an end to the harvest of "literature as falsehood," the literature of barren subtleties, ever new approaches and tastes, novels that might equally well be published or not, and pen-and-ink party games in which "serious" is a synonym for "boring." We go back to Solzhenitsyn and his like through unfortunately fleeting reference to their weight and substance. That is why this writer who is merely serious, merely fully conscious of the writer's calling, is sometimes accused of wanting to play the "prophet."

Overwhelmed by his enormous volumes, cycles, and "nodes," we are inclined to overlook his "slighter works." Who knows, they may give an even better idea of the class of writer Solzhenitsyn is. "Matryona's House," a story about "the righteous person without whom no village or city may survive." "An Incident at Krechetovka Station," a story about a human soul poisoned by the venom of "revolutionary vigilance." "The Easter Procession," a picture of the Feast of the Passion and Resurrection disturbed and reviled by young hooligans. In all three stories, Solzhenitsyn touches the depths of the depravity of Soviet life in the "raging torrent of epochal historical processes." He does it in a way that is modest and frugal, weighing every word, his voice subdued and solicitous, as if he wanted to caution "experts" on contemporary Russia: as long as you do not understand, as long as you do not see the actuality of my country in seemingly slight events and images, as Chekhov tried to see the truth about last-century Russia, your would-be "expertise" will be lifeless, soulless inking of paper that is too clever by half. This warning is no less timely today, when legions of "experts" glide over the surface of Soviet life, content to construct diagnoses and quick to project "prognoses," and make no attempt—God forbid!—to glance even a bit below the surface. Solzhenitsyn is the writer of deep Russia, which lies silent under the ice and rarely awakens. When it does awake, however, there will be a terrible icequake.

December 8 [Solzhenitsyn]

In our conversation we also talked about the artistic merits of Solzhenitsyn's prose. I quoted Pasternak's view that "art never seemed to me an object or an aspect of form but rather a mysterious hidden element of content. . . . Works of art speak in many ways: with subject matter, theses, situations, characters. But they speak chiefly through the presence of art. The presence of art in *Crime and Punishment* is more overwhelming than Raskolnikov's crime."

What is this "mysterious hidden element of content" that gives the sense of the "presence of art"? Whatever else we might try to say about it, it certainly does not depend on the inherent wealth or poverty of the narrative material. Flaubert dreamed of describing the basest things as if they belonged to history or epic. An apparently absurd undertaking (he added), yet the only one worthy of a writer's efforts and the one that determined the degree of originality and artistry. In a letter to Louise Colet he made a strange comparison. The artist must raise everything to a higher level; he is something on the order of a pump, which dips into the deepest layers of things, sucks up what is at the bottom, and brings to light something unremarkable and disregarded. The comparison may be too clever, but the meaning is sufficiently clear. To transform what is featureless, even banal, into the unusual; to elevate the gray quotidian and glut it with unexpected colors.

The "presence of art" makes it possible to set Flaubert's "A Simple Heart" side by side with Solzhenitsyn's "Matryona's House," two masterpieces of transfiguration that take earthbound realistic description into another dimension.

1 9 8 9

April 9 [A Stendhalian pope]

It was a delight and a relief, after long immersion in the immensity of the Cathedral of Siena, to enter the Piccolomini Library, originally a side chapel. Aeneas Sylvius Piccolomini, elected pope in 1458 as Pius II, was immortalized in the library by his nephew Francesco Todeschini Piccolomini, Archbishop of Siena, subsequently Cardinal, and finally Pope under the name of Pius III. So the library is a family monument. The original nucleus was a collection of illuminated manuscripts, and the crowning touch is the set of ten frescoes depicting the life of Aeneas Sylvius, which Francesco commissioned from the Umbrian painter Pinturicchio (or Pintoricchio). One of the assistants of the then-famous Umbrian, a follower of Perugino, was the young Raphael.

I had read a great deal about the frescoes in the Piccolomini Library, from Berenson's professorial censures to Zbigniew Herbert's beautiful description in *Barbarian in the Garden*. I have only one thing to say of my visit: anyone who considers Pinturicchio a mere "decorator of architecture," however qualified by a whole sheaf of the requisite superlatives, has missed the fairy-tale sensitivity and imagination of the painted biography.

I left the cathedral in urgent need of another look—after some twenty years, I imagine—at the novella Pius II wrote in his youth, the *Storia di due amanti*. But where in Siena could I find it right away? Destiny provided. It was on display in the first bookstore I passed, in a new and original edition from Sellerio, the Palermo publisher.

Original, because the jacket copy of the Palermo edition describes Aeneas Sylvius Piccolomini as a Stendhalian figure *avant la lettre*. A learned humanist, diplomat, and poet, he wrote his *Historia de duobus amantibus* before finally settling on an ecclesiastical career. He was still fairly young and exceptionally handsome, and he presumably drew inspiration for the *Tale of Two Lovers* from his own amatory experiences. The story of the passionate love of the German knight Eurialus and the Sienese lady Lucretia is full of charm, delicacy, and psychological insight, and it has its daring and racy touches as well. (When Eurialus lends his steed to Lucretia's husband, he laughingly thinks: "You mount my charger, and I'll mount your wife.") Aeneas Sylvius was surely the only (future) Holy Father in the history of the papacy whose brow was decked with the golden laureate of poetry. He received it from the hands of King Frederick III, and Pinturicchio immortalized the event in one of the frescoes.

Stendhal knew the *Tale of Two Lovers* only by hearsay; he makes passing reference to it in his *Promenades* in connection with Raphael, the Umbrian master's apprentice in the work on the wall frescoes of the Piccolomini Library. The frescoes evoked a curious response in Stendhal: the figure of the protagonist made him wish he had had a friend like Aeneas Sylvius. His intuition was not mistaken. *The Tale of Two Lovers*, a short work by an author who knew how much more intense and irrepressible woman's love is than man's, really is Stendhalian *avant la lettre*.

Naples, July 15 [After communism]

How leave communism behind? Recently the question has been coming up incessantly, and the newspapers and magazines have been harping on it with increasing, almost hysterical insistence. As if the emergence from communism—something wished for, after all—were at the same time a sort of troubling leap into the unknown.

In an interesting report from the USSR ("a journey among people who are no longer afraid"), Claude Roy quotes Tocqueville: *"Il n'y a qu'un grand génie qui puisse sauver un prince qui entreprend de soulager ses sujets après une oppression longue."* Here saving the prince obviously means saving Gorbachev.

Timothy Garton Ash quotes "one of the most intelligent Polish communist leaders" during a break at a roundtable discussion: "All the handbooks explain how difficult it is to acquire power; none of them tells how hard it is to get rid of power."

The threesome Timothy Garton Ash, Janos Kis, and Adam Michnik turned out *mille mots* on the subject *Sortir du communisme*. The upshot seems to be that the ticket for a safe departure (with the brakes on) from communism must be paid for in dollars by the capitalist West.

Revel suggested three ways of leaving a system in its death throes. One way was demonstrated by the Chinese in Heavenly Peace Square. It is the most direct way, but it entails not leaving the system at all; on the contrary, it leads right back to Mao's old tenet that "power resides in a gun barrel," and to Brecht's famous 1953 formula that "since the nation through its own fault lost the government's trust, the government must choose another nation." It is not an unfeasible objective: suffice it to shoot long enough, heavily enough, and blindly until power pops out of the gun barrel, and from under the mountain of bodies "a different nation will dig itself out and stand up firmly on its feet."

Another method applies to countries in which the totalitarian regime did not contrive to annihilate the forces communism left untouched at the moment it came to power and subsequently failed to prevent the community's reactions and spurts of independence and autonomy. The pluralistic democratic tradition remained so alive in these countries that a peaceful and evolutionary exit from communism seemed theoretically possible. For the time being this process applies to Poland and Hungary. Both countries are on their way, faster or slower as it may be, to unalloyed democracy and unalloyed political pluralism.

The third way, according to Revel, is what Gorbachev has done in the USSR, where glasnost is to serve as the motive force of perestroika. The motor acts to accelerate the number of revolutions, and

sometimes it seems to be dangerously overheating, while concrete social, political, and economic reconstruction is marking time or going
backward; the rusty, blocked, and heavy train of perestroika threatens
to pull the steaming locomotive of glasnost in the opposite direction.
So application of the Chinese method in extremis cannot be totally
ruled out.

Is the second, the Polish-Hungarian, method realistic? Is it possible to advance along the path to democracy and pluralism gradually,
in an evolutionary way? It is, as the results of Polish elections to the
Sejm and Senate show, results that far surpassed expectations (alarmingly so, it seems, for the leaders of the opposition). But with several
provisos. The opposition must go it alone, guard its identity for dear
life, and never for a moment forget to use the form of address, dear
to the hearts of Poles "in the national need," of "mass gentlemen"; in
other words, it must limit its goal to regaining full independence and
one day recovering all the power from the usurpers, especially because
the "mass gentlemen" (or "comrades") on the government side are as
keen as possible to get rid of them (and apparently do not have much
idea how to do it). On the path to democracy and pluralism the
opposition leadership must also break with the cabinet-caucus style of
decision-making by an elite and of reserving all essential prerogatives
to the leader and his intimates. Last but not least: it would be salutary
if the leader and his team were more cautious in their use of the rather
risible concepts of the big game and the major players and practiced
greater restraint in fostering an improved opinion of General Jaru-
zelski (at least out of respect for the unchanged opinion of Solidar-
nosc's "rank and file" and presumably of the distinct majority of the
June voters).

July 20 [Moby Dick]

Late afternoon the day before yesterday, I was walking home along
the street next to the Anjou Castle and the damp sultriness was too
much for me, so I sat down in the square facing the port and fell into
a doze or a fleeting swoon, indifferent to the noisy swarm of American
sailors and prostitutes around and ignoring the lightning flashes in
the direction of the island foreboding a violent summer storm. What

roused me from my swoon was a stench so intolerable that I automatically reached for my handkerchief and held it over my nose. People were running down to the port, and they too were holding
handkerchiefs to their noses. I kept hearing the word *balena,* and at
the very end of a long pier I saw a dense crowd of people shouting
and gesticulating.

I joined the runners, but before I reached the pier, a flood of new
arrivals had blocked the entry, and policemen were holding back the
throng. I managed to join two American navy officers, whom the
police let through. Together with them I got to the end of the pier,
consumed by a curiosity that was stronger than the stench. "God
Almighty," one of the officers exclaimed, "it's Moby Dick! Good old
Dick, dead as a doornail and stinking like hell." His companion leaned
forward in the darkness toward the sea and remarked matter-of-factly
that Moby Dick had turned from white to black between the last
century and this one. "Does that surprise you?" came the immediate
reply. "In a filthy damn bay like this! Why did he swim here in his
old age, what brought him here? Poor Dick. And poor Captain Ahab,
wherever he is, if he could see his enemy now, the enemy he thought
was eternal, the black carcass of the white whale that once incarnated
evil, he would certainly look away in disgust."

The whale's carcass was bound with ropes and strapped to the pier
and rocked in the dirty water, regularly dipping down and rising up.
Nothing remained of its natural form; it was a slab of rotting meat.
It had died about two months ago, and when some terrified fishermen
came across it in the vicinity of the island of Ponza, it still gave some
faint signs of life. How did it die? Shreds of nets in a couple of places
on the carcass told nothing. And there did not seem to be any deep
wounds. Did it die of poison? Had it run into a flow of leaked chem-
icals or a drifting patch of oil? Or like an old elephant, guided by the
instinct of a century, did it consume the last remains of its strength
to reach its cemetery in our bay?

It was hard to stay by the dead whale any longer; the stench grew
stronger and slowly swept people from the pier. I was agitated as I
walked along the breakwater in the direction of home. Moby Dick
dead! The American officer's joke suddenly stopped being a joke. It
was as if I literally believed that the unconquered hero of Melville's
metaphysical prose poem, the Biblical Leviathan, the ruler of oceans

and evil, had overcome his impudent adversary, had swum around the world hundreds of times, shattering all the whalers he met on the way, defenseless in the face of his might, and at long last reached his final harbor to give up the ghost like a vagrant, a beggar in a gutter. The setting favored such nonsense: the storm, instead of striking in the city, swept around it at a distance with dry cracks and fiery streaks.

The next day, that is to say yesterday, the local newspaper brought me down to earth. A "conflict of authority" had arisen: what was to be done with the corpse of Moby Dick, and by whom (just so, the article had a drawing of a municipal sanitation officer wearing a gas mask while immersed in reading Melville's novel). The city sanitation bureau proposed using a special flamethrower to burn the whale's remains, but the proposal was rejected for fear that it would leave a black toxic cloud hanging over Naples. Nor did the proposal of the port authority seem much safer, stuffing the carcass with dynamite, hauling it to the middle of the bay, and blowing it up. The resolution of the bureaucratic controversy was postponed to the following day.

Evidently the night brought good counsel, because today I read in the local paper that the earthly remains of Moby Dick (weighing eight tons) were taken outside the city by truck and buried in a grave ten meters long and three meters wide. The paper did not say where, and what is more, the participants in the burial proceedings were sworn to silence, which calls to mind the secret burial of vampires in Transylvania. (There, just to be sure, they also drove a sharp stake into the ground at the level of the deceased's heart.) *Requiescat in pace.*

Albori, August 16 [Camus and Dostoevsky]

In this year's, third volume of Camus' *Carnets* I was surprised by an August 1957 entry. It was very dramatic and—as a sworn admirer of Camus, I can scarcely choke out the words—rather hysterical and histrionic. "For the first time, after reading *Crime and Punishment,* absolute doubt about my calling. I am seriously considering the possibility of giving it up. I have always believed that art is a dialogue. But with whom? With our literary world, whose principle is mediocre spite, where insult takes the place of critical method? With society *tout court,* people who do not read us, a bourgeois class that reads the papers and two fashionable books a year? In reality the artist today can be only a solitary prophet, an artist possessed and consumed by an immeasurable drive to create art. Am I this kind of creative artist? I believed I was. To be precise, I believed that I could be. I doubt it today, I feel strongly tempted to reject that ceaseless effort which makes me unhappy in happiness, that barren asceticism, that calling which draws me I know not where . . . am I capable of making my dream reality? If not, why dream?"

This lament to the tune of "break the pen" comes out of the mouth of a forty-four-year-old writer who was to receive the Nobel prize a few months later, and whose life and astonishingly prolific career were to end tragically three years later. What does *Crime and Punishment* have to do with this? Did Camus suddenly realize he was not as great as Dostoevsky? He could have realized that equally well by reading dozens of other writers who were also greater than he. The very idea of "comparing oneself" is childish and unworthy of Camus. It is a self-regarding procedure of second-rate literati who frequent literary clubs and salons. Surely, the genuine writer is (and always has been) something on the order of a "solitary prophet." Surely, he must cultivate and consolidate bland indifference to the affronts of the "literary world" and evidence of coolness on the part of the reading public (which after all was not Camus' case). But if you accept the role of "solitary prophet," you become a monologuist, so you cannot also hope immediately and simultaneously for the boon of "dialogue" (which takes time to establish or not). Literally, unhappiness (solitude) in happiness (creation) is his natural condition. Barren asceticism! The calling drawing one who knows where! Renouncing dreams that cannot become reality! In his life and in his art, Camus was the antithesis of what he accounted in his *Carnets* entry as a supposedly intolerable burden.

So why this plaintive outburst? The explanation may be quite banal. The enthusiastic actor he had been in his youth suddenly longed to indulge in a spectacular theatrical gesture. Fortunately in the private theater of a notebook not intended for publication.

Naples, October 15 ["Incomprehensible Holocaust"]

In the course of half a century some two thousand books have been published on the Holocaust, so it would seem that it has been minutely described, analyzed, and explained. And yet the American historian Istvan Deak, recently discussing fifteen new books on the subject, gave his enormous article the title "The Incomprehensible Holocaust."

Incomprehensible? Yes, incomprehensible in the sense of how incomprehensible human behavior is under inhuman conditions. It strikes such horror that one's ability to comprehend is paralyzed by the effort of looking into the abyss of human nature exposed to the highest test in the world with such force that man's humanity is wrenched away. I shall always repeat the terrible observation of Shalamov the atheist: in Kolyma ninety-nine per cent of the people could not stand the test, and believers made up the majority of the remaining one per cent.

Incomprehensible then, or rather "incomprehensible." Quotation marks here serve to mark the conscious or subconscious refusal to say farewell forever to the hypocritical cry "how proud the name of man" and replace it with the true formula "people prepared that fate for people." But for many years the term "incomprehensible" has encompassed a wide range of accusations, charges, competing assessments of suffering and loss, catalogues of guilt, and degrees of responsibility. Not to mention the breast-beating, most often other people's, chiefly (aside from German) Polish breasts. Deak finally restores the proper proportions to this contest of cant. He points out, for example, that it is rank injustice to equate the war situation in Denmark and Poland, say, as it is generally to apply a single standard to the Holocaust in Western and Eastern Europe. Like Korbonsky, he reproaches Lanzmann for manipulative selection of Polish witnesses in the film *Shoah*. He notes that it is true that noble Dutch people hid Anna Frank and her family, while other craven Dutch denounced them and turned them over to Dutch policemen in the service of the Gestapo. The French, who take particular pleasure in beating Polish breasts, might, however, remember what Yehuda Bauer writes in his *History of the Holocaust*: "The French police, especially the *Garde Mobile*, who were very ardent in the pursuit of Jews earmarked for deportation, were not allowed to act in the Italian zone, because the Italians did not permit any anti-Semitic acts in their zone."

Beating other people's breasts, especially Polish breasts, is a favorite practice of American Jews, who did little during the war to help the victims of the Holocaust. Unfortunately, Deak passes over this aspect of the story in silence, he does not refer to the testimony of Karski, he does not mention Walter Laqueur's book *The Terrible Secret*, nor does he take even passing notice of David Wyman's shocking book, *The Abandonment of the Jews—America and the Holocaust 1941–1945*.

October 18 [Isaiah Berlin and Brodsky]

A long section of Isaiah Berlin's *Personal Impressions* is devoted to his meetings with Pasternak and Akhmatova. Berlin rightly observes that Akhmatova's entire life was "one uninterrupted indictment of Russian reality" ("what Herzen once described virtually all Russian literature as being"). Speaking about the legend of Akhmatova, about the legend of her life and her unyielding passive resistance to iniquity in her homeland, Berlin says that she became a figure not merely in Russian literature but in Russian history in our century, as Herzen was in the previous century, according to Belinsky's famous definition.

Joseph Brodsky called this figure the Keening Muse in his beautiful volume of essays *Less Than One*. A splendid name, and it is absolutely right for the author of *Requiem*. No one has ever written so acutely and wisely about Akhmatova, and many people have written about her. Brodsky has the gift of striking to the heart of a matter, like an exquisite archer, with a single arrow. The aged Nadezhda Mandelstam "looked like a remnant of a huge fire, like a small ember that burns if you touch it." About Akhmatova's *Requiem*, "the power of *Requiem* lies in the fact that Akhmatova's biography was all too common. This requiem mourns the mourners: mothers losing sons, wives turning widows, sometimes both, as was the author's case. This is a tragedy where the chorus perishes before the hero."

The Keening Muse goes rigid in her *Stabat Mater* and turns into a living monument of the revolutionary and postrevolutionary history of Russia. With the passage of time the awareness of this monumentality, this exceptional "tragedy" in which "the chorus perishes before the hero," took possession of her to such a degree that in Oxford in 1965 she told Berlin that she considered the repression and harassment she underwent after their meeting in 1945 in Leningrad (the second time since World War I that she had met someone from outside; the first was her meeting with Czapski in Tashkent during World War II) the start of the Cold War and thus a turning point in the history of mankind. "She meant this quite literally," Berlin says. Akhmatova "was totally convinced of it, and saw herself and me as world-historical personages chosen by destiny to begin a cosmic conflict. . . . I could not protest that she had perhaps . . . somewhat overestimated the effect of our meeting on the destinies of the world, since she would have felt this as an insult to her tragic image of herself as Cassandra —indeed, to the historico-metaphysical vision 'which informed so much of her poetry. I remained silent."

The keening muse and Cassandra in a single person. Brodsky and Berlin together give what is probably the most faithful likeness of Anna Akhmatova.

October 25 [*Hannah Arendt and the demons of our times*]

In 1963 I wrote a piece about Hannah Arendt's book *Eichmann in Jerusalem* and titled it "The Demon of Our Age" so that one of her main theses too, given prominence by the book's subtitle—*A Report on the Banality of Evil*—could be even more fully expressed. The banality of evil? The demon of our age: had the conscientious and scrupulous executor of "the final solution," the model bureaucrat of exactly planned crime been demonized? At the time I was not aware that the idiotic campaign against Hannah Arendt in America and in Israel, which went so far as to accuse her of being anti-Semitic, laid its main stress on the allegedly "scandalous" phrase "the banality of evil." I have just read about it in the correspondence of Hannah Arendt with Karl Jaspers. Gideon Hausner, the public prosecutor in the Jerusalem trial, bluntly accused the author of *Eichmann in Jerusalem* of defending a war criminal. For is it not a defense of such monstrous crime to relegate it to the region of the "banality of evil" instead of elevating it to the region of "the demonism of evil"? Hannah Arendt's indignant critics, evidently unfamiliar with the intelligence and resourcefulness of evil, did not realize how much more formidable and insidious is the banalization of evil than its demonization. The demon of our age tried to convince the Jerusalem judges and the whole world that he was merely an exemplary Clerk (with a capital letter), entrusted with the implementation of the mass extermination of millions of expendable people in the work of building a "new order." This is why the key statement in the *Report on the Banality of Evil* is that the reasons that suggest the possibility of a repetition of Hitler's crimes are real. They are more horrible probably than catching, judging, and hanging the devil himself in the guise of a German officer.

Comparable reflections might be spun on the theme of the temptations to demonize Stalin and Stalinism, with the covert or avowed need to shut and bolt the gates of hell after the defeat of the Soviet devil and his host of devilish helpers, though without the satisfaction of seeing them on the gallows. This tendency, rather weak (for now?) in the homeland of Dostoevsky's *Devils*, has a certain precedent in our literature. There is an inclination to demonize in Aleksander Wat. Once even, as far as I can remember, "cloven hooves" rapping on the roof awakened him in his prison cell. On another occasion he tried to explain to Milosz that Stalin communicated his peaceful intentions to Hitler by shooting Tukhachevsky and other Soviet generals. Which at times, as we know from demonology, is the way agreement is happily reached, in questions of exceptional importance, between Demons of the highest rank.

1 9 9 0

January

The Plague in Naples: A Report on a State of Emergency

I

The present report is a sequel to my story "The Miracle" (1983), which was a narrative, granted, a slightly embellished but historically true and exact reconstruction of the revolt led by Masaniello in 1647. Shrewd readers detected latent affinities between "The Miracle" and the chapter in the history of Solidarity that had recently been cut short in the wake of the declaration of martial law, a "state of war," as it was called in Poland. But it was only during the writing that any such awareness dawned on me and gradually became clear. If this awareness was there from the very beginning (as those inclined to be suspicious would have it), it was so obscure that it could hardly be called awareness. It would be nearer the truth to call it an inkling or something subconscious, since that is ultimately the source of most of the unpremeditated and, to begin with, obscure impulses of an author.

The case is different with the sequel to "The Miracle," namely "The Plague in Naples." Given the similarity of titles, I might have started with the same motto that Camus used at the beginning of his *Plague*, a remark from the introduction to the third volume of Daniel Defoe's *Robinson Crusoe*: "It is as reasonable to represent one kind of imprisonment by another, as it is to represent anything that really exists by that which exists not." Did Camus also use this motto because Defoe's is the classic description of plague (the London plague of 1665, which, however, he re-created from other people's accounts since he was only a five-year-old boy when it broke out)? I do not know. It is enough for me that Defoe's observation certainly applies equally if not more to "The Plague in Naples." I have drawn my material from contemporary chronicles and treated them with absolute and, at the same time, relative fidelity (after the example of Defoe). I borrowed my subtitle, for example, from a brief unsigned *Report on the State of Pestilence in Naples in the Year 1656*. I have taken the liberty of restricting my theme to the "state of emergency" indicated in the subtitle but not—as one might think—exclusively for "allusive" purposes. It is simply that the anonymous seventeenth-century author makes rather frequent use of the expressions "state of emergency" and "state of war," which carry more conviction, as it were, than "state of pestilence," the formula that was universally employed at the time.

Having made this clear at the outset, I ought to be ready to begin "The Plague in Naples." But what also needs clarification is why so much introductory clarification is needed at all. What sort of narrative is it (the reader may wonder, and not without a trace of irony) that needs so much help getting to its feet and moving on smartly? I grant that the reader is right, but I would also ask him to remember that no two stories are exactly alike. Not in the sense that they have the same artistic worth, God forbid! That is not what I mean. Rather, in the sense that my story (I ask the reader to take my word for the time being) has a particular narrative key, in that it will tread the narrow path between history and its pale reflection in actual fact, a reflection so pale that it is legitimate to wonder if any lessons flow from it (history). Do any lessons flow from history? I maintain that they do not, or if they do, they are extremely deceptive and misleading. But at the same time I maintain that sometimes—very rarely!—historical events draw a strange afterglow in their wake, almost a subtext obscurely written by some unseen hand. In such cases history is more than a lesson; it is a speck or grain of our vicissitudes reflected in the Eye of Providence. And in such case the need for constant preparatory clarification is evidence that an author—who cannot always trust his own associations, distant echoes, and manifold yet fleeting similarities—wants to bring this to the attention of the good and patient reader at the outset and make him aware of it.

II

And now to the sequel of "The Miracle." There is no reason, of course, to suppose that "The Miracle" left any deep impression in the memory of those who read it years ago, so I must preface "The Plague in Naples" with its own prologue, preferably a brief summary of my previous account.

The revolt of the common people led by Masaniello was a veritable earthquake for the Spanish Viceroy in Naples. Reports from the Duke of Arcos, Philip IV's governor general in Naples, are preserved in the archives in Madrid, and they express not only the alarm of the then-governor of the vassal colonial nation but his fears as the representative of the local aristocracy, which was devoted body and soul to the Spanish sovereign. Absolutist powers consider conflict and even war with "the external enemy" as natural phenomena; what makes their hearts pound, instead, is the "internal enemy," the revolt of their subjects. That is what Masaniello and his Neapolitan tatterdemalions were to the Neapolitan court, a threat to an established order buttressed by scepter and cross.

The Duke of Arcos (with the collaboration of the old Neapolitan nobility and cardinals) went to incredible lengths in attempting to tame the rebel and conjure away the tempest in the community: he appointed Masaniello "general of the people" and accepted his conditions for restoring order, conditions that were written into a "social contract." It looked as if the court had capitulated to the populace (the "rabble"), but it was only a stratagem to gain time, and the simple-hearted Masaniello, overconfident and giddy with success, failed to understand. He was outmaneuvered, arrested, and slain. His enemies also achieved what is most important in such situations: the rebels did not long continue their revolt, and they turned away from their leader. After the Duke of Arcos, abetted by the Neapolitan barons and the dignitaries of the Church, had secured the imperiled order, when, in other words, the tempest of the community had moved off and subsided on the far horizon, the people realized their error. But it was too late for them to do anything but bow their heads and content themselves with the legend of Masaniello.

It is a mistake not to credit the power of legend, especially for simple minds. A Masaniello of legend burgeoned, flourished, and became the hero of covert discussion, a symbol, an act of defiance, the object of a cult. He excited the imagination much more after his death than he did during the weeks of his living glory. (And, to tell the truth, more than he actually deserved.) It was not only the imagination of his own countrymen that he stirred. His spirit ranged far beyond the borders of the Kingdom of Naples, it soared above the whole of Europe as proof that the seeming power of sovereigns was fragile and that the real power was in the hands of their subjects and depended only on their courage and intelligence. They realized, however clearly or not, that Masaniello had been a forerunner of revolution, a flame that had briefly ignited thrones and been extinguished only a moment before the whole world caught fire. It was not only the throne in Madrid that quaked, not at all, though the royal court in Spain (along with the viceregal court in Naples) understood it best. The free and mighty were terror-stricken at the sight of the bloodshot eyes and clenched fists of the unfree. How frightened, how panic-stricken they are when they are suddenly faced not by familiar enemy arms but by a formless mass of furious insurgents!

III

The nameless author of the *Report on the State of Pestilence in Naples in the Year 1656* was probably a Neapolitan priest; such is the opinion of the archivists who, at the end of the last century, discovered his sole surviving report. There must have been others, because the Neapolitan priest—according to the archivists—was probably acting as agent and factotum for some influential figure in the Vatican, whose job it may have been regularly to provide the Holy Father with first-hand information about the "state of the pestilence" in the plague-ridden city.

The style of the report testifies to an ecclesiastic pen—full of things only hinted at or implied and a humbly feigned ignorance. For the addressee, who had the same kind of mind, the more cautious and discreet the report seemed, the clearer and more telling it would have been. It must have given the prelate in Rome pleasure and amusement to undo the knots that his sharp, perspicacious agent in Naples drew so finely and (to uninitiated eyes) innocently, with the air of a simple-hearted ignoramus. At the very end of his only report to survive, just before adding the date June 20, 1656, the anonymous soutane-clad figure dropped the mask of humility and ignorance: "I live shut up in my house, yet I know everything; and that is cause for some happiness in our adversity."

He did indeed know everything. He knew, which is most impor-tant for my account, whether the "state of pestilence" served to de-scribe a "state of emergency" in Naples or a "state of war." He realized that the Duke of Arcos had not been totally victorious over the re-bellion led by Masaniello. Somewhere deep down, live embers still glowed beneath the ashes. And the Duke of Arcos' successor, Count d'Ognatte, failed to stamp them out. On the contrary, his coarse bru-tality and ruthlessness kindled them all the more. As a result he was promptly recalled to Madrid, to be replaced by Count Castrillo, who boasted a host of titles (which I omit), with instructions to govern in a "gentle," not to say "paternal," fashion. But by 1653 it was already too late for that. The kingdom was in need of special laws, all the more so because French ships had appeared off Castellamare, perhaps intending armed action against Naples to exploit the suppressed tur-bulence stirring under the surface of the capital of the Spanish colony. Even the new viceroy, a man whose nature was not particularly warlike (despite several military decorations and a fancy for his rank as gen-eral), felt that something decisive and radical had to be done. But what? What seemed most urgent was to break the social bonds that united the people of Naples, bonds that the legend of Masaniello seemed to strengthen with every passing day. The dangerous prox-imity of the French fleet might dictate the proclamation of a state of emergency or a state of war, martial law. But Count Castrillo, valiant general that he was, saw this as an act of humiliation and a confession of weakness. His idea was to take steps tantamount to a state of emergency or a state of war but under a different name.

IV

There are two reasons why I want to go back to Daniel Defoe; let it be understood as a brief interlude in the story.

One: I should like to take a closer look at the meaning of Defoe's observation; it was helpful to Camus in his *Plague* and is helpful to me in "The Plague in Naples": "It is reasonable . . . to represent anything that really exists by that which exists not." Camus wrote an allegorical novel, his plague in Oran was a narrative fiction with specific aims. And my plague in the Kingdom of Naples? It is not a narrative fiction, it is based strictly on historical documents and evidence. Yet it too represents something that really exists by something that does not exist. In a different way, however. It may sound paradoxical, even absurd, but in my story it is the plague itself that exists and does not exist. It was a real plague for its victims—and how many they were the reader will learn at the proper time. But it was an unreal plague for its perpetrators, who used it to achieve certain ends. Ends? It is important to know this at once, hence I have no fear of risking what might at first glance seem an irresponsible allegation. Which is not to say that I intend to get ahead of the natural flow of events in my story.

Two: In the *Journal of the Plague Year*, the chronicle of the London plague of 1665, Defoe reports that "before the sickness was come to its height, people had more room to make their observations than they had afterward. But when it was in the extremity, there was no such thing as communication with one another." People stopped sharing their thoughts with each other: they simply fled from the city, or they bolted the doors and windows of their houses.

As the plague increased and spread, community life died away. Plague is first of all an illness that strikes the life of the community, the way leprosy is an illness that afflicts the cursed individual, the suffering of both marked by mystic signs. Let me be more precise: plague is synonymous with the decay of the bonds that link people, leprosy is synonymous with infinite aloneness; what towers over the plague is chiefly a dwarfing God; over leprosy no one rises.

The Vatican prelate's acute Neapolitan agent rightly stresses one particular in his report. The Neapolitan plague made its way into the capital of the Kingdom in January 1656. It was underestimated at the beginning, and despite the doctors, the authorities would not allow it to be called by name. In March, when the epidemic was fully rampant (but not yet at its zenith), it was forbidden and punishable to use the word "plague." The prohibition was lifted in May, but two euphemisms were still obligatory in official language: *ricorrente infermità* and *morbo epidemiale contagioso pernicioso.* What this meant the author of the *Report on the State of Pestilence* made unambiguously clear to his addressee: the hope was not only to avoid panic (which was understandable) but to turn attention away from the source and cause of the illness.

V

The source and cause of the illness varied with its manifold interpretations. The simplest interpretation, as usual, and the one the clergy at every level hastened to proclaim, from simple priests to bishops and archbishops, from ordinary monks to abbots and priors, was the Chastisement of God. Chastisement for what? There were few sins committed by the insufficiently pious and God-fearing that they concealed from their confessors! The Punishment of God, God's Scourge (they were all the happier and oftener to say it, because the image of the hand of the Wrathful Almighty, wielding whip or rod, so matched the torments of the illness), owed some of its popularity to the hope that the Wrath of God was something that might be propitiated, it was not something final and irreversible. So new churches and convents were built (only virgins were admitted to one of them, *Suor Orsola,* as if they were fitter than any others to beg forgiveness of the Lord of Heaven), flesh was mortified, fervent prayers filled the aisles of churches by day and by night, confession and communion were incessant, coins were stuffed into alms bags in church and on the street, and the faithful trembled as they listened to self-styled theologians who also threatened the end of the world to those who were indifferent and lukewarm in their faith. It is no exaggeration to say that the Church blossomed and constantly put forth new shoots on the dung of the plague. The Church offered asylum and the promise of a change for the better in one's fate. But in the name of strict truth, it must also be said that this was true only for those as yet spared by the illness. What burst from the lips of those already stricken by plague were blasphemous imprecations, which poured out together with the foam and slaver of the illness.

There were a host of other interpretations aside from the natural Scourge of God. The Viceroy loosed swarms of small-fry police spies and provocateurs on the city every morning, and they assiduously spread the rumor, which could not be proven or disproven, that the Anti-Christ, in the form of Masaniello, was responsible for the plague and plotted mischief against the welfare of the city even beyond the grave. Whoever it was in the Viceroy's palace that happened on this idea had a poor grasp of the psychology of the populace. The people did their own reasoning, and the rebellious humors of 1647 spread amid misery and death. All the more so, because the plague seemed to be guided by an invisible hand and reaped its richest harvest in the quarters that ten years earlier had harbored the main rebel strongholds. No better was the idea of arresting several old companions of Masaniello who had returned from exile to the Kingdom of Naples and trying them on charges of spreading the illness. Few people took seriously the allegation that the French fleet was preparing for armed intervention under the cover of the plague that had stolen into the city. The view of the populace was summed up in the words: the plague is the Spaniards' revenge for Masaniello's week of triumph and our government of Naples. It was not long before the words "plague" and "revenge" were uttered in the same breath in the backstreets.

There was only one undeniable truth, one that the Viceroy's palace tried to hide at any cost: the plague had been brought to Naples by a fifteen-man detachment of Spanish soldiers from Sardinia, where the plague had long been decimating the population. Efforts were made not only to hide that truth but in any case to offset it with the "powder theory." The real hotbed of the pestilence was alleged to be certain powders that the enemies of the Kingdom of Naples were pouring into reservoirs and wells. Two would-be powder-pourers were caught at once and hanged in the main square of the city. Both men had belonged to the old Masaniello "gang." The plague took on the character of a renewed struggle between the court and the people, but its real purpose was, in the masked form of a "state of emergency" or "state of war," to break the back of the people with one strong stroke.

VI

It is time to sketch with at least a few strokes a portrait of Count Castrillo, viceroy and general. He was physically ugly, slimy, almost repulsive. What was striking was his stiffness, as if he were corseted from neck to haunch, a stiffness that sometimes made him look like a rag puppet held erect by a stick or wires. He had a disproportionately small head, like a shrunken skull covered with sleek yellowish skin. His face was totally expressionless, nor did a sign of life ever flicker in his queasy eyes. He did not know how to smile; in his rare moments of good humor what took its place was a peculiar grimace the meaning of which was undecipherable: satisfaction or barely assuaged bitterness. He preferred to listen rather than speak, seemingly attentive but actually absent. He seemed chiefly preoccupied with his own thoughts, but they could not have been either pleasant or interesting, because from time to time he would shake them off like someone plagued with vermin. He was full of contradictions, but, judging by his appearance at least, he was certainly not suited to play the role of a "pleasant" or "fatherly" viceroy.

He owed his career to his exalted birth, his valor on the battlefield, and a gift for diplomacy. It is legitimate to wonder what was the prime consideration in Philip IV's decision to appoint him to the viceregal throne in Naples; probably faith in the count's diplomatic talents together with the certainty that in any event he had valuable military experience. It was Madrid's opinion that, after Masaniello's revolt, the Kingdom of Naples was in need of two medicines to be administered simultaneously: cunning and "paternal benevolence" backed up by military force. Philip IV had this to say about his representative in Naples: "A good tactician, a brave soldier *contre coeur,* and a faithful servant of the crown. The only way he might disappoint me is through excess of zeal." As we shall see, the king turned out to be a good prophet.

The Count came to the post of royal governor general in Naples with his recently married young bride, Isabella, who was thirty years his junior. The jewel of her beauty took the place of the jewel of nobility: she was of rather common descent. But she was an ornament to the viceregal court, she aroused admiration, perhaps more than admiration, among the Neapolitan aristocrats in the palace, and she was greeted with applause in the streets during carriage outings with her husband. She was also distinguished by natural goodness. It had happened in the past that viceroys' wives would occasionally look in on the backstreets, but so much was false and forced that the well-meaning visits left behind more exasperation and irritation than any intended gain for the court. Whenever Isabella visited the backstreets, she was afterward mentioned with feelings of gratitude and fascination. Those who were privy to Philip IV's intentions had reason to suspect that the duty imposed on Count Castrillo of "paternal benevolence," so at odds with his appearance and disposition, was to be implemented by the vicereine on behalf of her husband. In any case she succeeded in surrounding the palace with an atmosphere that was somewhat less hostile toward foreign rule (among the people). That was no mean achievement.

After five years of marriage, the couple were still childless. In the opinion of the court and the common people of Naples, it was obviously the Viceroy's fault: aside from his age, he must have had some sort of organic defect. Dislike for the Count was enhanced by an admixture of contempt.

VII

Shortly after midnight between December 12 and 13, 1655, carriages started arriving in the palace courtyard. It was probably the first time in Count Castrillo's vice-royalty that at such a late hour he summoned all the Neapolitan grandees in any way connected with the administration of the vice-kingdom. They stepped out of their carriages or were helped down by servants, and the expression on their surprised faces shifted between shock and concern. Princes, dukes, marquesses, and barons whispered to each other on the stairs, wondering if there was something serious, perhaps even dangerous, behind such a sudden summons in the night.

The Viceroy sat at his desk gloomier and more inscrutable than ever. When the party was complete, the ministers of state and members of the Royal Chamber all in their usual places, he began to speak—reluctantly, often breaking off, as if he had a stammer, staring at the ceiling, stiff and motionless in his red armchair. And not so much bored as simply absent.

He demanded that the entire company immediately send their families to their country estates, or in any case far from the capital of the vice-kingdom, and that they themselves move into the palace, where they would be duly attended by the Viceroy's servants. For the time being, the palace was to become a fortress, and all its portals and exits would be bolted and patrolled by guards. The cavalry detachments, normally garrisoned in the provinces, where forage was abundant, were to be brought to Naples and quartered in the barracks on the outskirts of the city. The civilian population was forbidden in the strictest terms from infringing on their terrain and the soldiers from entering the city. From that moment and for an unspecified time, Naples was to be divided in two: the court with its dependencies, including the military garrison, and all the rest, that is to say, the populace.

The assembled company watched him attentively and then looked at each other, making no secret of their amazement, even astonishment and alarm. It was Prince San Severo who broke the deadly silence; he was the boldest member of this company because he was the highest born, related by blood to two royal families. Would His Highness be so kind as to explain to those present the reason for these measures?

The Viceroy looked at him as if he had just awakened from sleep. Still neither bored nor absent, without the slightest change in his stiff bearing, he remained silent for some time. Finally he drawled easily in a soft voice: "There are two dangers threatening us. The plague is raging in Sardinia, and every week ships from Sardinia dock in our port with important freight. French warships are grouping off Castellamare as if they were preparing to attack." The Duke of Atri asked if they might not suspend sea communications with Sardinia and prepare the Neapolitan fleet to repel any eventual French intervention. The Viceroy looked at him long with a cold queasy eye, and then he replied succinctly: "No, we could not." At which point he considered the meeting adjourned. They broke up, still bewildered, troubled, and averse to conversation or comment. About one in the morning the courtyard of the palace began to empty out. The Viceroy, contrary to habit, stood on the balcony and swung his hand back and forth in farewell to his departing guests.

Only when the palace gates had been bolted did he withdraw from the balcony and motion to Captain Mermoz, who had been waiting in the dark by the wall. Diego Mermoz, a thirty-year-old giant known for his furious courage, was a distant cousin of Isabella, and it was at her behest that the general had brought him from Madrid as aide-de-camp and officer for special missions. The Viceroy had a very special mission for him now. He was not to remain at the Viceroy's side, in the palace turned into a fortress, but was to quit it without delay for the poor Spanish Quarter (so called because of the buildings where Spanish soldiers had been quartered). There he was to find or requisition an apartment, and every three days he was to send written reports to the palace about the mood of the populace, particularly the poor. The orders were that the reports be delivered to the guardhouse after dark, addressed to the personal attention of the Viceroy. And during this time, for no reason was the captain to dare approach the threshold of the palace.

The captain paled as he listened: that a combat officer should be turned into a spy and informer! But he drew himself up to attention and took his leave without a parting word. The Count walked down the long corridor to his bedroom with a barely perceptible grimace of satisfaction in the corners of his small clenched mouth.

VIII

One of the earliest chronicles of the time—albeit chaotic, verbose, and in some places rather hysterical—gives an account of December 13, 1655, in the life of Count Castrillo. It seems unlikely that the author of the chronicle could have known of the secret night gathering in the palace, so why did he attach such importance to that particular day? And why did he describe it as if he had glimpsed a preestablished scenario? I asked experts on the history of the plague in Naples about it, but unfortunately no one was able to offer an unambiguous answer. Two hypotheses sounded most sensible: either the author of the chronicle was a member of the Viceroy's inner circle and wrote it anonymously, solely for his own use with no thought of future publication; or the chronicle came into being several years after the plague, when a good deal more was known about the events, and the author illegitimately predated it to 1657 in order to attract the interest of scholars and readers. This is actually of little importance to me, since I am writing a contemporary "report on the state of emergency," which can only benefit from a description of the Viceroy's activities on the day following the nocturnal assembly in the palace.

About noon the Viceroy rode out on horseback to a poor quarter and dismounted in front of the "miraculous image" of Nostra Signora del Carmine, which the people of Naples held in particular reverence. He made a low bow, genuflected, and put his lips to the pane protecting the sacred picture. A goodly crowd gathered and broke out in applause (though not very loud). Count Castrillo gave a quick and brisk nod of his head, which the Neapolitans recognized as his "general-like" response to any sign of homage.

He got back on his horse and, with an escort of two officers, then proceeded to the as yet unfinished Convent of Suor Orsola, where devout volunteers were still helping in the work. The crowd was large, motley, and busy, but they immediately made room for the Viceroy. He dismounted smartly (considering his stiffness), consigned his horse to his companions, and reached for a shovel that was stuck in a heap of sand. He did not stop with a symbolic sweep of the shovel but actually worked for several minutes. The crowd rewarded him with an ovation that did not go silent for some time.

The next stop was a small harbor near the main port. He waited patiently for a ship due from Sardinia at that hour. For some time the crew of the ship from Sardinia had been allowed only to unload its cargo (raw materials, chiefly), obliged to go back on deck at once and not leave the ship again before it sailed from Naples. This time, in addition to the usual cargo, the ship was carrying a detachment of fifteen Spanish soldiers from Cagliari. The Viceroy whispered something to one of his companions, who bounded to the detachment commander: "You have been on heavy duty for a long time, you have earned a holiday in the city, report back to barracks after New Year's Day."

It was early evening by the time Count Castrillo was back in his study to receive an old fortune-teller named Rossana, commended to him by his predecessor when he assumed the throne in Naples. In his private thoughts he referred to her as "the witch," but more than once he had been convinced that it was worth taking her auguries seriously. He had made the appointment with her the day before, as was his wont in times of emergency. He was stretched out in his armchair, plainly tired. The old woman put a large crystal ball on the table and covered it with a yellow cloth, and then with a lightning-quick movement she uncovered it again. She gazed into the heart of the crystal with an expression of painful exertion in her wrinkled face and a gurgling murmur of her toothless mouth. At length she looked him in the eye: "Your victory will be in the cemetery—" She broke off as if hesitant to say anything else. Finally he heard her somewhat lowered voice: "And in the grave." He did not venture to ask for further clarification. He knew from experience that it was pointless to make such requests, he knew that the poor wretch from the backstreets could not be bribed even with a purse full of gold. He held a coin in the hand he extended for her kiss and then dismissed her. The scornful glint in her old eyes sent a sudden, strange shudder through him.

IX

There is no doubt that the Spanish soldiers brought the plague to Naples from Sardinia. And this raises two questions: Why did the Viceroy send them into town instead of sending them to the military hospital, knowing that some, if not all, of them must have been infected? And what became of them in the city? It is easy to give a brief response to the second question, but the answer to the first one is the substance of the narrative fabric and will only emerge by degrees. Well, all we know of the fate of the fifteen Spanish soldiers from Sardinia is what Captain Mermoz reported to the Viceroy. Three of them infected the prostitutes with whom they took up lodgings and soon died, together with their temporary partners. The hotbed of the plague arose there, in that small bordello, and in the month of January it spread to the neighboring sidestreets in the Lavinaio quarter. There was nothing to report with any certainty (according to Mermoz) about the other twelve soldiers: either they were swept away by the first wave of the epidemic, or they were lynched as the guilty parties after the plague appeared. In any case they all disappeared without a trace.

The scrupulous historian Salvatore De Renzi had this to say in his 1867 book *Napoli nell'anno 1656*: "It was the general opinion at the time that the plague was brought from Sardinia to destroy the people who eight years earlier convulsed Spain and were still not wholly subdued. It was universally considered tantamount to murder." De Renzi quotes a chronicler of the time, Canon Celano: "Our poor city was murdered."

Hence De Renzi, reasonably I think, makes a connection between the plague and Masaniello's revolt ("eight years earlier"). Other historians (of the nineteenth century) are more cautious: they point to Spain's decline as a colonial empire and thus explain the growth of blind absolutism. They recall that the plague mowed down two hundred thousand people in Spain itself in 1648, and this might have been a latent source of a need for "irrational retaliation" against the vice-kingdom of Naples. These arguments are not very convincing, however supported by relevant premises, especially in the matter of the blind absolutism that often accompanies the dissolution of colonial powers. These arguments should be kept in mind, but most heed should be given to the insight of Salvatore De Renzi, because it is backed up by the Spanish archives and the opinion of contemporary Spanish historians, who focus on the person of Count Castrillo.

Reviewing Elias Tejada's several-volume *Napoles hispanica* for the Madrid quarterly *Hispanidad*, the well-known essayist Jorge Turga half jestingly espouses Professor Tejada's main thesis, that under Spanish rule the city of Naples was more Spanish than the cities of Spain itself. "Surely," Turga says ironically, "it was undeniably so, since it is equally easy to detect the *locura hispánica,* Spanish madness, in the revolt of the half-naked barefoot Neapolitan proletarians under the leadership of Masaniello and in Viceroy Castrillo's plan to use the noose of the plague to strangle any thought of rebellion once and for all."

It is all but incredible that a scholar of Jorge Turga's stature could be ironic about a truth, or rather the shameful part of a truth, that seventeenth-century historians of his own country took quite seriously and in substance tacitly accepted. Forget the "Spanish madness" of Masaniello and his comrades, but certainly Count Castrillo was a Spanish madman in his *actual* intent. The reports he prepared for the king, which are still in the Madrid archives, do not constitute irrefutable proof of crime, but for the attentive student they contain quite a bit of glaring circumstantial evidence.

The Viceroy was totally obsessed by the matter of *sentido de la comunidad,* the "sense of community," which in his opinion Masaniello had implanted in the common people of Naples. "If we wish to continue governing this city, if we consider it—and rightly so—as the pearl in the crown of the vice-kingdom, as a veritable mine of manifold wealth; we must use a blazing brand to cauterize this sense." And he constantly repeated this theme. At the same time he gradually convinced the king (clearly in responses to suggestions from Madrid), that the proclamation of a state of war or a state of emergency would be read by the inhabitants of the city, particularly by the "inherently rebellious rabble," as a sign of weakness, however much it might be justified by the aggressive nearness of the French fleet. "Something more is needed," the Viceroy repeated, "even something terrible, but as decisive as a surgical operation." These reports date from *before* the coming of the plague. Afterward the main theme of Castrillo's reports was the equally maniacal argumentation that plague is not something spontaneous, that it can be "controlled," and that despite all its horror ("with which we are familiar from our own past") it can be "steered in the right direction." This is close to that *locura hispánica*. But it is madness with a logic to it, because in several reports the Count stresses "the splintering effects of the plague on the life of the community" in language quite close to that of Defoe's inferences and observations.

No, I have no hesitation in stating that the Viceroy coolly and deliberately brought the plague to Naples and counted on it to accomplish its assigned tasks. What were these tasks? To drive a part of the Neapolitan population to the grave and to bring the rest, those who survived, to their knees. De Renzi and Canon Celano were right to speak of intent to murder the city. I, who consider any state of war or state of emergency a crime, think with horror of the manner in which Count Castrillo's satanic idea condemned "Spanish Naples" to unimaginable agony from January to early September 1656.

X

In our century, in the "age of ovens" and "white crematoria," in times when mass graves have been unearthed, the sheer number of victims does not have much effect. What is more, large numbers somehow blur and banalize the human tragedy and deaden the mind to the extent of the suffering. Perhaps that was also true in the past, because what is too enormous generally tends to become routine. But independently of the effect that large numbers had or have, they cannot be disregarded. In the seventeenth century Naples was the second largest city in Europe. Between high and low estimates, it counted about seven hundred and fifty thousand inhabitants. In the course of eight months of plague more than half of them died.

There is no dearth of exact, sometimes minutely detailed descriptions of the plague-stricken city, but I shall not draw on that abundant material. It would be like copying or at leasting imitating Defoe's incomparable journal, although, despite the basic similarity between the plague in London and Naples, there were differences worth noting: the London and Neapolitan plague-stricken fell ill and died in the same way, but (and this is surely due to specific features of their national character) the Neapolitans more often than the Londoners lost their minds before they lost their lives. People twice afflicted was not an uncommon sight, people afflicted by bodily illness and extreme mental disorder. Pasquale, a scrupulous and trustworthy chronicler, compiled a copious list of the different forms of insanity. And the list he compiled makes one shiver: one man rushes forward with a piercing scream and leaps off a precipice or into the sea; another one is strolling along the street and suddenly with the same kind of scream tries to climb up the wall of a building only to plunge to his death on the pavement; yet another has a sudden burst of energy, breaks into flight like an escaped prisoner, and falls dead at the foot of a wall, his face still turned to the wall.

In this brief account, the words of Canon Celano will have to suffice to give an overall view of the plague in Naples: "There was no room in the cemetery, and nobody was willing to dig graves. My poor eyes saw Via Toledo, where I lived at the time, so full of corpses, that carriages going in the direction of the Palace crushed baptized human flesh deeper and deeper into the ground."

Meanwhile behind the walls of his fortress, the Viceroy had reason to rub his hands. What he wished for had come to pass, and he made no secret of it, even in the reports prepared for Madrid: all the bonds of family and community were broken. This is what the contemporary historian Florio had to say about it: "It was impossible to see friend consoling friend or rushing to offer help, a relative extending a hand to a sick relative, or a husband saying farewell to a dying wife. The doctor touched the sick person and fled. The maidservant brought her master dinner and fled. The father shunned his sick son, the wife locked the door of her bedridden husband's room. The son did not take the trouble to bury his dead father but carried him outside at night wrapped up in a sheet and left the body outside the door, until the gravediggers' cart noticed the corpse and took it away." The "dissociative" virtues of the plague filled Count Castrillo with satisfaction. The city was at his mercy.

The plague reached its greatest intensity and reaped its largest number of victims in July and August. Especially blazing August, *agosto di fuoco,* accomplished more devastation than all the preceding months. It soon became clear that the plague had reached its peak just before it expired.

One dawn in the middle of August the corpse of Captain Mermoz was found between two columns of the palace cloister. How he got there, whether ill but still alive or already dead and dumped there by someone else, and how he penetrated the locked and guarded palace, was a mystery. The chronicles of the time make no mention of it. They are equally silent about the circumstances of the death, the following week, of the beautiful Isabella, whose belly was swollen as if she were pregnant. The Viceroy ordered her body sealed in an underground vault of the palace, and the two Spanish maids who served the vicereine in her bedchamber were turned out in the streets. How and of what did Isabella die? Only her two chambermaids might have had something to say about it, had all trace of them not soon disappeared as it had of the twelve Spanish soldiers. Could it be that the germs of the plague finally penetrated, or were smuggled into, the palace? The chroniclers of the era evidently lacked the information to answer this question, all the more so that soon after the plague subsided, all thoughts were turned in another direction.

XI

The rain of God followed close on the scourge of God. The early September rain deserved that name. Nothing like it was ever seen before or since in Naples. It really seemed that God, having cruelly scourged the city, mercifully opened the floodgates of heaven to cleanse the wounds that had been inflicted on it. Black churning clouds burst over Naples, raging torrents flooded through the streets and alleys, lakes formed in the piazzas, and a broad river rumbled along the seafront promenade. Noah's flood, the *diluvio universale,* to use the chronicler's term, lasted four days and four nights. People did not go out of their homes, but they felt that the end of their torment was at hand. No sooner did God's cleansing rain cease, and the sun somewhat dry the city in the course of a single day, than the place of water was taken by flames engulfed in clouds of smoke: everything that might be infected was burned, furniture, bedding, old clothes; Naples shed its sick skin, certain by now—although it dared not express this in words and cries of joy—that its health would soon be restored.

The following month the Viceroy—who for reasons unknown was now everywhere called the General, *il generale,* as if like Saint George he had taken up his lance, speared the dragon of the plague, and driven the French fleet from Castellamare—took his place at the head of a retinue and led a thanksgiving procession to the Church of the Immaculate Conception. And crowds followed his entourage. To the sound of fanfares and church bells, the Viceroy advanced slowly, his head held proudly high, a votive candle in his right hand, and his left hand resting on the hilt of his sword. What did he most feel? Pride or the holy fear of God, *il santo timor di Dio?* Pride, says De Renzi, for "after the fashion of Nero he had refashioned our city." Enigmatic words, but in the spirit of my "report on a state of emergency."

Philip IV, long childless and unhappy on this account, was finally expecting a son. The Viceroy celebrated the birth of a successor to the throne in Madrid with a ball in the palace in Naples, a ball attended by a countless host of people, and for the first time representatives of the common people were invited (including a couple of Masaniello's former comrades), whom Count Castrillo had appointed to the city senate immediately after the plague. It was no easy matter to reach the Viceroy's red armchair and "kiss the General's little hand," *baciare la manina del Generale.* The Viceroy had never before enjoyed even a jot of the attention shown to him now, after the plague, in a city shorn of half its inhabitants. Why that was so, none of the chroniclers of the time nor later historians could ever explain. But so it was, and so I must take note in my report.

The fact that the Viceroy organized a ball at the palace without waiting till the end of the period of mourning for his wife was a signal for Naples to curtail all mourning for the dead, despite the wrath and fulminations of the clergy. Less than three months had passed since convalescent September, but Naples was awhirl in a frenzy of entertainment, carousal, general feasting, illuminations and fireworks, and unbridled licentiousness (wilder than ever before, according to the chronicler).

There was a touch of vainglory in Count Castrillo's report to Philip IV that the subjects of the vice-kingdom, "although seriously diminished in numbers by the will of heaven, are happy with their lot, and after experiencing all that has befallen them, they have consigned to oblivion and resignation the dreams and demands that formerly threatened the throne, thanks be to God and to his faithful servant." By way of full recompense, the monarch summoned the faithful servant of God to Madrid, conferred on him still another honorary title, and recommended a long, well-deserved rest on his family estate near Burgos, and to the viceroyal seat in Naples he appointed Count Pegnaranda.

XII

At the end of his *Journal of the Plague Year*, Defoe could not refrain from the melancholy conclusion "that for the generality of the people, it might too justly be said of them as was said of the children of Israel . . . when they passed the Red Sea . . . viz., that they sang His praise, but they soon forgot His works."

When the euphoria of salvation subsided after the Neapolitan plague, when life a step from death had been tasted to the full, the true and deep effects of those ghastly eight months came to be known. The same note of grief runs through the vast majority of historical works: for nearly half a century, until the end of the seventeenth century, demoralization was rampant in the vice-kingdom of Naples, corruption, contempt for the laws of God and man, aversion to labor, indifference, apathy, and atrophy of resistance to foreign domination. What the plague killed in the survivors, in their children, grandchildren, and great-grandchildren, was any taste for, appreciation of, and enjoyment of community life with all its splendors and miseries.

"Plague?" As long as Count Castrillo still lived in gilded exile on his estate, he received these tidings from his once subject country with a shrug of his stiff shoulders. "Plague?" He smoothed his forehead in silent meditation and kept his thin lips from forming a triumphant smile. "My state of war, my state of emergency."

Naples, May 5 [Flaubert]

In September 1849 Flaubert invited two friends to Croisset: Maxime Du Camp and Louis Bouilhet thus became the first to know and *hear* "The Temptation of St. Anthony." Flaubert spent three years gathering material for the "Temptation," and eighteen months writing it: he wrote five hundred pages with a sense of relaxation, lightness, and ease. This was the first (and last) time anything of the kind happened to him, so it is no wonder that he was euphoric. He seated his guests in easy chairs with the words: "If you are not bursting with enthusiasm after the reading, then nothing can stir you." The sole reader was Flaubert himself. He read aloud for four days, eight hours a day, modulated his voice like an actor, and sometimes almost chanted. Du Camp and Bouilhet listened in silence. Flaubert read the last lines of the manuscript the afternoon of the fourth day, slammed it shut, and hoarsely said: "It is your turn, now. Tell me sincerely what you think about the 'Temptation.'" Bouilhet answered for both of them: "We think you should throw the manuscript in the fire and never mention it again."

Flaubert agonized like a wounded animal. The conversation about "The Temptation" lasted all night; Flaubert defended the book, his friends criticized it with increasing severity. Finally he capitulated: "Perhaps you are right. The theme so gripped me that I could not see clearly. I agree that the book has the faults you point out, but they are faults inherent in my nature. What am I to do?" They replied that he should seek themes he could truly master, avoid excessive lyricism, check his appetite for ornamentation, eliminate his tendency to constant digression and elaborately embellished "trimmings": they provided an outlet for his own need for display but were boring to the reader. Flaubert, *plutôt vaincu que convaincu*, muttered: "It won't be easy, but I will try." The next afternoon the three of them took a walk, they were all embarrassed and loath to converse. Bouilhet suddenly turned to Flaubert: "Listen, why don't you write a novel about

Madame Delamare's story?" "What a splendid idea!" Flaubert exclaimed. The story of Madame Delamare, which was common knowledge in Rouen and its environs, was probably the germ of *Madame Bovary*. Flaubert is known to have fought for every word with his editors and publishers, but in 1874 he published "The Temptation" shortened by half. He salvaged it, as much as it could be salvaged, for scholarly opinion is that the first "Temptation" was indeed illbegotten, to say the least.

The Peruvian writer Mario Vargas Llosa described the vicissitudes of "The Temptation" in a book about the role of *Madame Bovary* in Flaubert's art.

Louise Colet, surely out of obligation as the writer's mistress, found "pearls" in "The Temptation." Flaubert replied: "It is not pearls that make a necklace; it is a thread that makes it. I was Saint Anthony in the Temptation and I forgot that. First you have to create the figure. . . . Everything depends on a plan, and there is none in The 'Temptation.' " Reconciled to the judgment of his friends, Flaubert was already organizing his thoughts for Madame Bovary, and he treated "The Temptation" as a negative model. He wrote to Louise Colet: "I am in a completely different world now, in a world of exact observation of the most boring details. My eyes are concentrated on the slightest flutters of the soul. Far from the mythological and theological flashes of 'The Temptation.' I do not want my new novel to contain just one reaction, just one reflection of the author. . . . I am Madame Bovary!" Yes, but he was Madame Bovary in a totally different way than Saint Anthony. At a level that precludes personal "ecstasy" and metaphorically embroidered style. In an objective way, cool, thoughtthrough, and experienced in the deep recesses of the heart, in a way that sets the writer's "realism" far above "actuality."

Vargas Llosa called his book *The Endless Orgy*. The title comes from a letter of Flaubert's of 1858: "One can learn to bear existence through immersion in writing as if it were an endless orgy." The word "orgy" is certainly an overstatement on the part of Flaubert, who was rather a galley slave than a hedonist as a writer. But what is important and insightful is the idea of "writing" as a form of "being."

May 15 [In the shadow of Vesuvius]

The day before yesterday I went to the Angevin Castel Sant'Elmo to see an exhibition, *"All'ombra del Vesuvio,"* three hundred pictures by European painters from the fifteenth to the nineteenth century that originated "in the shadow of Vesuvius." The title of the show is a good one, but it might have been more accurate to borrow the title of Malcolm Lowry's novel *Under the Volcano*. Because we do not have a shadow here, we do not live "in the shadow," we live "under" the volcano. Under the rule of a sovereign who has been merciful or relatively merciful these many years (the last, mild and rather theatrical eruption, which I saw in March 1944, caused little damage), but Vesuvius is an unpredictable and fierce tyrant, the thundering master of fifty eruptions in the subconscious mind of the inhabitants of Naples and in the more or less conscious mind of passing tourists. Leopardi referred to the volcano as *Sterminator Vesuvio*. I once read the opinion of an expert on the city and the psychology of its inhabitants, that the subconscious of the average Neapolitan is still, after two thousand years, frequented by the ghost of "the last days of Pompeii." The Osservatorio Vesuviano on the slope of the volcano, equipped with every possible measuring instrument, candidly admits that very little can be predicted. In people's imagination the lava is certainly a dragon lurking in impenetrable darkness. Occasionally, as in 1944, one sees his flashing eyes, but his presence is felt every day through the wall of sleep.

Outsiders who move here feel his presence more strongly and glaringly than the natives (atavism serves to mitigate). I am an example of this myself. Tomasz Burek's observation about my writing may be quite right: "One would like to call it, in a metaphorical and at the same time the most exact sense, 'notes from under the volcano.' "

But alongside the mortal strand of the volcano, Naples has another life-giving strand of "instinctive, downright pagan joy in living . . . a human throng that is happy just to be alive." This is what Pawel Muratow writes about Naples in *Obrazach Włoch* [Pictures of Italy]. He goes on to say that "nobody more than the Neapolitan loves the world with such a strong, stubborn animal love." Muratow wrote his two-volume work before World War I. He certainly would not have recognized Naples today, nor would all those travelers of the past who were lured here in pursuit of the "earthly paradise." And yet, despite all, the formula of the "two strands" is also true today. Which, in the distant past, through the centuries, is just what the exhibition "In the Shadow of Vesuvius" is about!

Jan Brueghel (the Elder) opens it: *Christ During the Storm on the Sea of Galilee.* What does the sea of Galilee have to do with the bay of Naples? What is Christ (with the Apostles) doing "in the shadow of Vesuvius"? For the simplest of reasons, because Brueghel had our bay "under the volcano" before his eyes. He treated the bay as synonymous with storm and dread. He did something similar when he used the bay and the volcano as the background to his *View of a Port, the Departure of Saint Paul from Cesarea.* It is wholly possible that Naples in the fifteenth and sixteenth centuries aroused a feeling in foreign painters that they were in touch with some deeply hidden level of the world where mythology and nature came together.

Subsequently there was a boom in likenesses of the volcano with no metaphorical entanglements. There is a vast array of portraits of Vesuvius plumed with dense clouds of smoke, wrapped in a shawl of smoke negligently draped around the peak, sheathed in evening dress of fire and glowing lava, nightcapped with clouds and what might be a wisp of pipe smoke. The supplicant processions on the shore opposite gradually gave way to idyllic scenes. It is as if the Neapolitans of the "other strand" failed to notice the eruption or, enraptured by their love of life, turned their eyes away from the fiery tempest of death. An interweaving of the "two strands" prevailed in the seventeenth and eighteenth centuries, and this may have been what led art historians to coin the term "existential baroque." Frenchmen (Didier Barra and Vernet, Diderot's favorite painter), Spaniards, Dutchmen, and English (Turner's evocative, somewhat pastel-like *Bay of Naples*), Germans, and Italians wallowed in dramatic effects enhanced by bucolic landscape.

For me Corot's small painting *Vesuvius* is the most beautiful; a reproduction has been hanging on the wall of my room for years. It expresses the same thing in an uncommonly clear and discreet way by combining the lifeless black volcano with a solitary white sailboat. In the nineteenth century Vesuvius draws away from, or rather is slowly drawn out of, the shadow. The less shadow there is, the more it becomes what is called *vedutismo,* "view painting," softened, groomed, often saccharine. The Neapolitans like to look at it. But at the same time they know that the *Sterminator Vesuvio* is, as always, looking at them.

November 12 [The Pope's visit to Naples]

Yesterday (it was a sunny, almost springlike day) I stood in the crowd in Piazza Plebiscito during the Mass celebrated by John Paul II. The Pope's five-day pastoral visit to Naples, and so long a visit to a sole Italian city, is an unprecedented event. It was probably conceived as radical treatment in extremis for a critically ill patient suffering from a cancer that has spread to almost every organ of the body (for such is the case of Naples). Before the Pope arrived in the square, some priest acted as master of ceremonies and kept shouting the word *"Speranza"* on the loudspeaker and vainly exhorted the crowd to join in singing the church hymns as the first notes were struck. I looked at the people standing around me: they had tired gray faces, with not a whit of the festive or of religious fervor, faces that could not have been farther from *speranza*. They quickened somewhat the moment the Pope's glass cage entered the square. The burst of applause ended quickly and then silence. When solemn words began to come from John Paul II's lips—rule of law, dignity, responsibility, courage, solidarity, love—the faces around me again dimmed and turned gray. No, there was no trace of "hope" in them. The miracle of rousing Naples and delivering it from the cancerous pincers of illness, the miracle expected from the curative medicine of the papal visit to a city for centuries accustomed to waiting for miracles, soared up, spun a while in the air, and burst like a punctured balloon. The reason for Naples' inexorable decline in recent years is that it has stopped believing in miracles. For some time I have doubted that there is anything to inject that might instill in its veins even an illusion of recovery.

1 9 9 1

Maisons-Laffitte, October 3
[Conrad and the banality of good]

There is a striking passage in Conrad's *Heart of Darkness*: "I've seen the devil of violence, and the devil of greed, and the devil of hot desire; but by all the stars! these were strong, lusty, red-eyed devils, that swayed and drove men. . . . But as I stood on this hillside, I foresaw that in the blinding sunshine of that land I would become acquainted with a flabby, pretending, weak-eyed devil of a rapacious and pitiless folly." Evil lurks in the heart of darkness. Conrad presents it in the form of madness brought about by the monstrosity of the tropics and isolation among savages. Our more highly civilized century introduced a new concept, "the banality of evil." We owe it to Hannah Arendt, who at the Eichmann trial caught sight of not "a flabby, pretending, weak-eyed devil of a rapacious and pitiless folly," but a bureaucratized devil so dominated by a rapacious and pitiless folly that it might have been a matter of running a large efficient factory with a planner-devised schedule for delivering an assortment of cadavers.

Fortunately the banality of good also exists. That is the title Enrico Deaglio gave his book *La banalità del bene*, and he makes no secret that it was conceived as a modest counterweight to Hannah Arendt's report. The hero is Giorgio Perlasca, an Italian merchant and—interestingly enough—a combatant in Spain on the side of General Franco, although it is hard to tell if he was a volunteer. In civilian life he was in the cattle trade, and his business often took him to Hungary. He was in Budapest during the last phase of the "final solution of the *Judenfrage*," when Eichmann was bringing his death factory to peak production efficiency and Raoul Wallenberg was trying to rescue some of those marked for the gas chamber. Perlasca, who came back from the civil war in Spain with a good knowledge of Spanish and a letter of commendation from his Franco-ist superiors, wangled his way into the Spanish consulate in Budapest, and when the consul left, took his place with the agreement of the staff. Pretending to be a consul, he began to provide Budapest Jews with "letters of guarantee" (in the sense that Spain would accept them because of "family and relatives") that were respected as safe conduct by the Hungarian authorities successors to Admiral Horthy and even by Eichmann's subordinates. In this way Perlasca saved five thousand Jews from certain death. After the war he returned to Italy, settled in Padua, lived in retirement, and told nobody (except his wife) about what he had done in Budapest. Until after much searching the people he saved finally tracked him down. And then a flurry of high awards, travel, and honors. Perlasca was bewildered, as if it were all slightly embarrassing, and maybe somewhat pleased by the disturbance of his silent, peaceful, regulated old age. "Anyone in my place would have done the same," he felt sure. It is legitimate to doubt that, but how inspiring this uncommon example of "the banality of goodness"! The Orwellian counterpart to the "banality of good" was "ordinary human decency."

1 9 9 2

There is a species of large African ants that live on their own and each other's excrement; they have created their own autarchic circulatory system, which in its peculiar *perpetuum mobile* loop makes them independent of the outside world. I suppose that in fifteen to twenty years the new adepts of "Sovietology," after the breakup of the USSR and the crash of communism, will operate in comparable fashion. Until the day "the country of the victorious revolution" is completely effaced from readers' consciousness and memory. Looking at the work of the new wave in Sovietology, I had a sense of déjà vu: someone already wrote, ruminated, and excreted all of this before, and now the ant tribe in its autarchic inner loop is settling down to eat the excrement. The joke is that as long as the "Soviet and communist myth" prospered, its analysts and critics were ignored and treated with unconcealed distaste if not hostility. Just a minor example: when Maria and Bohdan Paczowski lived in Milan, and I was writing for the Milan papers, their Italian acquaintances greeted every article of mine with the words *il solito Herling*, "the same old Herling," in other words, another helping of humbug. Now, in what Broniewski calls the "little

245

burial place of ideas," the "Sovietology" ants have something with which to begin their ruminations and excretion. They will certainly find a bit of nourishment in the hundreds of my scraps in the *Corriere della Sera* and the *Giornale*.

These reflections were evoked by the recently published *L'immagine dell'URSS* [The Image of the USSR], subtitled *L'Occidente e la Russia di Stalin 1927–1956* [The West and Stalin's Russia, 1927–1956]. The author, Marcello Flores, a "politocologist" at the University of Trieste, has industriously collected probably everything that went into the West's "image of the USSR" in the course of the thirty years mentioned in the subtitle. I would not want the ironic tone of my reflections to dim Flores's monastic efforts. But I cannot help noting that everything he has "discovered" on the tomb of "the Soviet and communist myth" has been said dozens of times in the past by people seriously concerned with these matters, to the almost total indifference of the so-called "thinking public." Now that the "myth" is lying in the rubble, the "thinking public" will presumably read Flores's book, which is useful in its way, with such exclamations as "incredible," "never heard that before," and "I can't believe it!"

I was pervaded by deep sadness mixed with irritation as I turned the pages of this image of the USSR under Western eyes. So-called intellectuals and luminaries of European culture (with few exceptions) prostrated themselves before the divine "myth." The clamor of rapture drowns out the voices of the few exceptions. It has something of the bigotry of new converts about it. It is true that as early as 1920 Bertrand Russell passed sobering judgment on the prospects of Bolshevism. But his skepticism (to say the least) did not carry much weight against the raptures and ecstasies of the Webbs, Wells, and Shaw. Shaw caught the "myth" in the act of lying on his trip to Soviet Russia, but it did not weaken his positive "global view." Gide retracted the initial hurrahs of his *Retour de l'U.R.R.S.*, but this had no subsequent influence on the euphoric idiocy of Sartre and his "intellectual" wards (in Poland, the Kotts, the Brandyses, etc.). Walter Benjamin made no secret of his shock or maybe indignation at Joseph Roth's sensible misgivings. One could go on quoting forever, which is exactly what Flores does with admirable scrupulosity and patience. But what for? The only interesting feature of the Western "cult" involves the question: What was the main reason for the blindness?

According to me it was twofold: "intellectuals" were puffed up and ballooned like toads at the thought that they might play the role of a priestly caste (a highly investitured elite) in the "new order," which was unthinkable under democratic governments; and for good reason, the life of ordinary people did not interest them, although it might seem that is precisely what ought to attract the attention of people who are "fascinated by revolution." Koestler's autobiography *The Invisible Writing* is an amazing book from this standpoint: as a communist he traveled throughout the Soviet Union, republic by republic, gathering material for a long reportage, *White Nights and Red Days*, and almost never caught sight of—he would not or could not catch sight of—everyday reality. Only someone so color-blind could, after breaking with communism, write the "intellectually" flashy trash of *Darkness at Noon.*

February 23 [Churchill and Stalin]

Churchill talks in his memoirs about his meeting with Stalin in August 1942. He asked him if the war being waged against Germany was harder for him than forced collectivization, in other words, than the war against the peasants. "Oh, no," replied Stalin, "collectivization inflicted a much more terrible war on us. We had ten million peasants against us. It was a terrible war, it lasted four years."

To be precise, "that" war was waged against twenty-two million peasant families, which at the end of the 1920s meant about eighty per cent of the Soviet people.

By now the bloodstained horrors of forced collectivization are sufficiently well known, from scholarly works and from literature (Vasily Grossman's novel *Everything Flows*, for example). Nevertheless a relatively short book, *Lettere da Kharkov*, is astonishing and horrifying. It is a collection of reports the Italian scholar Andrea Graziosi found in the archives of the Italian Ministry of Foreign Affairs from consular staff in Kharkov and Novorossiysk and from officials of the Italian Embassy in Moscow. The reports refer to the period from 1930 to 1933 in the Ukraine and northern Caucasus. They are enormously valuable for their information and analysis and show that Mussolini sent the best of the diplomatic corps to the USSR. What unfolds before the reader's eyes are succinct, factual descriptions of peasants enslaved by the nation, epidemics, banditry, cannibalism, markets offering slaves, abandoned children, masses of peasants in flight, regions governed by sovereign authorities, villages in the clutches of little despots, assaults on bakeries, death barracks, mounted patrolmen with clubs in their hands, life and death struggles for a handful of grain, and uprisings mercilessly suppressed. And looming over all the reports is hunger, hunger, hunger, hunger. It really was a harder war than the war against Hitler's invaders. One report, from Kharkov in February 1932, quotes an appeal found in the post box for letters addressed to the Polish consulate. "We are bound in a sack and cannot untie it by ourselves. We are ready to follow anyone who would deliver us. . . . We are ready to fall on our knees before him, let him trample on our corpses, only save our children. . . . But if our letter falls into your hands, you guardians of 'the land of freedom,' may you be damned, executioners of a Russia destroyed, destroyers of our families, child murderers." The authors of the appeal identify themselves as a group of village teachers, workers, and farmers. What must certainly have led them, subconsciously, to choose the Polish consulate was the recollection of Pilsudski's Kiev campaign. But I suppose that similar appeals were tossed into the letter boxes of German consulates.

Graziosi says that the Italian, German, and Polish consulates were the ones that most carefully monitored hunger in the Ukraine and were the best informed. France and England did not have a network of consulates in the Ukraine and northern Caucasus. Why? Did they prefer not to know? Probably. In the summer of 1933 Edouard Herriot, the then French minister of foreign affairs, visited Ukraine in the peak period of hunger. He rode along city streets where bakery windows displayed loaves of bread made of painted plaster. The foxy (and at the same time donkeyish) old parliamentarian evidently had a more than normally cultivated sense of smell, because when he returned to Paris he described to journalists the "splendid smell of freshly baked bread in the cities of beautiful and fertile Ukraine."

1 9 9 3

A Venetian Portrait

I read the following death notice in yesterday's *Corriere*: "Countess Giuditta Terzan has died at the age of eighty-seven at her home in Calle San Barnaba in Venice. She went to her eternal rest at peace with God. This announcement of death is made by her sister Giovanna Olindo in Rome. Friends are requested not to disturb the deceased's quiet departure with condolences."

I came across the death notice by chance last evening when I was looking for the television program listings. I never moved from my chair. How do distant memories suddenly come pouring back? Probably differently for each of us; in my case they come storming back in violent tumult. It was only the next day, after a night of restive dreamless sleep, that events, people's faces, and dates fell into place the way a jigsaw puzzle does as the picture pattern is gradually reconstructed.

In the spring of 1946, as April turned to May, I went to Venice on business that was important for me (and for my superiors in the army office in Rome). I expected the trip would take two weeks at most, and that was how long I told my wife I would be away. I had to make a brief stop in Florence as well in connection with those matters.

Trains and long-distance buses were readily available by then, but those of us in uniform trusted only military transport. The drawback, if you were in a hurry, and the attraction, if you were tempted by sightseeing, were the frequent long stops. My errand was urgent, but not so urgent that it could not be extended on some pretext. The first jeep (American) took me to Orvieto, and there I spent the afternoon and night, after making arrangements with a British passenger truck (army excursion) for the next stage to Florence.

I regret that it is not possible in reminiscence—after so many years!—to recapture the atmosphere of my *first* encounters with the marvels of Italian architecture, painting, and landscape, the discoveries made by virgin eyes that are effaced by time or altered by successive encounters. All that I remember is the state of numbness and inner trembling, which had nothing to do with aesthetic experience, in which I spent several hours sitting and kneeling by turns in the Duomo, in the Chapel of the Last Judgment, to be precise. Something about it seemed to cleanse away the war and all the experiences of the six years past, something like a voiceless prayer for grace. It is odd that Rome did not have that effect on me.

In the evening I got drunk on Orvieto wine in a tavern near the Duomo, after which, indifferent to the spring chill, I slept the night on the stone benches on the other side of the Cathedral Square, and every reawakening sated me and again lulled me to sleep with the slightly blurred contour of the front of the Duomo, a facade that in the vernal darkness looked like an enormous pipe organ in stone.

I quickly settled the personal and office business I had in Florence, walked around the monuments in the center of town, and, disheartened by the crowds of soldiers and tourists, fled to the Arno. And there in a dusty little used-book shop, I spent a pittance on a large-format *Album di ritratti*. It was with this *Portrait Album* in my knapsack, after a night spent at an address I had from Rome, that I stood at the city gates at dawn waiting for a vehicle to Venice or thereabouts. The only ride that turned up was for Padua.

In Padua I ran into some Polish officers I knew, and with them I reached Venice about noon. The city military command post in a small street near St. Mark's Square was already closed but reopened in the early evening. For the time being I had to forgo assigned lodgings, to which I was entitled, and was prepared to try one of the few non-requisitioned hotels. They were supposedly all full; supposedly—the truth was written in the unwelcoming looks of the desk clerks.

So I returned to the square, where by a lucky stroke I managed to get the last free table in a café facing the basilica. And I took the book out of my knapsack.

The *Portrait Album* was clearly a commercial enterprise of the thirties, without so much as a mention of a scholarly editor or art historian. But the selection was large, the reproductions were good, and the notes on the artists were taken from serious biographies and monographs.

In anthological publications of this sort the whole effort is to capture the substance of the main subject. In the case of the *Album* it was the presentation of the widest possible range of nuances in the art of portraiture. There is an extremely fine line separating the good conventional portrait from the portrait the artist intends to be *read*— for the character, psyche, mind, and accumulated experience of the sitter (or of the artist himself in the self-portrait). I would roughly distinguish three categories of portraits, aside from the conventional portrait, of course, where resemblance and attire are the main concern. (1) There are portraits in which the artist immediately captures the essence of the facial expression (for example, Holbein and Rembrandt), which is why, at least for me, there is no doubt that every meaningful and rightly observed face speaks in full voice from the first glance. (2) There are emotional-poetic portraits that are as revealing and intense as a good poem (Van Gogh, say). (3) And there are portraits that are explorations of psychology, where the approach to the face is highly individualized (Lorenzo Lotto), in contrast with Titian's handling of facial types.

Lorenzo Lotto! There was the name of that long-familiar great painter from Venice—primarily a portraitist. I write the name with some chagrin. Will the reader believe—and I am anxious that he should—that at the very beginning of my journey (and my story) I immediately happened on a thread of such importance to the "Venetian Portrait." If the reader blinks in skepticism as he continues, I ask only that he remember it is not the author who is responsible for the way destinies capriciously and unexpectedly intersect and branch out every which way; the author is just as surprised by the hand that guides his own.

The note about Lotto in the *Portrait Album*, backed up by very authoritative references, described a life dogged by misfortune. Lotto was born in the late fifteenth century in Venice. Our century and the end of the last finally saw him as an artist who sometimes even surpassed his contemporaries—Titian, Michelangelo, Raphael, and Dürer—but throughout his long life was barely noticed and never fully appreciated by patrons and connoisseurs. He painted a great deal but was not a success; he was a vagabond in constant pursuit of even modest commissions. He earned a pittance from churches and for his portraits. The best evidence of his character is the exclamation of the venomous Aretino: "as good as goodness itself, as virtuous as virtue!" Contemporary accounts refer to his "spiritual darkness" and "religious unrest," which aroused suspicions that he secretly favored Lutheranism. He passed for a student of Bellini (it is now known that his master was Alvise Vivarini). His frescoes on religious subjects suggested a connection with Coreggio, and in portraiture Lotto outshone Stendhal's favorite. He never married, and his itinerant life deepened his penchant for solitude. He was said to be "rootless." He wanted to be buried in his native Venice, but he was too poor to go back before he died. He spent the last years of his life as an "oblate" in the sanctuary of Loreto, where he could count on a daily bowl of soup. And there he died in his eightieth year (or thereabouts). Twenty years after the publication of the *Portrait Album* Bernard Berenson wrote a major monograph about the artist. Berenson's opinion was that never before or since Lorenzo Lotto had any artist captured so much inner life in his sitter's face.

It was getting dark, so I could go to the city military command post.

My official authorization was unreservedly accepted at once. The British sergeant in the housing section asked if I wanted a room in a hotel or in a partially requisitioned private home. I chose the latter. He looked down the list with a sorrowful air. With relief he finally pointed his finger at one of the addresses on the list and said I could have the whole ground floor of a small house in Calle San Barnaba. "But I have to tell you honestly," he added, "that the place is terribly run-down and neglected; it belongs to a Venetian countess who occupies the whole upstairs. And she's a bitch and a witch."

That evening I found the little house without much difficulty, although it was back behind a row of buildings and connected to the calle by a dirty narrow passageway. The Contessa (that is how everyone in the neighborhood referred to her, without using her name or surname) took the slip from my hands, looked me up and down with barely disguised repugnance and a spark of anger in her black eyes. She brightened slightly on learning that I was Polish, gave me the key to the entrance door, and told me in advance that she "did not do housekeeping." She took sheets and towels from a chest of drawers and threw them on the bed, warned me that the stove did not work, likewise the bathroom, so I could take only a cold shower. And coffee was served at the bar in Campo San Barnaba by the church. She told me that she was a picture restorer and copyist and often worked nights, so she appreciated peace and quiet. "It would be best if we just ignored each other's existence. I would also ask you not to conduct your social life here" (a euphemistic way of describing the military habit of bringing prostitutes home).

The British sergeant was right: the two rooms on the ground floor with kitchen and bathroom were appallingly neglected; fortunately, in addition to the wide bed, there was also an armchair by a bookcase full of books and painting portfolios. The rest—a table, chairs, and a chest of drawers—was thick with dirt, rickety, and out of place, as if there had been some sort of commotion. The house itself was almost in ruins, there were holes left by fallen plaster, and an iron staircase fastened to the wall outside led to the upper story. (The inside stairs were evidently not often used, and they creaked alarmingly when the Contessa came down to open the door for me.) But it was obvious that someone had been living in the other room not very long before. There were photographs and reproductions of paintings on the walls, and near the now-blocked glazed doors leading to the outside staircase stood a large, stylish, locked clothes cupboard (with no key in the lock). As it turned out the next morning, three fluffy cats dozed on the outside iron staircase during the day and scared off the rats that used the passageway to get from the calle to the canal.

Years later, when I became an admirer of *The Aspern Papers*, I thought of the little house in Calle San Barnaba every time I read the Henry James novella. It was truly wretched in comparison with the home of the two heroines of *The Aspern Papers*, but there was a similar air about it—how describe it?—surely, secretly creeping dissolution. And notwithstanding the fact that my Contessa was a good-looking woman, she looked forty, while old Miss Bordereau, in her youth the mistress of the famous poet Aspern, standing jealous guard over her highly prized love letters, was on the verge of the grave.

I collapsed from fatigue on the bed, and when I awoke the clock said ten o'clock. I felt hungry. I went out of the dark passageway on to the calle; the *campo* was nearby. The bar by the church was still open but empty (before the summer season, ten is a very late hour for Venice). I went into the little room at the back, where I was given something cold to eat and a bottle of wine. The owner lowered the shutters in the entrance, turned out the light in the bar, and sat down with me. He already knew I was staying at the Contessa's.

He needed no urging to speak: an evening chat "after hours" with a glass of wine is every *barista*'s delight. The Contessa was not born a countess. As a young student at the Academy of Fine Arts she was seduced by an older man, Count Terzan. She got pregnant. Terzan agreed to give her and the child his name and title, but on condition that after the wedding she would never try to see him again. He bought her the little house in Calle San Barnaba, which was still in good repair at the time, and he retired to his estate near Sondrio in the Valtellina. Nothing was ever seen of him again here; he did not even come for the boy's first communion.

When the boy finished secondary school, he went to study architecture at the university. Alvise, he was called Alvi for short. The mother earned a living for the two of them by restoring old pictures and copying masterpieces in the Accademia to order for wealthy customers. She was in love with Alvi (and he with her), he was her whole world, yes, yes, a good boy and nice-looking. She lived alone, like a nun.

"You saw for yourself that she is still young and pretty. She neglects the house, she neglects herself. She can barely make ends meet—for nowadays who is interested in restoring old pictures and ordering expensive copies in the Accademia—she owes so much that the grocery stores have stopped giving her credit. I give her a *cappuccino* and *cornetto* in the morning, I put a good face on it, because she tells me to put it on her tab. Contessa! She's the illegitimate daughter of a school janitress (that janitress later got married and had a second daughter, who is now a rich woman in Rome), but she acts like a real countess."

For three years she had lived alone: her son was drafted in the army early in 1943, and after a year in the service he stopped writing. "Did you notice how she runs out morning and afternoon to her mailbox outside? Nothing, two years and not a word, everybody knows, and since the war ended a year ago, a lot of Venetian soldiers have come back to their families. You see, you can see for yourself: in the morning out to the mailbox, then to the Accademia, in the afternoon back to the mailbox, and in the evening and sometimes all night the lights blazing in her room. She certainly spends most of what she earns on light. She rarely leaves the house. Only to the antique dealers and the stores that sell canvas and paint, they say. One day that little house of hers is going to fall down. It will fall down, I swear, and bury the Contessa together with her pictures. Well, it's time to close, it's midnight already. I've given you all the gossip I could, but I thought you ought to know who you're living with. I suspect that what little money the army pays for the room must be a big item in her budget. The catch is that it will hardly last her more than three or four days."

I settled the official business and my own in a couple of days, so I could actually have started looking for transportation back to Rome. But you do not come to Venice for the first time in your life only to say farewell as soon as you have said hello. So with a sense of light-heartedness and ever-increasing bedazzlement, I became a tourist. Besides, the day I originally expected to leave was still far off.

Venice was the third big Italian city I saw just after the war, after Naples and Rome; I omit Florence, because that was a lightning visit to the museum-city with no chance for a deeper look.

Each of the three cities came out of the war different. Naples wore a pained smile (but a smile nevertheless) and a foxy gleam in the eye, which befitted a city that had never in its history met a single invader or any foreign domination that it could not tolerate and overcome with the secret weapon of sly, derisive submission. Rome grimaced in desperate panic with the meek and dazed look of a wretch who has suddenly lost most of what he had and is ready to give up all the rest just for the chance of ordinary life. Venice (perhaps because a year had already gone by since the end of the war) had an incomparable elegance and dignity and the mysterious hauteur of the sacrosanct, a city so proud that no one would ever dare to raise a hand against it.

The hardest pitfall to avoid is trite repetition when you are trying to express wonderment. But it is like lovers' confessions and declarations. What happens is something on the order of absolving yourself of banality, you stop noticing it, because—or so it would seem—the hackneyed shopworn words begin to shine with a new light and all by themselves start to transcend their ordinary meanings.

So it was as I started falling in love with Venice. I fell deeper in love every day with the city that, to quote a poet, is made of the stuff of dreams, a city I marveled at for a particular connection that needs mentioning: the conjunction of dream with waking. That brief moment before waking while the evaporating dream is still present but is already being dispelled by the light of day. Such for me was the stuff of Venice. Is it still so? Still unreal? On the bridges over the canals I lingered long, very long, as if I expected the mirror of dark water to preserve the sight of things gone by, the reflected flux of time. In the streets and squares I listened intently to steps, going away or just coming? I did not use the boats, I had to go everywhere on foot. Gondolas seemed like ghosts to me. I knew, and I readily accepted the fact, that never, even if I lived there or returned again and again over the years, would I ever get to the heart of Venice, the way you do with other cities. Because it does not have one. There is no heart or core to Venice, it is too liquid and fleeting, palpable yet elusive. I did not like St. Mark's Square and its overly haughty basilica, I did not like the Ducal Palace, I did not like the overly concrete city sustained by a shred of hard ground. I preferred the Venice balancing on an edge, because it proved that dreams were real. Even on the serpentine Canal Grande (which is how most visitors describe it), crammed, God only knows how, with palaces as brittle as fantasies, Venice was and was not. The mere idea of Venice towered over Europe and at the same time threatened to disappear, the city was crumbling.

That is what I loved about Venice with bitterness and simultaneously with rapture, as I trod every possible route through the city from dawn till dusk. But the truth, which I cannot deny, is that from the first moment the Venice I loved was also the woman in whose house I lived.

It was ordinary military practice for British and American soldiers to apply the term "bitch" to women generally, especially to women they knew only by sight or not at all; so it was a form of conventional insult like spitting on the ground. But when the British sergeant at the command post applied the term "witch" to the Contessa, whom he had met only briefly on business, he accidentally struck home, there was something of the witch about her. It *also* showed when anger flashed in her lustrous black eyes, which were such a contrast to her very fair long hair. Then she looked dangerous without losing the least of her good looks—nay, her rare beauty. But the next moment her face darkened to soft velvet, and the flame in her black eyes did not so much subside as go elsewhere far away, somewhere known only to her. Tall, slender, and willowy, she did not look her age, probably forty. She had the gift of lightning transformation, as if she relied on constant mutation to confuse the observer. She was conscious of her beauty but without a trace of vanity. And omitting the violent outbursts she occasionally voiced, she was angelically mild, languorous, and composed. She adored two things: her son and Venetian painting. (The subject of her son was taboo, but the terrain of Venetian painting was always open for conversation.) She asked no questions herself, and she parried the most circumspect attempts at inquiry with a pucker of her brows and a tightening of her lips. She seemed consciously and purposively to guard her enigmatic quality. This profile after the fact is drawn from the time when, at her invitation, I clambered upstairs in the evenings. A delirious thought soon took shape in my mind: somehow she was Venice personified, no, no, not in the sense that she was (as they say) a worthy daughter of the city on the lagoon, sharing in some of its attributes, but in the sense that she *herself* was Venice, the object of admiration wholly enveloped by the marvelous city, like the world captured forever in the mirror of the canals. She was a plebeian child, and the acquisition of an aristocratic patina turned the humbly born into a pure resonant alloy.

For several days I walked "far" and "wide" exploring the city, plumbing the twisting calles, floundering over canals, lingering in the sun in small campos, leaning on parapets and low-walled bridges until the time came for the paintings. I would return home late, exhausted, and before going to sleep I would stare at the photographs of the Contessa's son. There were four of them, framed under glass, hanging one over the other on the wall: a baby picture, then a boy, and two as a young university student. There was only one word for them, cherub. The childish curls and coils of ringlets gave way to a luxuriant mop of hair, but the eyes, the plump and then oval face never lost their look of goodness and ineffable sweetness. The face in the last photograph was somewhat harder but not enough to mar the angelic expression. There was a slight resemblance to his mother in the girlish lineaments of the mouth.

I knew, as I walked to the Accademia, what I most wanted to see. I glanced absently at the pictures in the first rooms, I looked into the side rooms, and I was beginning to think my search would come to nought when, in a corner of the collection of Venetian masters, I spotted my landlady. She was copying Lorenzo Lotto's portrait of a *Giovane nel suo studio*. She was so absorbed by her work that she did not notice that someone behind her to one side was carefully observing her punctilious embroidery on a canvas of the same size as the original. Ah, Lotto! The left hand turning the pages of a book, a beautiful counterpoint to a somewhat ascetic, sleekly brushed head that did not exactly fit the *giovane* in the portrait's title. The youth was leaving, rather he had already left his youth behind. I came a little closer and looked over her shoulder to see how she was managing with that splendid hand turning the pages. It was only then that she turned her head and responded to my greeting. Leaning against the wall and ready for sale was a copy of Giorgione's *Tempest*, startling in its precision and nuances of aged color, almost surpassing the original in the figure of the naked woman with the infant on her knees.

We walked along the canal in front of the Accademia. It came as a surprise to her that I knew quite a bit about painting, especially about the art of portraiture. For her no one could compare with the Venetian portraitists, and she considered Lotto the finest. I might have raised a mild objection, but I had no wish to; I just gazed at her as if she were a living portrait. I nodded automatically, but she perceived that I was not giving my whole attention to the conversation. She smiled, and the barest trace of coquetry did not escape my notice when she said: "Do come upstairs this evening, I have to go back to my easel now."

Once my visits upstairs began, I would return evenings from my wandering around the city excited and impatient; actually I spent the whole day waiting only for the evening, and Venice became increasingly confused and perhaps identified with the Venetian woman. I hoisted myself up the creaking stairs with a bottle of whisky and canned food from the military store in Venice. What a pleasure it was to talk to her about painting after supper, with a glass of whisky in my hand! I forgot about Rome, about my wife, about my military duties. The "scheduled" two weeks of my stay in Venice went by, then a third week and a fourth. The mailbox, which the Contessa actually checked twice a day after the postman had come, now produced letters to me, reminders, summons, and reproaches. I replied with euphoric picture postcards but no word of explanation, like a drunk who does not hear what is said to him.

The upper floor was the same size, except that the partition between the workroom and the bedroom had been torn down, and the kitchen and bathroom on two sides had been widened. The whole floor was essentially one large workroom overwhelmed with canvases, sketchbooks, portfolios, and unbound reproductions everywhere, even the couch disappeared under their weight, so no cleverness was required to slip away to either of the wings. The actual workroom, which was also a little sitting room with two armchairs, was distinguished from the bedroom by the decoration of the walls. The walls of the bedroom were hung with photographs of her son, while the main wall of the workroom bore two very large, excellent, and duly framed Lotto reproductions: the *Giovanetto* in Milan's Sforza Castle and the *Triple Portrait* in the gallery in Vienna. An easel stood by the window giving onto the passageway, which also had a view of the calle and the canal. There was a medium-size canvas on the easel covered by a Venetian patterned scarf. Lotto had portrayed the Milan *Youth*, wearing an ornamented cap and a striped doublet and holding a book on his knees, in a position halfway between profile and full face; sitting sideways, he turned his ephebic face halfway to the observer. His features were remarkably regular, and his beauty was heightened by one large, deepset eye (the other eye was barely visible). The Vienna *Triple Portrait* looked like a *jeu d'esprit* on Lotto's part. The man, perhaps thirty-five, has a wispy beard, one hand on his breast, weighed down by solemnity and the vicissitudes of life, and on each side his profile, the one to his right is sharper, the one to his left is not very expressive. The juxtaposition of the Milan portrait and the Vienna triple portrait on the same wall was striking: you might have thought the same person sat for the artist in early youth and in adulthood.

Was I in love with her? Could that fascination have been an illness, a beautiful illness? As far as I remember Stendhal's tract *De l'amour* (I do not have it at hand), that great connoisseur of the human heart identified and described the position of collateral affections to the primary love, which is not expelled or imperiled by enchantment or fascination, what Italians (and Stendhal had total mastery of the Italian language of love), speaking about anyone so infatuated, express with the words *è stato stregato,* "he has been bewitched." What is clear is that an infatuation branching off the trunk of one's feeling for another, truly beloved, likewise reaches what Stendhal calls "crystallization." In my case it was not so. It was blocked just before it was reached.

It was probably a month after I began paying my evening visits upstairs. (That morning I received an official letter from my military headquarters in Rome with the warning that further delay in Venice might be considered desertion; my office colleague added that my wife was beginning to "express serious concern.") About eleven o'clock, while we were talking and finishing a bottle together, the Contessa put her hand on my knee. I put my hand on hers. She did not withdraw hers; instead she closed her eyes. The next move was up to me; I felt my throat go dry, I knew that the nature of our relationship would change; that certainly was the "crystallization," ardent and prolonged. Suddenly someone called to her from the gateway, and the voice was clearly impatient. She broke away and went to the window: "Thank you, I'll be right down, sorry." And to me: "I'll be right back, there's a telephone call for me at the neighbor's." (Whether it was "on principle" or concern for the expense, she did not want a telephone of her own.) She ran down the rickety steps, and from above I saw that she left the downstairs door open.

When I cooled down a bit, I was overcome by the temptation to uncover the canvas on the easel. It was not just a canvas. It was a picture in an old, worm-riddled gilt frame. There was the youth in Milan, already clearly outlined in half-profile, but with the face of a cherub; yes, it was Alvi's face, I recognized it from his photographs. And to the right Alvi was seen full face, an even more striking image. The composition was conceived as a double portrait.

Just in time I threw the scarf back over the picture; I had heard the gate slam. The Contessa was trembling and all aflutter, she could barely speak. She finally managed to utter a few words, stammering slightly: "I beg you, please leave tomorrow, I need the downstairs flat, please, please, please."

I left early the next morning with my knapsack over my shoulder, but instead of rushing to the square by the station, I plunged one last time into Venice. Marvelous Venice, wonderful Venice, would I ever see you again? At dusk I realized that I still had the house keys in my pocket, and the *Portrait Album* was missing from my knapsack. In the evening I stole into Calle San Barnaba like a thief and noiselessly opened the door. I did not turn on the light in the room and gropingly tiptoed to the little table by the bed where the album lay. At that moment I heard steps on the gravel, and a tall man went up the iron steps wearing a military tunic and forage cap; the Contessa ran down the steps, threw her arms around him, and sobbed softly. I watched them without being seen. The man's face was unshaven, and when he looked through the window into the room where I stood flattened against the wall, I caught a momentary glimpse of a hard, cruel face with two blazing little coals instead of eyes. That is my recollection of the "cherub's" return from the war.

I was lucky. In the square next to the station a New Zealand military truck was getting ready for a night run to Rome with its freight of tarpaulin-covered crates. There was room in the wide cabin to wedge in a third passenger between the driver and his partner.

In Rome—what I didn't have to listen to from my colleagues in the office and my wife at home!—an odd feeling overcame me, a cross between euphoria and disquiet. It was easy enough to attribute both to Venice. I had fallen in love with Venice, hence the euphoria of love; and doubt aroused disquiet, would I ever see her again, for the Polish army was already preparing to move from Italy to England.

That summer I went to Capri with my wife for a week's leave.

There, on the beach, I found a discarded copy of *Stars and Stripes*, the American army newspaper, which I almost never looked at, since I saw the Polish II Corps newspaper as well as the Italian papers, which were particularly important for improving my Italian. *Stars and Stripes* had a whole spread on Venice with photographs, and I immediately recognized two blurry photographs of the Contessa and her son. For reasons which I still do not understand, the Italian papers (much less our modest Polish newspaper) had not a word about the events described in the American report. Perhaps the Italian journalists, despite their weakness for *cronaca nera,* considered the story an embarrassment in the atmosphere of postwar Italy.

The bare facts of the story went like this. In the last stages of the war, Count Alvise Terzan, son of the Countess Giuditta, joined a special detachment of the Fascist Republic of Salo, a unit that quickly distinguished itself for cruelty; the American report referred to it as "the torture unit," and the Italians stigmatized it as *la squadra fascista degli aguzzini e dei boia.* After the defeat Terzan went home to Venice, where his mother hid him in her house in Calle San Barnaba. They had the habit of going out for a walk late at night, well after midnight, when the city was totally deserted. The day before yesterday, July 27 (the correspondent was reporting from Venice), a masked man leaped from the doorway of a house on Campo San Barnaba, ran after the couple, and without a word shot the young count three times. After which he fled in the direction of the Canal Grande, where a motorboat was probably waiting for him. The reporter could not have "imagined" the final scene. One, there might be someone who actually saw what happened from a window on the campo. Two, it agrees with *my* imagination. Before the police appeared in response to a call, that is to say, for twenty minutes after the shooting, Giuditta first knelt in silence over her son's corpse, and then she lay on top of it "as if it were her lover and not her son" (the reporter's words). She did not move until the police arrived, and two strong men had their hands full to drag her away from the dead man.

Oddly enough, I did not want my wife, who was lying next to me on the beach, to read that issue of *Stars and Stripes*, so feigning absentmindedness I leaped into the sea with it in my hand and with brisk strokes I swam far from shore. The soaked newspaper gradually began to sink; I kept afloat on the surface without moving and stared at the two washed-out photographs.

"The torture and execution squad" was what the Italians called it. It was still too soon for any report or even proper information about it. But fragments, chaotic fragments, yes. Participants and witnesses of the battles in the north poured into Rome. They were not very talkative, the truth is that the final phase of the war fostered cruelties on both sides; fascist and partisan alike; the word most frequently used at the time was "escalation." Nevertheless, with some wine or a bottle of liquor, tongues sometimes loosened. Twice in my cautious inquiries I heard the young Count Terzan mentioned by name. Both times he was referred to as a *belva,* a "beast." But one man went farther: *belva umana* sounds even worse.

I thought about him all the time, about the "cherub" called Alvi, about him and not about his mother. The war was not sparing of examples of bestiality and hitherto unimaginable cruelty. Especially in my own country. Hearing tidings from countries conquered by Hitler's armies, and likewise occupied (partially at first, and then more and more) by Soviet armies, we sometimes acquiesced in an instinctive, stupid, and egoistic reaction: "People can get used to anything." But the germ of totalitarian "reeducation" lurked in that remark. It was a lie that poisoned the soul. I was sure of that as I walked around Rome, but I knew full well that the end of the war, which promised the revival of elementary human feelings, might make it hard for me not to relent. Besides it was all there in the face of Alvise Terzan. I remembered the soft boyish, almost girlish face of the photographs; as well as the face outside the windowpane, when he looked toward his room the evening he came home, a hard face clotted with undiluted hate. What had happened in the meantime? How did that astonishing change take place?

Obviously, the crumbs of information that came my way could not provide an answer to those questions. He was glimpsed but twice, and fiercely, in connection with the torture of "suspects," the shooting of children and old people, the rape of women, and the torching of the homes of people considered "enemies." His name aroused terror. Wherever his squad passed, few were left to mourn.

In the festive throng on the streets of Rome, or strolling nights along the Tiber (alone or with my wife), the face of evil always walked faithfully by my side. Born of need, the irresistible need to give pain.

The Polish army had already been transferred from Italy to England, except for soldiers who had decided to return to Poland or to remain in Italy for personal reasons. I was one of a small number of people obliged to extend their stay in Rome. The time eventually came for discharge, and the formalities were carried out in England. I was informed that I could not stay in Rome beyond the end of autumn 1947. I made arrangements for me and my wife to move at the beginning of October. In September I kept a promise to my wife to take her to Venice. And for me, it was presumably my farewell to Venice.

We went by train, for life in Italy quickly returned to normal after the war. The privileges of the recent "liberators" were now abrogated, so we had to find a place to stay for ourselves. I remembered from my first trip that what was once Ruskin's home on the Zattere had been turned into a modest hotel. It was in rather pitiable shape after being requisitioned by the military, but the manager or owner, a slightly scatty old Englishwoman, warmed to us at first sight and arranged a decent room for us with a lovely view of the Giudecca island.

I did not keep the story of my first stay in Venice a secret from my wife, omitting only that I was all but infatuated with the Contessa. Just like me now, her whole attention was concentrated on the tragedy of the son, which was so significant for the tempestuous years after the fall of fascism. We had arrived late in the evening, and the next day she went with me to pay a visit to the barman in Campo San Barnaba. He remembered me, to my surprise, and at midnight we invited him to our table in the empty bar. I should mention that the day we arrived, I rushed alone to the little house in Calle San Barnaba. I rang the doorbell several times to no response, after which I wrote a note on my knee and tossed it into her mailbox, realizing that *nowadays,* in all likelihood, the Contessa had stopped looking in it. It was probably one or maybe two o'clock when the barman motioned us to the front, where the lights were already out, and told us to stand by the window facing the campo. The Contessa was crossing the square with a regular, vigorous stride and then disappeared from sight for a quarter hour. She evidently had a fixed route for her nightly walk, because she came back across the campo at the same regular pace on her way home. I could not restrain myself; I rushed into the square and ran after her. She turned to me with a spent colorless look (where had her flashing eyes gone?) and said softly: "There must be some misunderstanding, I don't know you. You shouldn't bother a woman alone." I was speechless and stepped to one side.

She was all alone (according to the barman), she left her house in the morning to go to the Accademia and at night for a short walk, she no longer stopped at the bar for her morning coffee. She continued her copying in the Accademia and painted at home (the light in her room was on all night), and she sold some of her reproductions, not so much as a fine copyist but as the famed heroine of the previous year's drama. It seems that on Sundays, very early and whatever the weather, she visited her son's grave.

As I was polishing and correcting what I have written so far, the autobiographical weft of my story stood out in all its flagrancy. I am not sure if that is good or bad. As a rule I like first-person narratives, but they usually involve a narrator who only occasionally and tentatively might be identified with the author. But here the autobiographical element is glaring and indiscreet. Why? My writer's instinct tells me it could not be otherwise, but at the same time I plainly feel it behooves me to make some explanation.

There are different kinds of events in our life. There are events that flow by us and attract our attention without drawing us directly into the mechanism of their "happening," as if they did not sufficiently touch the deeper levels of our sensitivity. That is the simplest kind, and the writer may or may not "enter" imaginatively into the course of occurrences. There are also intermediate encounters where the external distance fluctuates constantly and occasionally stops being a distance at all, and there is a degree of participation (then it is a matter of "empathy"). And finally it may happen, albeit rarely, that there is a strong sense of being a part of events that actually get under the skin, a peculiar and even absurd sense that our participation is much more meaningful than it might seem. That is when the autobiographical note can be heard louder and louder. And that is the case with the *Venetian Portrait*.

In November 1947 we moved to England. I will skip over the details of demobilization and the proceedings for settling in a foreign country and go at once to our dark room in an apartment building near the Gloucester Road Underground station. From the perspective of many bygone years, I associate that room with the idea of a deep well. Indeed, at that time—but not in our subsequent apartment near the beautiful old park—when I was not at work I would look down at the wall of the damp closed courtyard and fall victim to nostalgia and moon about Venice. How was that possible? How could I descry, or rather evoke, a picture of Venice on a shabby patch of dirty wall? I do not know, but what is certain is that the more our life in that dark room became a drowsing nightmare, the more often euphoric illusions flashed before my eyes. Later the phenomenon spread beyond our building, and I would succumb to similar fantasies on squalid little streets veneered with the yellow light of streetlamps. It was inconceivable how I could bring back fragments of the Venetian landscape and two faces, the woman and her son, and keep them alive in memory. (I would go so far as to say that they grew more vivid with every passing day.)

This mechanism of fleeting escape to Venice from the well of London functioned almost till the end of my five-year stay (albeit with long interruptions in the new apartment). The word "almost" spans a half-year period of gradual but irresistible descent to lower levels or deeper bottoms of the well of our life in London (how many there were!). Suddenly visions of Venice ebbed, and London was just London. We both thought that never again would we emerge from the thickening gloom into the light of day. After my wife's death, I spent three years in Munich. I married a second time and settled in Italy.

A year after I moved to Naples, the newspapers were full of stories, not to mention specialist articles and reproductions, about the big Lorenzo Lotto exhibition at the Ducal Palace in Venice. The official inauguration was announced for the day after Christmas 1956 with the President of the Republic and members of the government in attendance. The exhibition was scheduled to run until May 1, the following year. And Berenson's bulky tome *Lotto* appeared in the bookshops. The press devoted a lot of space to the mystery of the rather odd timing of the show. For a variety of reasons, foreign tourists usually skip Venice in the winter, which must have been why the organizers decided to offer the exhibition first to the Italian public and then, toward the end, to visitors from other countries. One journalist took flight on the wings of "poetic license" and toyed with an original explanation: since the "mysterious" Lotto was "unappreciated in his lifetime," "adopted in his poverty by the sanctuary of Loreto," and "ignored by his native Venice," he was obliged five centuries later to return home "in the clouds of Venetian winter fog." What the papers gave most attention was the painter's neglect by most of his contemporaries ("the exquisite portraitist!"), his wanderings in search of work, his frequent hunger, and his loneliness. "Venice bows its head and beats its breast, the world has discovered the Master," was how the headline of one article put it.

All the reports had a few lines about an item of mystery: the highlight of the exhibition would be an unknown Lotto painting recently discovered in the garret of a house in Loreto, where centuries ago the city's richest merchant had lived, a *collezionista di oggetti preziosi,* a collector of precious objects, and a benefactor of the painter. The picture was found by chance and purchased in 1954 by a Venetian antique dealer, Marini, and identified as a Lotto by a specialist, Countess Terzan, who also did the restoration work.

I went to Venice December 20 alone, because my second wife had to look after our baby son. I had been invited to spend Christmas Eve in Padua by a Polish friend from the army and his Italian wife, but my early arrival did not make it any easier to find a hotel room in Venice. The hotels were all full, booked at least a month in advance, because the clamor in the press had made Lotto the "cultural event of the year." In extremity I could have taken advantage of hospitality in Padua for a few days, but I was anxious not to be away from Venice for an instant (with the exception of Christmas Eve in Padua). I did not have high hopes when I tried the Ruskin House, but the old Englishwoman remembered me. She also remembered my first wife and made so much of our meeting after many years that she immediately packed me off to a cluttered room, our room from the postwar Venetian trip, that had been booked by a couple from Bologna only from the day the exhibition opened. I promised her that I would be taking the night train back to Naples as soon as I saw the exhibition and would leave my bag at the reception desk that morning.

I spent the night without closing an eye, wrapped in a blanket (Ruskin House did not have central heating) and sitting at the window. I stared motionlessly at the dome of the church on the Giudecca, as if I expected someone to sit down next to me, the ghost of someone with whom years before I had shared that very same fragment of the nightscape of Venice; as if I were firmly convinced that the dead come back to life, in unmaterial form, if you can fix an image in which they once long sank their eyes.

The night was clear, chill, and windless, the sky shimmered with pale stars, and the dark canal puckered delicately like a length of velvet. Near dawn a mantle of fog fell all unawares over the city, dense and pervasive; all it took was a quarter of an hour for Venice to disappear so completely that you might have wondered if it had even existed a moment before. Boat horns resounded, and the cloud of white began to be slashed by lightninglike blades unsheathed somewhere from beacons and lanterns. The fog lasted my whole stay, occasionally clearing for a brief moment. But what those moments were like! Venice became a series of quick purloined pictures. Revealed to the eye only to disappear at once were portraits of passersby, yes, portraits, it was only then—as if in preparation for the Lotto exhibition—that I learned to descry in human faces their natural reflexive aptitude to "sitting for a portrait." Each of us is a living portrait, especially when the face momentarily emerges from the fog; such moments are the subject of the great portrait painters.

A long line crept slowly to the Ducal Palace, drawing shreds of fog behind it into the crowded hall where ticket counters and kiosks were set up. The exhibition rooms were beyond the row of ticket turnstiles. I walked at a brisk pace, glancing superficially at the Lotto pictures I knew from reproductions, and hurried on to the "jewel of the exhibition," to what the previous day's newspapers called a "sensation."

Finally, at a distance, in what seemed to be the last room, I saw a spotlighted alcove with a crowd of people standing in a semicircle in front of it. That was where I had to go, if my visit to the exhibition was to start from the new acquisition, from the hitherto unknown and miraculously discovered Lotto portrait.

I could see that both sides of the alcove were draped with dark red or purple cloth, perhaps brocade, spotlighted by stylized candle-shaped lamps set horizontally above and below. There was a panel hanging from the upper light with a detailed description, but it was unreadable at a distance. I am allergic to crowds, so the only thing to do was wait. But I had miscalculated. Every time the semicircle around the alcove started to thin out, newcomers immediately replaced those who left. Like it or not, I had to forget my allergy, approach the throng, and watch for a sudden opening. The moment finally came when I could see the whole alcove, albeit between the heads and over the shoulders of the people in front.

The first thing I saw was the Contessa. She was sitting in a wheelchair, her legs wrapped in a blanket down to her feet. From the waist up she was still as beautiful as ever; her face had not grown older with the years, but it seemed darkened by a shadow of what might have been madness. Her eyes flashed as never before, indeed, the fire in her eyes seemed even brighter and a bit disquieting. "She is paralyzed," a man standing in front of me told his female companion. "She lost the use of her legs four years after her son was shot." She answered the questions of those who managed to get near her. I listened to her responses—the same soft, deep voice! Her replies were thorough and businesslike, and I noticed (perhaps the only one who did) a trace of pride in her voice. When I managed to get close enough to her that she could not but see me, she fixed her eyes on my face for one brief moment, and then, without a quiver of her noble features, she went back to answering the questions people asked her. I was absolutely sure that she recognized me, but she did not want to acknowledge it. More—she expected me to do the same.

Not without some effort, I elbowed my way forward and approached the portrait. I am anxious to avoid cheap dramatic effects, but, for the sake of exact description, I cannot omit the details of my first impression: it was like a sharp blow between the eyes, my heart suddenly palpitated, my knees went weak, and my face flushed as if struck by a hot blast from an open furnace, and I could not breathe. I recognized the composition of the picture, entitled *Double Portrait* and similar to the Vienna *Triple Portrait*, from the canvas on the easel in the Contessa's workshop that I had intentionally unveiled. But only the composition. The time I removed the Venetian silk scarf from the canvas, I stood before a painting that had just been started but was clearly a portrait, full face and in profile, of the painter's young son seen as a beautiful cherub. Now I stood in front of a *Double Portrait* of Alvi as he was back from the war, the Alvi I had fleetingly glimpsed (probably the only one who had) through the windowpane between his room and the outside stairs. It was a hard manly face with a bold and fearless look, yet there was no trace of that fiercely cruel expression in this young warrior's face. It was beautiful (indeed it looked like the face of a warrior who had just won his spurs), how beautiful his double portrait was!

The panel on the upper light detailed the circumstances of the discovery of the painting, gave the year 1555 (with a question mark) as the probable date of the portrait, reported that it had been impossible to establish the identity of the sitter, and explained that it was in the "fully mature and perhaps even a bit overripe" *(pienamente maturo e forse anche un po' stagionato)* style of Lotto's portrait art, suggesting it was done a year or two at most before the artist's death. How the Contessa had fathomed that art, in the nuances of color, in the set of head and arms! How her boundless love for the real sitter gave wing to *her* art!

When I pulled myself together, I passed by her wheelchair once again before proceeding to the remaining rooms of the exhibition. But I must have sensed that she was looking at me, and I did not glance in her direction.

Several years went by. I bought art magazines regularly, and more than once I was able to admire color reproductions of Lotto's *Double Portrait*, with learned commentary by art historians and complimentary remarks *en passant* about the restoration done by Giuditta Terzan. When the picture was acquired by the Accademia in Venice, the prestigious quarterly *Il Mondo dell'Arte* published a lengthy interview with the Contessa, together with photographs of the restorer, her home, and her workshop. I marveled at the interview, and several times over I avidly read the Contessa's adroit and intelligent balancing act and her expert reflections about the painting of the Venetian-Loretan Master, but most of all I marveled at her sangfroid. I knew the truth, perhaps the only person in the world besides the Venetian antique dealer Marini, and kept the secret deep in my heart. And I racked my brains wondering where that paralyzed woman found the strength to play with fire. For I never doubted that the forgery would not remain long undiscovered, however remarkable and near-great her hitherto hidden and suddenly revealed talent was. I was right, although I did not suppose it could last so long, until 1975. As to the source of the Contessa's strength and astonishing composure in her awesome daring, the trial was to shed a fleeting light on something of it.

The first flash of the impending storm came in October 1975, an article by a Lotto expert in a major paper with the perfidious headline "La Contessa Van Meergeren?" No reference was made to the Venetian *Double Portrait*, and the Contessa was not mentioned by name. But the writer alluded to her under the name of the brilliant Vermeer forger (albeit with a question mark) and spoke in general terms about the particularly risky case of the unfortunate and destitute Lotto, "who scattered his masterpieces at random, without the slightest protection of his rights as a painter—easy for imitators (which is no felony) and forgers (which is a crime)."

I do not know if Giuditta Terzan's letter to the newspaper was a mistake or rather a bold rational move. After all, she could have refrained from comment, for it was only her title that had been used and not her name, and not once in the text was the *Double Portrait* mentioned. Evidently she judged that the tactic of immediately dotting the *i*'s would pay off. "I surmise," she wrote in her letter, "that in his article Professor Salimbeni, a justly renowned connoisseur of Lotto's painting, while preferring not to name names out of some consideration, had in mind the *Double Portrait* from the celebrated Venetian exhibition, of which I was the restorer. The very hint, or rather the hint of a hint, of insinuation is sufficient reason for me to demand a ruling from a commission of experts, including Professor Salimbeni of course."

Salimbeni's reply was dry and matter-of-fact. Yes, out of some consideration (here a delicate allusion to the Contessa's personal tragedy) he preferred to hedge around the subject rather than take the bull by the horns. The Countess Terzan's letter freed his hands. Indeed he considered the Lotto *Double Portrait* a very skillful and in a certain sense even praiseworthy fake. Without a moment's hesitation he agreed to calling a commission of experts and proposed a roster of six names, including his own. It was his opinion that the commission be appointed and operate as a representative of the law courts. Moreover, the Accademia, as owner of the portrait, had the right to have the courts subpoena Countess Terzan and the antique dealer Marini.

And that is what happened. However, before the matter went to trial in Venice, the six-member commission split in half: three experts judged the portrait authentic, they believed the painting was Lotto's work; three considered it an immensely skillful forgery. Their stance remained unchanged throughout the week-long trial. There would have been no sentence, that is to say, the Contessa and Marini could have walked out of the courtroom with heads held (half) high, and the portrait would have returned to a room or a vault in the Accademia, had it not been for the statement by Giuditta Terzan. The press gave a lot of space to wondering why she made it; for me, I must admit, it came as no surprise. She confessed to forgery and described the circumstances in exact detail, nor did she forgo the easy satisfaction of pointing to her half-success. When asked why she had done it, she said she had been tempted by substantial gain. "But that was not all," she added, and then her calm even voice broke slightly. "I also wanted to leave the world a lasting portrait of my lost beloved [*amatissimo*] son."

The Venetian antique dealer was sentenced to five years in prison without parole. So was she, but with the difference that as a cripple she was sent to a penal institution for invalids in the vicinity of Lake Como. The portrait, the corpus delicti, was confiscated by the court.

We sat by the open window on the fourth floor of a building on the Tiber. The sky was limpid and blue with a clear view across the bridge to the other side of the river and the monument to the master of sonnets in *romanesco* dialect, Gioacchino Belli, who scoffed at love's excesses, a poet Gogol loved and tried to translate. The building was outside the old ghetto, at no great distance from the synagogue, and its tenants were wealthy people. Across from me sat Giovanna Olindo, the Contessa's younger half-sister, several years a widow of an extremely rich builder. She resembled an old, plucked turkey: she blinked her eyes constantly, and every so often this wizened figure disgorged a comment, squeaky and sharp and plucked as bare as herself.

It was not easy to obtain that visit. I allowed myself a fib ("I was connected to your sister by something more than a fleeting wartime acquaintanceship"), of which I hereby make confession and likewise self-absolution: I saw no other way of getting to the one person who might have told me about the Contessa's fate from her conviction until her death.

Giudi (she used her family nickname) served her full sentence in the penal institution for invalids. She was apathetic, as if her spirit were elsewhere, and had no wish to do anything, not even take advantage of the painting materials her sister sent. She expected only one thing of her sister: to pay lawyers for her ever-renewed efforts to ransom the picture the court had confiscated. All efforts proved vain; it was quite plain that the court feared a repeated attempt to exploit the fake. Constant refusal drove Giudi into deep neurasthenia. When she finished her sentence she was taken, at her sister's expense, to an institution in the Aosta Valley for people with nervous disorders. She spent eight years there, "dead to the world" (as Signora Olindo put it). It was only the court's decision to release the picture that lifted her from total prostration. She came back to life. She went to Venice at once, to the house that had been locked and abandoned for years. Her sister paid for her support and found her a permanent house-keeper, a distant relative of their mother, an iron-willed old spinster. The Contessa spent several years, until her death of a heart attack, bristling with suspicion and ever standing guard over her treasure.

So my intuition was not mistaken. The whole story was at least to some degree a modern version of Henry James's Venetian novella *The Aspern Papers*. Down to the tiny detail of the Contessa's relative, corresponding to the old spinster Tita, Miss Bordereau's niece.

We went into the next room for tea. On the wall, under a small crucifix and untouched by the light of the sun, hung the *Double Portrait* by Giuditta Van Meergeren. I gazed at it so long that Signora Olindo had to remind me, with a note of irritation in her voice, that the tea was poured. The Venetian portrait was certainly a masterpiece; who knows if Lotto could have painted anything like it? The author of the forgery had painted two splendid, adamant, and captivatingly beautiful faces of evil.